Child Psychology & Development

FOR

DUMMIES®

Child Psychology & Development

FOR

DUMMIES®

by Laura L. Smith, PhD,
and Charles H. Elliott, PhD

WILEY

Wiley Publishing, Inc.

Child Psychology & Development For Dummies ®

Published by
Wiley Publishing, Inc.
111 River St.
Hoboken, NJ 07030-5774
www.wiley.com

For general information on our other products and services, please contact our Customer Care Department within the U.S. at 877-762-2974, outside the U.S. at 317-572-3993, or fax 317-572-4002.

For technical support, please visit www.wiley.com/techsupport.

Wiley also publishes its books in a variety of electronic formats. Some content that appears in print may not be available in electronic books.

Library of Congress Control Number: 2011920892

ISBN: 978-0-470-91885-2

Manufactured in the United States of America

10 9 8 7 6 5 4 3 2 1

WILEY

About the Authors

Photo by Matt Foster of Kim Jew Photography

Laura L. Smith, PhD, and **Charles Elliott,** PhD, are co-authors of *Overcoming Anxiety For Dummies,* 2nd Edition, *Borderline Personality Disorder For Dummies, Obsessive-Compulsive Disorder For Dummies, Seasonal Affective Disorder For Dummies, Anxiety & Depression Workbook For Dummies,* and *Depression For Dummies* (all from Wiley Publishing, Inc.); *Hollow Kids: Recapturing the Soul of a Generation Lost to the Self-Esteem Myth* (Prima); and *Why Can't I Be the Parent I Want to Be?* (New Harbinger Publications). They are members of the board of directors of the New Mexico Psychological Association and affiliated training faculty at the Cognitive Behavioral Institute of Albuquerque. Their work has been featured in various periodicals, including *Family Circle, Parents, Child,* and *Better Homes and Gardens,* as well as popular publications such as the *New York Post, Washington Times, Daily Telegraph* (London), and *The Christian Science Monitor.*

They have been invited speakers at conferences including: the National Alliance for the Mentally Ill (NAMI), the Association for Behavioral and Cognitive Therapies, the International Association for Cognitive Psychotherapy, and the National Association of School Psychologists. They have appeared o" television networks such as CNN and Canada AM. They have also been featured as experts on various National Public Radio programs, as well as "You The Owner's Manual," "Doctor Radio," "The Frankie Boyer Show," and "The Four Seasons Radio Show." They have committed their professional lives to making the science of psychology relevant and accessible to the public.

Laura is a clinical and a school psychologist. Previously, she was a special-education teacher, an educational diagnostician, a psychologist at a juvenile detention center, a child psychologist in private practice, a clinical supervisor at various rural school districts, and a consultant to Head Start programs. Throughout these years, she has raised three kids and enjoyed her four grandchildren. She is often asked to provide consultations to attorneys, school districts, and government agencies.

Chuck is a clinical psychologist and a founding fellow of the Academy of Cognitive Therapy. He has written many professional articles and book chapters on the topic of cognitive behavior therapies and pediatric psychology. He has been a director of mental health consultation-liaison at Children's Memorial Hospital in Oklahoma City, a faculty member at the University of New Mexico School of Medicine (programs for children), a clinical psychologist in private practice, and a faculty member at Fielding Graduate University (psychology).

Drs. Smith and Elliott are available for speaking engagements, expert interviews, and workshops. You may contact either or both of them at www.psychology4people.com.

Dedication

To children everywhere and those who care for them.

Authors' Acknowledgments

We want to take this opportunity to thank our outstanding editors at Wiley Publishing: Acquisitions Editor Michael Lewis; Project Editors Sarah Faulkner, Danielle Voirol, and Linda Brandon; and Copy Editors Kathy Simpson and Sarah Westfall. We also want to thank our publicity and marketing team, which includes David Hobson and Adrienne Fontaine at Wiley, and Technical Editor Angela Tomlin, PhD.

We appreciate Trevor Wolfe, Sara Rodriquez, Allison Wolfe, and Brian Elliott for achieving the four goals of growing up. And of course we're grateful to our grandchildren — Lauren, Alaina, Carter, and Cade — for keeping us amused and reminding us about what's really important. Thanks to Kate Guerin for interesting conversations and information about public relations. Thanks to Nathan Rodriguez for putting out fires.

We want to thank Deborah Wearn and Pamela Hargrove for their help in keeping everyone together and willingness to embark on adventures. We appreciate Barbara Warren, Bob and Jeanette Elliott, Tracie Antonuk, Kathy Desmarais, and Geoff Smith for their continued interest and support. Thanks to Betsey, Marty, and Andrew Chavez for being an inspirational family. A special thanks to Judy Frenak for her sisterly interest. Thanks to Sadie and Murphy for taking us on much-needed walks and jogs through Corrales.

Appreciation goes to Jaime J. Diaz, chief operating officer/Midwest New Mexico Community Action Program (NMCAP) and president of the New Mexico Head Start Association, and Pauline Binger, center director/Midwest NMCAP, for their interest and support of research on improving teaching methods and caring about the mental-health needs of the children of New Mexico.

Thanks to Drs. Brad Richards and Jeanne Czajka of the Cognitive Behavioral Institute of Albuquerque for including us in your affiliated training faculty. We look forward to another training session in Santa Fe. Thanks to Mathew Raikes at www.darn-computer.com for his timely, patient expertise on computers. To Dr. Brenda Wolfe and her husband, Ken, thanks for helping us uncork our creativity across the globe.

Finally, we are especially grateful to the many children and parents we've seen over the years in our practices. They helped us understand child psychology and development. They also taught us about resilience, courage, and persistence as nothing else could.

Publisher's Acknowledgments

We're proud of this book; please send us your comments at http://dummies.custhelp.com. For other comments, please contact our Customer Care Department within the U.S. at 877-762-2974, outside the U.S. at 317-572-3993, or fax 317-572-4002.

Some of the people who helped bring this book to market include the following:

Acquisitions, Editorial, and Media Development

Project Editors: Sarah Faulkner, Linda Brandon

Acquisitions Editor: Michael Lewis

Copy Editor: Kathy Simpson, Sarah Westfall

Assistant Editor: David Lutton

Technical Editor: Angela Tomlin, PhD

Editorial Manager: Christine Meloy Beck

Editorial Supervisor and Reprint Editor: Carmen Krikorian

Editorial Assistants: Rachelle S. Amick, Jennette ElNaggar

Cover Photos: © istockphoto.com/ Stefanie Timmermann

Cartoons: Rich Tennant (www.the5thwave.com)

Composition Services

Project Coordinator: Patrick Redmond

Layout and Graphics: Joyce Haughey, Lavonne Roberts

Proofreaders: John Greenough, Sossity R. Smith

Indexer: Silvoskey Indexing Services

Special Help: Danielle Voirol

Publishing and Editorial for Consumer Dummies

    Diane Graves Steele, Vice President and Publisher, Consumer Dummies

    Kristin Ferguson-Wagstaffe, Product Development Director, Consumer Dummies

    Ensley Eikenburg, Associate Publisher, Travel

    Kelly Regan, Editorial Director, Travel

Publishing for Technology Dummies

    Andy Cummings, Vice President and Publisher, Dummies Technology/General User

Composition Services

    Debbie Stailey, Director of Composition Services

Contents at a Glance

Table of Contents

Introduction

• •

*W*e love kids. Fact is, we used to be kids. We've had kids, and they've had kids. Also, we've devoted much of our professional lives to assessing, teaching, and treating kids. We've worked with kids in the class-room, in the hospital, and our offices. We've seen kids of all ages from infancy through young adulthood. We've helped kids deal with learning problems, anxiety, depression, autism, deficits in attention, and behavior problems.

So when the editors of the *For Dummies* series asked us to consider writing *Child Psychology & Development For Dummies,* we were delighted. We soon engaged in lengthy discussions and a few sleepless nights about the content and organization of this book. Take a look at most any college textbook on either child psychology or development, and you may find it daunting. Frankly, much of the material is esoteric and as difficult to follow as twisting country roads before Google Maps.

In collaboration with our editors, we took some time deciding on an approach to this book. We realized that most people who are interested in this topic are probably teachers, parents, child-care providers, grandparents, and others who are interested in kids. Thus, you'll discover that we don't follow a textbook approach to *Child Psychology & Development For Dummies.* Rather, like most books in the *For Dummies* series, this book takes compli-cated theories and ideas and turns them into practical information that can be applied to the real world of children and those who care about them.

We could have filled these pages with endless details about theorists such as Sigmund Freud, Erik Erikson, Lawrence Kohlberg, Jean Piaget, B. F. Skinner, Albert Bandura, Lev Vygotsky, John Bowlby, and Mary Ainsworth (among many others). Instead, we took a different tack, weaving science, theory, and our own clinical experience into a sensible look at child psychology and development.

About This Book

This book is about kids from A to Z. We start with the big picture of what makes kids tick and reveal the four major goals of a successful childhood. We also discuss how development proceeds normally with respect to each of those goals at different ages. We describe how families, schools, and commu-nities can optimally support child development.

We also take a look at what can go wrong during childhood. We describe the most common childhood disorders and disabilities. Fortunately, much can be done about these problems, and we tell you about the treatments and interventions that work.

This book is meant to provide lots of information about child development and the problems kids encounter. If you have concerns about a child, we recommend checking with either the child's pediatrician or a mental-health professional. Don't attempt to diagnose or try your own treatment ideas without guidance from professionals.

What Not to Read

Most books are intended to be read from cover to cover. If you like doing that, by all means feel free to do so. But you can actually approach this book in almost any way that you want. You can use the comprehensive table of contents to choose what you want to read and in what order.

If you're looking for text to skip, we recommend that you don't read the sidebars (text within those gray-shaded boxes) or any paragraph attached to a Technical Stuff icon. Although both items are interesting, skipping them won't take away from the practical knowledge you gain from the rest of the book.

Conventions Used in this Book

Throughout the book, we use the following conventions:

- ✔ We use case examples to illustrate our points from time to time. Please realize that these examples represent composites of children and their caregivers confronting all sorts of issues. None of these children actually exists as described. Any resemblance to a particular person is entirely coincidental. We boldface the names of people in our examples to indicate that a case example is starting.

- ✔ We do our best to avoid using technical jargon. But when we resort to using a term that you may find unfamiliar, we usually italicize the word and give you a brief definition. We try to keep technical terms to a minimum.

- ✔ All Web addresses are set in monofont to help them stand out. Also, if a Web address had to break across two lines, we didn't add any extra characters (such as a hyphen) to indicate the break. Just type the address as you see it on the page, ignoring the line break.

Foolish Assumptions

We're going to go out on a limb here and assume that if you've picked up this book, you probably have an interest in kids. Or maybe you're curious about children because you're expecting or you have a brand-new grandchild. Perhaps you're a teacher, parent, counselor, or other type of child-care provider. Maybe you're looking for ideas about how to manage or discipline kids, or you want to know about a certain type of disability or disorder. It's also possible that you want to know what types of treatments are available for various kinds of childhood problems.

In other words, if you want to know something about kids, you've found the right book. Enjoy.

How This Book Is Organized

Child Psychology & Development For Dummies is organized in 6 parts and 22 chapters. Here's a quick overview of each part.

Part I: Understanding Children: The Big Picture

In this part, we introduce the topic of child psychology and development. Chapter 1 provides a broad-brushstrokes overview. Chapter 2 tells you what goes into the soup of kids' development, including biology, psychology, learning, environment, and culture. Chapter 3 lays out the four major goals of childhood — what kids need to master to become well-functioning adults.

Part II: Watching Kids Grow

In Part II, we describe what normal childhood development looks like. Chapter 4 starts with what happens before a kid becomes a kid — at conception — and then describes birth and the rapid developments during the first year of life. In Chapter 5, we discuss the preschool years, ages 1 through 4. Then, in Chapter 6, we review what happens during the middle-childhood years, ages 5 through 12 — years that revolve around making friends, acquiring skills, and developing better self-control. During adolescence, described in Chapter 7, kids go through tremendous changes. Their bodies develop, their sense of who they are matures, they learn to think abstractly, and the importance of peers increases. For parents and teens alike, surviving adolescence is quite an accomplishment.

Part III: Growing Great Kids

This part reviews how parents, families, schools, and communities can give kids the best chance to grow up successfully. In Chapter 8, we describe ways that families can optimize kids' development. Next, in Chapter 9, we review what schools and teachers can do to help kids achieve their highest potential, as well as show parents some of the various day-care and educational options available to them. Finally, in Chapter 10, we discuss the role that communities can play in helping kids reach adulthood intact.

Part IV: Spotting Troubled Development

Sometimes, troubles pop up in spite of everyone's best intentions. Kids can be born with problems or develop them over time. This part alerts you to early signs of problems that could lie on the horizon so help can be sought early.

In this part, we discuss common physical challenges, problems that may affect school achievement, emotional disorders, the autism spectrum, and behavioral disorders. We also review the sometimes-horrific effects of child abuse, trauma, and accidental injuries. Our intention is to help those who care about children understand the nature of childhood difficulties.

Part V: Getting the Right Therapies

Perhaps you have or know a child who has one or more of the problems discussed in Part IV. If so, this part reviews the kinds of therapies and interventions that can help. These interventions have been studied and shown to be effective. We don't want you to waste your time and money on miracle cures that don't work.

We also discuss how parents, teachers, and professionals can collaborate for even better outcomes. We tell those who care for kids how to communicate effectively. Finally, we tell parents how to work with and assist the efforts of treatment providers.

Part VI: The Part of Tens

If you're looking for a quick reference, take a look at these helpful lists. Read about ten ways to calm kids, ten signs of gifted kids, and ten signs that a kid needs help.

The Appendix

The Appendix provides a quick overview of major milestones of child development, showing what kids generally should be doing at various ages.

Icons Used in This Book

This icon is intended to grab your attention. It indicates something that we think you'll find important and want to remember.

The Tip icon alerts you to specific useful actions you can take or interesting insights for your consideration.

These icons appear when you need to be on the lookout for a potential problem.

Not everyone wants to know everything about every topic. This icon indicates material that you may want to delve into further, but you really don't have to read it.

Where to Go from Here

Child Psychology & Development For Dummies offers you the best, most-up-to-date information we have on what makes kids tick and how normal development usually proceeds. It discusses the problems children encounter and how everyone can help them do better.

Reading this book will help you understand kids better. If a child you care about has a specific problem, however, we encourage you to seek professional guidance from a pediatrician or other health-care provider or a mental-health professional.

Part I

Understanding Children: The Big Picture

The 5th Wave   By Rich Tennant

"He should be all right now. I made him spend two and a half hours on a prisoners' chat line."

In this part . . .

We look at why child psychology matters. We tell you why anyone who's interested in kids needs to know something about child psychology. We explain how biology mixes with the environment, culture, and experiences to determine how kids turn out.

We also discuss the four goals all kids must master to do well in life. Specifically, they must learn how to relate to others; they need to figure out how to control their emotions and impulses; they need to develop a healthy view of themselves; and they must find the motivation to learn and achieve.

Chapter 1

Exploring Child Psychology

- -

- -

Child psychology and development captures the interest and imagination of anyone who cares for kids. Kids grow, develop, misbehave, play, learn, and love in rapidly changing yet fascinating ways. Parents, educators, grandparents, health-care providers, and child-care workers also wonder and worry about the kids they care about. Raising a child in today's world requires more than just good intentions. It calls for a comprehensive knowledge about kids, what motivates them, what goes right, and what can go wrong.

In this chapter, you can discover compelling reasons for diving into the topic of child psychology and development and take a look at the wide range of influences that determine how kids ultimately turn out. Here, you can also find an overview about the nature of normal and abnormal development, which we discuss throughout this book. You can find information about how all people involved with caring for kids can maximize good outcomes.

Good outcomes for kids means mastering four key objectives of childhood — the goals of growing up:

- ✔ Forming good attachments and relationships
- ✔ Controlling emotions and impulses
- ✔ Developing healthy self views
- ✔ Achieving one's potential

Last but not least (this may be the first section you jump to), you can read about getting help for kids when they need it.

Although this book takes a heavily practical, applied focus, those of you interested in theories of child development may want to review the sidebars in this chapter.

Why Child Psychology? Exploring Some Compelling Reasons

Understanding children helps teachers become better teachers, parents become better parents, child-care workers become better at taking care of kids, grandparents do a better job of grandparenting, and health-care providers give more compassionate and competent health care. Understanding children just makes the world a better place — and that's the bottom line. The next two sections point out two important reasons why having a basic understanding of child psychology is beneficial.

Reviewing realistic expectations

Knowledge about child psychology helps you have realistic expectations for kids. Educators and parents alike always have expectations — whether they realize it or not — for children's behavior, learning, emotions, and physical capacities. Yet, sometimes these expectations don't fit reality. For example, a girl who is taller than most kids in her age group may be out on the playground struggling to follow the rules of a game of baseball. She manages to hit a ball, but then doesn't know she's supposed to run to first base. An adult watching her confusion may think that she's delayed, or not really caring about the game like she should. In reality, the girl has not mastered the skill because she's only 5 years old and most kids that age don't understand the rules of baseball.

Unfortunately, kids sometimes become the brunt of bullying or abuse when their actions fail to meet the expectations of others. Furthermore, many disabilities (such as mild autism or learning disabilities) are not readily apparent to the untrained eye and may also lead to inappropriate expectations of the child. Therefore, having an increased knowledge of child psychology and development can really aid concerned adults with helping children in the best manner. Knowing about the challenges of childhood can help adults intervene when problems occur.

Understanding worrisome trends

Kids today have more troubles than their parents or grandparents. For example, the diagnosis of autism has skyrocketed over the past several decades. Attention deficit disorders, learning problems, and behavior problems are all on the rise. Today, anxiety disorders and depression occur at much higher rates than in past decades. The diagnosis of bipolar disorder, in the past a very rare diagnosis in children, has demonstrated a 40-fold increase in the last decade. Some of these increases are no doubt due to improved awareness of these issues in children among professionals, but most experts believe we are nonetheless observing significantly more troubles among kids than ever before.

In addition, pediatricians find that about half of all patient visits involve questions about emotional, developmental, and behavioral issues. Worried parents want to know more than vague reassurances that their kids will outgrow their problems or "your child seems within normal limits." This book should serve as a valuable resource for tackling those issues.

Reviewing the Recipe for Child Development

A lot more goes into making a kid a kid than the joining of a sperm with an egg. From that moment of conception onward, influences bombard developing children from all directions — media, culture, genetics, and the list goes on. How much any of these influences determine how a given child turns out is utterly unknown (Chapter 2 takes a look at different influences). However, when any of these factors are at extreme levels or endure for a long time, the degree of influence increases.

See Figure 1-1 for an overview of the factors that can influence the development of any particular child.

Note that in Figure 1-1, the arrows run from "outside" the child to the child. In truth, most of these influences run both ways; not only that, these influencing factors affect each other. For example, a school influences kids, but the kids in that school influence the school and its teachers as well. A really good school may succeed in decreasing the impact of learning disabilities or premature birth for some of its students.

Plus, some genes lie dormant and don't become expressed unless a child has certain experiences or encounters other important triggering events such as toxins or illnesses. Poverty may have a devastating effect on one child, but another child responds to poverty by ultimately finding creative ways to change it. Oppression usually causes children to feel helpless and angry, but the right combination of other influences may allow some kids experiencing oppression to turn into productive leaders.

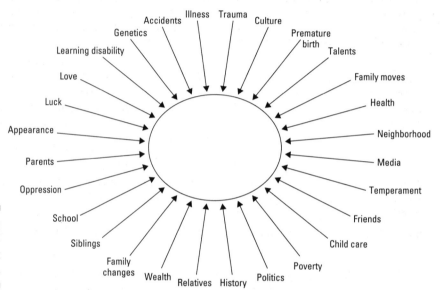

Figure 1-1: Child development factors.

Noting Normal Child Development

Across the world, children develop with striking similarity when things go right. They typically begin to take their first steps around their first birthday at which time they also begin saying their first few words. Kids form strong attachments to their parents quickly and then slowly form attachments to other kids and adults. They come into the world with almost no ability to control their emotions and will cry and scream at the slightest discomfort. Gradually, they acquire the ability to regulate their emotions.

Part II describes normal childhood development in detail. You may wonder why we provide this much information about normal development. For one, if you know what's supposed to be happening and at what ages, it's easier to determine when things aren't proceeding smoothly. When children fall seriously short on developmental milestones, they may need further assessment and help from a professional. Plus, knowing what to expect helps caregivers provide kids with optimal experiences and guidance.

Finding Freud's perspective

Sigmund Freud (1856–1939) was a physician and prolific writer who developed one of the early theories of child development. Freud believed that all humans possess basic drives and motives. People, for the most part, are unaware of these forces that guide their lives. He wrote that babies are born with *libido,* which is a sexual pleasure-seeking energy or drive.

During the first few months, the baby gets pleasure from sucking. Thus, Freud labeled this stage the *oral stage* of development. Sometime after a child's first birthday, the child gets pleasure from having bowel movements and then controlling bowels. This stage, that lasts until about age three, is called the *anal stage* of development. During the preschool years (roughly ages three to six), the child falls in love with the parent of the opposite sex and realizes the parent of the same sex is a rival.

The child then represses those sexual feelings and identifies with the same sex parent during what Freud called the *phallic stage.* During the school years, ages 6 to 12 (also called *latency*) sexual feelings are repressed. Finally during the *genital stage* of adolescence, sexual feeling reemerge and are directed toward opposite-sex peers.

Freud's theories of child development have been very influential. Among his enduring contributions to the field of child and developmental psychology are his basic contentions that adult psychopathology is connected to childhood experiences and that people aren't always consciously aware of why they do what they do. However, his concepts also have been criticized as possibly sexist and lacking in sufficient scientific validation.

However, normal isn't as black and white as you may think. When it comes to child psychology and development, you can find a lot of gray that may or may not be considered "normal." Here are two reasons why that's the case:

- *Abnormal* **isn't that abnormal.** When kids have emotional or behavioral problems, it usually involves a normal reaction to abnormal events. Thus, kids become anxious because their worlds are unusually scary; they become depressed when there are people and events that would make anyone sad. They act out when their parents, families, or peers have inadvertently encouraged bad behavior.

- *Normal* **isn't all that normal.** Almost all parents say they want their kids to be happy and normal. Terrific sentiments. But what's normal anyway? No one gets through childhood without a few significant bumps and bruises. In fact, if you review most people's lives you'll almost always find problems — substance abuse, struggles over weight, emotional problems, divorces, traumas, tragedies, serious losses, troubles in school, money worries, relationship problems, and much more. How many people do you know who have never struggled with issues like these? Face it: No one is perfect. Normal isn't normal at all.

Although we use the conventional terms normal and abnormal development in this book, we do so with some reservation. These terms help communicate information about general expectations and common childhood problems. But, be aware that children's strengths, weaknesses, and struggles cannot be neatly categorized as normal or abnormal.

Analyzing Abnormal Development

Knowing the signs of abnormal child development allows teachers, parents, grandparents, counselors, and health-care providers to intervene quickly and appropriately when problems start to emerge. When problems are addressed early, outcomes usually improve.

No one other than a trained health professional should attempt to diagnose disorders in children. However, knowing the signs can alert you to the need for a more thorough assessment, which is how this info comes in handy.

The following sections outline some of the basic areas of abnormal child development, but for a more detailed overview, check out Part IV.

Focusing on physical problems

Kids' bodies don't always work the way they should. For example, babies can be born too early, have birth defects, or struggle with bodily functions such as elimination, sleep, or eating. Sometimes kids get sick with serious or chronic illnesses. Other times symptoms in the body stem from emotional distress. A child's pediatrician needs to check out any symptoms involving the body.

Taking care of children who have physical problems can create considerable stress. Caregivers armed with sufficient information deal with the child's physical problems more effectively. See Chapter 11 for details about these various sorts of physical problems and suggestions for addressing them.

Looking at learning

This book describes one of the four goals of childhood as achieving a child's potential. For most kids, much of that achievement occurs in school. Learning disabilities, attention problems, and intellectual challenges all can stand in the way of reaching this goal. However, much can be done to partially or fully overcome these obstacles in many cases. But first, identifying kids at risk for learning problems as soon as possible is crucial.

Elucidating Erikson's views

Erik Erikson (1902–1994) was a follower of Sigmund Freud (see sidebar "Finding Freud's perspective"). Erickson's developmental theories also acknowledged the relationship between adult problems and unresolved issues of childhood. He viewed the life cycle as a series of challenges that when successfully met, lead to good adjustment. When challenges are not successfully negotiated, these issues can harm later adjustment. He differed from Freud in that his stages more closely tie child development to social and environmental factors.

Here are Erikson's psychosocial stages of development:

✔ **Trust versus mistrust:** During this stage, babies figure out to trust that others will take care of their basic needs. When care is poor, they discover how to mistrust.

✔ **Autonomy versus shame:** Toddlers discover skills during this time such as independent toileting, walking, dressing, communicating, and feeding. Success during this stage leads to feelings of competence. Failure leads to self-doubt.

✔ **Initiative versus guilt:** Preschoolers continue to catch on to new skills. They may also have some conflict with others and can experience guilt when they do not meet the expectations of their caregivers.

✔ **Industry versus inferiority:** During the elementary school years, children develop more feelings of competence as they negotiate how to get along with others and master school-related tasks. If they do not meet demands adequately, they are likely to feel inferior.

✔ **Identity versus role confusion:** Adolescence is the time to develop sexual identity and self-concept and begin to explore occupations. Teens who fail to find their way often become confused about who they are.

✔ **Intimacy versus isolation:** Older teens and young adults begin to form partnerships or find themselves lonely and isolated.

✔ **Generativity versus stagnation:** During the adult years, having activities such as raising children or having a vocation leads to contentment and a sense of having made a contribution. Those who do not have these sorts of activities stagnate.

✔ **Integrity versus despair:** As life comes to an end, some look back at meaningful lives; others look at back with regret.

Erikson believed that people evolve over time. Stages were not discreet but overlapping. His theories have enjoyed popularity for their optimism and belief that humans can age gracefully.

Children at risk for learning problems often show early signs of struggle. Such symptoms can include disinterest in reading, low muscle tone, late talking, delayed motor skills, and impaired self-care skills. Caregivers who are alert to these issues can advocate for prompt assessment and treatment. Chapter 12 gives you considerable information about what to look for.

Analyzing autism

The possibility of autism strikes terror in the hearts of many prospective parents. In part, that's because the most serious forms of autism are quite debilitating — such children who have profound problems relating to others and the world. However, many of those kids with autism exhibit much milder problems, and all children can benefit from intensive intervention. Like all childhood problems, the earlier the intervention, the better the results.

See Chapter 13 for detailed information about autism, its early signs, and what can be done about it. You can also discover that many children with autism are quite fascinating and a good number of them exhibit extraordinary gifts.

Examining emotional disorders

One of the four goals of childhood highlighted in this book is discovering how to control one's emotions and impulses. Children come into the world with almost no ability to control their crying, distress, and behavior. Gradually, they acquire the ability to soothe themselves and delay their need for instant gratification.

Because little kids lack self-control skills, many parents find it difficult to tell the difference between a child with normal emotions from abnormal. Signs to look out for include changes in sleep and appetite, increased moodiness, spikes in irritability, withdrawal, listlessness, age-inappropriate fearfulness, and bouts of crying. (See Chapter 14 for information about normal versus abnormal fears, early warning signs of emotional problems, and descriptions of the various types of childhood emotional disorders.)

Investigating behavior disorders

All kids misbehave. They all have temper tantrums and meltdowns. They all refuse to do what they're told. And they all talk back. (Sounds like quite the pep talk for soon-to-be parents!) However, when tantrums and meltdowns persist and disobedience becomes the norm, you have a potential behavior problem emerging.

Left unchecked, minor behavior problems can easily evolve into more major issues, including shoplifting, serious problems at school, animal cruelty, fire setting, aggression, and even violence. Chapter 15 describes the risk factors for developing behavior disorders and the signs to look out for. It also describes the types of behavior disorders found in children and adolescents.

Being clear about behaviorism

Behaviorism rose out of a need to be able to study psychology and people with greater objectivity. Because unconscious thought is hard to measure or quantify, behavioral psychologists began to look at how science could measure human activity. John Watson (1878–1958) was one of the early proponents of psychology as the study of human behavior. His belief was that children could be molded by their experiences to turn out to be just about anything from street person to professor. Although his work was based on scientifically validated rules of behavior, his opinions about children's behavior being completely malleable have not been substantiated.

Later, B.F. Skinner (1904–1990) expanded the theory to include other forms of learning based on consequences of behavior influencing future behavior. Albert Bandura (1925–) developed social learning theory that included observational learning and modeling as a way that children learned through interactions with others. See Chapter 2 for information about specific forms of learning — such as operant conditioning, classical conditioning, and modeling — based on these theorists. These learning principles have had strong, enduring influence on the field of child and developmental psychology as well as education, although they have been criticized as insufficient to explain all outcomes.

Tracing trauma and abuse

Tragedies and traumatic events happen to kids. Kids get abused and neglected by parents, caregivers, family members, and strangers. They suffer from the effects of car accidents, natural disasters, and crime. They also witness traumatic events happening to others, such as domestic violence, and when they do, they often suffer effects similar to that of the one who actually was the direct recipient of the abuse.

Chapter 16 reviews the common sources of childhood trauma and describes the various diagnoses that are generally thought to result from traumatic experiences. You can also find information about the factors that appear to help kids get through traumatic experiences relatively unscathed.

Finding Help for Troubled Kids

When children hurt, most adults passionately want to help. That passion sometimes causes them to lose objectivity. They hope for miracle cures and may buy into seductive, but empty promises. However, you can find sources of effective help abound if you know where and how to look.

Chapter 17 reviews the therapies that are known to work and for which problems. This chapter also warns about a few things to look out for when seeking help for kids' problems. Go to this chapter if you have concerns about a child with emotional disorders, behavioral problems, learning disabilities, problems resulting from trauma or symptoms of autism.

When kids have trouble, schools can do a lot to help too. For that to happen, parents, caregivers, teachers, school administrators, therapists, and counselors all need to communicate and work together. If a child's problems are interfering with her ability to learn, schools will provide evaluations and assessments. Chapter 18 provides tips on effective communication, information about tests and evaluations conducted by schools, and appropriate accommodations that schools may make.

Parents and family members also have a crucial role to play in helping troubled kids. They can implement a wide variety of strategies with guidance from a child's therapist. In order to do so, they may need to work on overcoming fears and other obstacles that sometimes interfere with effective parenting. Chapter 19 lays out the ways parents can support and enhance professional efforts for helping their kids.

Covering Piaget's cognitive theory

Jean Piaget (1896–1980) started as a biologist and later studied children's thinking. He came to believe that children's thinking developed and changed over time. During the first two years, infants move and experience their worlds primarily through their senses. This stage according to Piaget's model of development is called the *sensorimotor stage.* Around the ages of 2 through 6, children begin to use language and begin to have conscious thought. During this stage, called *preoperational,* children tend to view themselves as the center of the universe. The *concrete operational stage,* roughly ages 6 to 11, involves logical objective thinking. *Formal operational thinking* occurs after age 12 and beyond. During this stage, children are able to think abstractly.

Piaget's ideas have exerted a lasting influence on the way psychologists look at how children discover how to think. However, most of his work was based on observations of his own children and children from well-to-do, highly educated backgrounds. Thus, his ideas about children's stages of thinking have undergone significant revisions by others over time. Later research has indicated that Piaget likely underestimated young children's abilities.

Chapter 2

What Makes Kids Tick?

Figuring out all the components that go into making a child is a bit like putting together a 10,000-piece puzzle of a cloudless blue sky. Minute differences in shading, shape, and size confuse and bewilder. The solution lies in looking closely at tiny details and in applying determination, persistence, and patience.

Children, like complex puzzles, consist of thousands of pieces connected to make a whole. Unlike puzzles, however, children can be put together in infinite ways.

In this chapter, we delve into the puzzle of human development. We look at the reasons why kids laugh a lot, cry too easily, work hard, seem lazy, enjoy good relationships, or remain friendless. What children ultimately become involves heredity, biology, luck, learning, and effort.

Highlighting Heredity's Influence

At the moment of conception, biological forces begin that strongly influence what a person becomes. A child's genetic blueprint starts with a single cell that reproduces miraculously into the trillions of cells that make up a human being. In this section, we highlight the basic biology — sometimes referred to as nature — that explains the process of becoming human.

Glancing at genetics

All living things consist of cells. Each cell contains *chromosomes* — structures within cells that carry genes. *Genes* are essentially a string of chemicals that provide the detailed set of instructions for the biological makeup of life. Each species has unique sets of instructions. About 25,000 genes go into the blueprint for human life. People across the world are more similar than different, in that about 99.9 percent of their genetic codes are identical.

The set of instructions that go into making a person is called a *genotype*. The genotype is determined when 23 chromosomes from the biological father combine with 23 chromosomes from the biological mother. This combination of genes, which is unique for everyone except identical twins, immediately starts to send orders to cells, telling them how to grow into a human being.

Building a unique person from a genetic blueprint

The way that genes are actually expressed in a person is called a *phenotype*. Think of the genotype as a blueprint and the phenotype as an actual building created from that blueprint. Although genes exert powerful influences, some of their effects can be modified to one degree or another, as we discuss in the next section. Even identical twins, who share a genotype, have subtle, important differences in their personalities, interests, and phenotypes.

Even though all human beings start from a single cell, the transition from that cell to human adult takes many pathways. Again, think of a blueprint. The same plan can be used to make many houses, but the houses would vary because of the quality, kind, or makeup of their raw materials (such as straw, wood, or brick). In addition, the varying skills of carpenters, electricians, and laborers may result in variations in the foundation and the completed structure. Furthermore, unexpected accidents, random events, and changes in the weather can influence the soundness and even the appearance of a building.

Following the blueprint (or not)

The genotype starts a complex process of construction, but like any other construction project, it isn't perfect. During the construction project, dividing cells ignore some genetic instructions, follow others to the letter, amplify some directions, and mute others. What happens to any particular genetic instruction depends on many factors, including the following:

- ✔ **Interaction of genes:** When two genes contain conflicting information, one gene usually wins out over the other, which means that gene is expressed in the phenotype. Dominant, as opposed to recessive genes, typically end up expressed. For example, if one gene is dominant, such as the one that produces brown eyes, when a genotype contains genes for both brown and blue eyes, brown eyes will be more common than blue.

- ✔ **Multiple influences from the environment:** Genetic codes can be challenged or changed by a variety of environmental influences. Thus, a pregnant mother could be exposed to toxins such as alcohol during pregnancy, or the child could lack adequate nutrition; either of these environmental challenges could cause developmental delays.

- ✔ **Learning experiences:** Children who are genetically predisposed to developmental delays can sometimes change or overcome them with early intervention.

Sometimes, genetic instructions go significantly awry. Genetic problems can be caused by abnormalities in the chromosomes. The most common disorder caused by an extra chromosome is Down syndrome, which usually causes intellectual disabilities and produces characteristic facial features. Some disorders occur only in males or only in females because the defect is contained in the chromosome that determines gender; others involve genes from both the father and mother. See Chapter 11 for more information about genetically caused disorders.

Investigating the link between genes and temperament

Most folks understand that genes strongly influence physical characteristics, but you may not know that genes also help determine people's temperament. *Temperament* refers to general patterns of emotional and behavioral responses that can be detected in infancy and sometimes continue into adulthood. These patterns appear to be strongly influenced by genetics, although other factors may modify them.

How do we know that genes influence temperament? Numerous studies have demonstrated that emotional and behavioral patterns show up early. They also show that even when identical twins are raised apart by different parents, they tend to have the same temperament style.

Researchers have identified three temperaments in particular:

- ✔ **Easy:** Infants with this temperament style usually are in good moods, sleep regularly, eat normally, and adapt to new experiences readily. Parents find them easy to take care of.

- ✔ **Difficult:** These babies cry and fuss a lot. They don't have regular, predictable sleep patterns; they awaken more than other infants do, and they aren't easy to soothe when they're upset. Parents know when they have a baby with a difficult temperament, because the infant is stressed and stressful to take care of.

> ✔ **Slow to warm up:** These babies are less active than easy or difficult babies, shy, and withdrawn. They take a while to adjust to changes but eventually adapt.

Not all infants are easily categorized into easy, difficult, and slow to warm up. Some may shift from one category to another from time to time. Others seem to have some characteristics from more than one category.

If you're the caregiver for a baby with a difficult temperament, that pattern isn't your fault. You may be able to do some things to help improve your baby's long-term outcome, but the difficult temperament isn't due to your poor parenting; it's more likely the result of the influence of unfolding genes. Conversely, if you're lucky enough to have an easy infant, you can't take all the credit!

See Chapter 4 for information about other factors that also contribute to babies' behavior and development.

Putting genetic predispositions in perspective

Genes can create predispositions, but environment can also have a strong or weak influence. Intelligence, depression, anxiety, impulsivity, aggression, and happiness are all states or traits that are influenced by genes but modified by experience. (The following section, "Emphasizing Experience," tells you more.)

Because so many people struggle with obesity, weight is a good example of this effect. Research on the ways that genes influence weight is still in its infancy, but several studies of twins — identical and fraternal, living apart and living together — indicate that obesity is caused, at least in part, by genetic influences. These tendencies may relate to factors such as how food is metabolized in the body and how appetite is controlled.

To see how genetics and environment interact in children, consider four girls who inherited a genetic tendency for obesity, but had different environments that interacted with that inherited tendency:

> ✔ **Annabelle:** Annabelle, age 15, weighed 9 pounds at birth. As a toddler, she appeared solid and a bit chunky, but the doctor didn't worry. She continued to be on the heavy side and put on excess pounds as an adolescent.

✔ **Brenda:** Brenda, age 14, also inherited a genetic tendency to be over-weight. However, in addition, she had a genetic predisposition to be hyperactive. She couldn't seem to hold still. When she sat, her legs bounced up and down, and her hands fidgeted continually. Because of her increased activity, Brenda ate about the same amount as Annabelle but remained thin throughout childhood. Her genetic tendency toward obesity was canceled by the influence of her hyperactivity genes.

✔ **Candice:** Candice, age 17, was born 10 weeks prematurely with the same genetic tendency for obesity as the other examples. However, due to prematurity, she weighed a little less than 3 pounds at birth. Her worried parents were told that she must remain in the hospital until she gained weight and became physically stronger. During her first few years, Candice was sickly, a picky eater, and somewhat underweight. Her family constantly encouraged her to eat. She continued to stay underweight until she reached puberty, when she developed a hearty appetite and couldn't stay away from carbohydrates. As a teen, she started to look pudgy.

✔ **Dianna:** Dianna, age 14, had a genetic predisposition to become over-weight. She was a solid and somewhat overweight child. Her parents spoiled her. Unfortunately, Dianna's mother, herself morbidly obese, had a severe heart attack when Dianna was 10 years old. The doctors explained to the family that her mother's extra weight and lack of exer-cise certainly contributed to her serious health problems. Dianna, now 14 and terrified of losing her mother, begins to restrict her food intake and loses weight rapidly. It's possible that Dianna could overreact and develop an eating disorder (see Chapter 14).

Emphasizing Experience

From the minute they're born, babies observe the world. They learn through sight, smell, touch, and exploration, and they learn from what the world does to them. They start out with a set of genes and a brain that's prewired to explore, make associations, and acquire knowledge. In fact, sometimes brain function itself may unfold rather differently depending upon the types of experiences encountered by the infant in its first few years of life.

The developing brain is inherently designed to explore and acquire informa-tion about the world. The three major ways that kids learn are

✔ **Modeling and observational learning:** Modeling and observational learning refer to the process of acquiring information from what chil-dren see in the world around them. Children observe parents, siblings, peers, and even fictional characters on computers and television. They also explore and observe how things happen and work, such as how to find balls that roll behind couches and how milk spills out of a cup. They learn specific social skills, and they see what actions result in good or bad outcomes.

- **Classical conditioning:** Classical conditioning refers to learning that occurs by associating the emotional response to one event with another event that occurs at about the same time. The human brain is designed to make associations between events. An infant readily associates the sight of a baby bottle with alleviation of hunger, for example, so just looking at a baby bottle may quell distress for a while. Also, many fears are acquired through classical conditioning. If a child slips and falls in a bathtub, she may develop a fear of taking baths.

  Interestingly, some fears appear to be prewired, requiring no learning at all. Thus, infants appear to be innately fearful of heights, snakes, and loud noises.

- **Operant conditioning:** *Operant conditioning* is a general term that describes how consequences influence later actions and behaviors. In a nutshell, behaviors that are rewarded usually start increasing in frequency, and those that are ignored or punished, or that result in a loss of a reward, usually decrease in frequency. See Chapters 8 and 9 for more information about how operant conditioning works with kids.

All types of experiences affect the manner in which genes ultimately express themselves, including the influence of parents or caregivers, health, unanticipated events, and plain dumb luck (both good and bad). We discuss this topic in the following section.

Note to teachers, parents, and caregivers: You can make a big difference in the way kids turn out, but it's not all up to you.

Recognizing the experiences provided by caregivers

Parents and caregivers provide crucial experiences that help determine what happens with any given genetic tendency. The good news is that even with genetic challenges, kids can still turn out well.

To see how different approaches to parenting can affect development, consider a hypothetical child named Gary, placed with two different sets of parents. In each scenario, Gary is assumed to carry the same genotype (genetic code) but turns out quite differently (phenotype) due to having different experiences.

No two babies with different sets of parents can possibly have identical genetic code, so our example is obviously fictional!

Both versions of Gary are born healthy but start out fussy and irritable due to a genetically determined difficult temperament (refer to "Investigating the link between genes and temperament," earlier in this chapter). Unknown to the parents, both versions' fathers passed on the genetic potential to develop a severe reading problem called dyslexia.

> **Gary Version 1** was born to teenage parents. His dad dropped out of school and worked to support his unexpected family; he made minimum wage, earning barely enough to feed the family, and hated his job. His mother stayed at home with Gary, bitter and depressed about losing her freedom. Overwhelmed by their responsibilities, the parents argued a lot. Gary, a baby with a difficult temperament, added to the chaos. Gary spent many hours in front of a television set, watching videos over and over because his parents used the television as a surrogate babysitter. He continued to be fussy and demanding, and as he entered kindergarten, he had frequent temper tantrums.

> **Gary Version 2** was born to parents in their early 30s who desperately wanted a baby. Gary was fussy and needed a lot of attention. Although sometimes tired of his inability to settle down, his parents found ways to comfort him. He eventually calmed down when swaddled and rocked. Gary's parents read books to him every night after he was born. Gary attended preschool and seemed to be bright and happy. He learned to control his temper and looked well prepared for school.

Both versions of Gary received reasonable love, nutrition, clothing, and shelter, but by the time they enrolled in school, they were in very different places. Gary Version 1 was ill prepared for the classroom, whereas Gary Version 2 was ready to learn. Recall that both hypothetical Garys had the same genetic code. We continue the story of the two Garys in the next section.

Examining education

Many factors continue to influence kids beyond their genetic code and their first few years of life. Schools and neighborhoods stand out. Sometimes, parents can influence the selection of schools or neighborhoods, although admittedly, that's not always possible. Economics, circumstances, options, and luck vary from one family to another.

In this section, we return to our two versions of Gary from the preceding section and show you what happens when they enter school.

Gary Version 1 runs into some luck. His now-single mother is admitted to a special vocational program at the local university, and the university's education department offers an advanced school and day-care program for teacher training and research purposes. The teachers immediately recognize that Gary struggles to identify letters and sounds and that he gives up too easily. They design an individualized plan for addressing these concerns as well as his behavioral problems. Gary thrives; by the end of first grade, he's reading at second grade level, and his self-control has improved.

Gary Version 2 attends his neighborhood school. He's cheerful and bright verbally but doesn't seem to be very interested in learning to read. His teacher isn't concerned because he's so socially skillful and active. At the parent/teacher conference, she tells Gary's parents not to worry, because boys are often delayed in reading. By the end of the school year, Gary has memorized a few words but cannot sound out the first-grade reading list. The teacher encourages his parents to continue to read to him but still expresses no serious concern.

Interestingly, Gary Version 1 began his education ill prepared, but his learning accelerated rapidly when he started attending a great school. Gary Version 2 arrived at school better prepared, but he languished because the teachers failed to notice his reading problems.

The two versions of Gary still have many possible outcomes in the ensuing years. Schooling really matters. So does early detection of learning problems. And, of course, parents matter too. See Chapters 8, 9, and 12 for more information about parenting, education, and learning disabilities.

Peeking at peers

As they grow, children's experience expands beyond the home into the neighborhood and the playground, so the kids who live next door or down the street and attend the same school exert considerable influence on the developing child. How well children get along with their peers greatly affects their self-concept and happiness. Children can be terrific companions for one another; unfortunately, they can also be cruel tormentors. A nice neighborhood is no guarantee that the children who live next door are nice kids. One bully can ruin a childhood.

Children discover moral values first from their families but later from their friends. Especially after they start school, most kids try to be like other kids. Fitting in with a peer group becomes increasingly important over time and sometimes conflicts with values learned at home. See Chapters 6 and 7 for more information about the role of peers in child development.

Absorbing the truth about health and nutrition

Life is full of potential dangers, such as bacteria, viruses, toxins, and physical accidents, which can cause anything from minor bumps in the road to life-threatening conditions for children. Furthermore, children's physical health affects their development in myriad ways over time. Children with chronic diseases face unusual stressors and challenges, some of which have enduring psychological effects even if the physical condition clears later. (See Chapter 11 for more information about chronic illness and kids.)

Women who are pregnant or even considering the possibility of pregnancy should be up to date on their immunizations and mindful of their general health, in part because much of an infant's immune system depends on what the infant receives from the mother during pregnancy.

Poor nutrition during pregnancy, infancy, or childhood can prevent children from reaching their true genetic potential because brains need good nutrition to develop normally. Children without adequate, balanced diets are at increased risk of having learning problems. In addition, both younger and older children who arrive at school hungry are likely to focus more on their hunger than on their lessons.

Height is also affected by nutrition, even though it's usually thought to be largely determined by genetics. In fact, the average heights of men and women have increased over the past few centuries in most countries because of improved nutrition. Interestingly, two countries with similar genetic backgrounds have witnessed the evolution of huge differences in height: Today, South Korean men are about 4½ inches taller than North Korean men. This remarkable difference is attributable to the greater affluence and improved diet of South Koreans compared with those of North Koreans.

Understanding the influence of unexpected events

Most people cling to the idea that kids become what they become because of a combination of their genetic potential; the environments they grow up in; the parenting they receive; and their own individual efforts, with substantial emphasis on the individual-effort part of the equation. The roles played by unexpected environmental events and luck are often given short shrift. The following sections point out how much these other factors influence ultimate outcomes.

Trying to make sense of trauma

Unfortunately, traumatic events happen to kids and their families. Car accidents, domestic violence, serious injuries, and natural disasters can occur at any time. If such traumas occur in the first year or two of life, the impact on a child may be variable and more difficult to measure. In any event, traumatic events after the first few years of life (and probably before) can exert powerful, enduring effects on children in various ways. (See Chapter 16 for more information about the effects of trauma and abuse on kids.)

The ten leading causes of death in infants and young children include drowning, motor-vehicle accidents, falls, choking, and ingesting poisons. If you care for children regularly, be sure to make your car, home, classroom, and general environment as safe as possible. No one can provide 100 percent security, but do all that you can.

See the U.S. Consumer Product Safety Commission's Web site at www.cpsc.gov for more information about childproofing environments and avoiding unsafe products.

Delving through the impact of divorce

Divorce is an unfortunate reality in almost 40 percent of households with children younger than 18. Most studies find that the effects of divorce on children are negative, especially in the first year following the divorce. Problems may be caused by parental conflict and unhappiness as opposed to the divorce per se, however, so some studies suggest that those who put off divorce "for the sake of the children" may cause as much stress and harm to their kids as those who choose divorce.

The bottom line? If you have a marriage with problems, try to seek marital therapy to improve the relationship. Your kids will probably profit and thrive if you succeed. If counseling doesn't work, it's important to work on letting your kids know that your marital problems aren't their fault and to make any transition as conflict-free as possible. Children do best when both of their parents stay involved in their lives and cooperate in parenting. Sometimes, help from a mental health professional can assist in this process.

Looking at luck, chance, and circumstance

The order in which you happen to be born seems to have some influence on how you turn out. Most presidents of the United States, for example, were firstborn sons or firstborn children. The oldest child of a family tends to be slightly more successful, studious, eager to please, and conscientious than his or her siblings. On the downside, they may also be a tad more fearful and stressed than their younger siblings, who tend to be a bit more relaxed, flexible, and innovative.

Packing up and moving on

Lots of families have to move their households due to circumstances of all sorts — sometimes, quite often. Parents may change jobs, go away for educational opportunities, change relationships, or get transferred by the military or another employer. Such moves are often viewed as representing exciting opportunities.

Moving creates special stresses for children, however. In an article, *Residential Mobility, Well-Being, and Mortality*, by Shigehiro Oishi and Ulrich Schimmack (published in 2010 in the *Journal of Personality and Social Psychology*), the authors discuss research indicating — that kids whose families move frequently perform more poorly in school and exhibit increased behavioral problems as compared to children who do not move frequently. Their study looked at a sample of over 7,000 American adults that they followed over a decade. They found that those adults who experienced frequent moves as children were less happy and had more psychological problems than adults who had moved less frequently during childhood. Interestingly, the frequent movers were also more likely to die early. The researchers ruled out the effects of age, gender, education levels, and race in these findings. They speculated that the impact of moving was largely due to stress and lack of social ties which has been shown in many studies to have very deleterious effects on health, learning, and adjustment.

It's difficult to isolate any given factor from other possible influences. For example, some research suggests that birth order effects may be at least partially a result of overall family size. Thus, many first born children are also only children. So it may be that smaller family size accounts for some of the apparent benefits of being a first born child.

The month in which a child is born can also make a difference. The oldest children to start school (usually, those born in the fall) are often developmentally more mature than those who are almost a year younger. Thus, the older kids tend to be a bit more successful in those early years, and their success is rewarded with praise and attention. These kids often get advanced work, which makes the gap even greater.

Moreover, the particular decade or year in which a child is born matters. If you were born during the baby boom (1946–1964), you encountered overcrowded classrooms and more competition than people born in other times. Boomers who wanted to attend graduate school had to compete against a much larger pool of applicants. Another example of how the year you happen to be born in matters can be found in those young adults who graduated from college at the start of the Great Recession that began in 2008. A couple of years either out of the job market or at a job below one's potential can profoundly affect later success.

Too many people in one place

Dr. Gary Evans, an environmental psychologist at Cornell University, has made a career of studying the effects of early-childhood environments on kids. He has discovered that high *density* — the number of people per room in a child's home — exerts a wide range of damaging influences on children. According to Evans, children raised in high-density homes tend to become overstimulated and withdrawn, demonstrating increased psychological and behavioral distress, along with declining motivation and achievement. Furthermore, the parents in these environments tend to be less responsive to their kids and to talk with them less often than parents do in low-density homes. Interestingly, income level of these families does not appear to make a lot of difference because these findings still held even when the researchers statistically removed the effects of income.

Noise, which often accompanies crowded living environments, appears to exert a similar influence on kids. High-noise environments seem to cause lower cognitive development, reading scores, and delayed speech. Blood pressure and stress hormones tend to go up as well. Studies have demonstrated that these effects heighten following the opening of airports near a child's home. (The next time you think about buying a home right next to a busy freeway, think again.)

Can parents do anything about these effects? Fortunately, yes. They can work hard to reduce noise levels, have their kids spend some time in quiet places such as libraries and parks, and even use earplugs if need be. They can also attempt to engage with their children more actively. Finally, the more they use the parenting techniques discussed in Chapter 8, the more they may soften the blows inflicted by crowding and excessive noise.

Considering Class and Culture

A family's social and economic class significantly affects a child's physical and mental health. Poor children are more likely to suffer from lack of adequate medical care, poor neighborhoods, inadequate schools, crime, and poor nutrition than kids from middle-class families do. These burdens aren't insurmountable, but they do pose a significant barrier to optimal development.

In addition, it's important to realize that some of our most cherished beliefs and attitudes about child rearing are just that — beliefs, not facts, and beliefs that vary widely from one culture to another. Cultures share values, customs, foods, and expectations. Experts talk about different types of culture based on ethnicity, location, religion, age, and gender; lots of people belong to more than one cultural group.

Cultures may profess widely differing attitudes about child-rearing practices. In some cultures, for example, parents carry infants on their backs for many months; other cultures encourage babies to actively explore their environments as early as possible. Interestingly, babies brought up in both types of cultures start walking at about the same age — usually around 12 months.

Experts and parents debate the pros and cons of such cultural differences, but no one really knows what the "right" approach is. One of the loudest debates has occurred over the issue as to whether babies should sleep in their parents' bed and for how long. Cultural differences also occur in regard to degree of competitiveness versus cooperativeness encouraged in children, the use of spanking, and ideas about expected chores and responsibilities for kids and teens. Whatever culture kids grow up in, they do best when they feel loved, appreciated, and supported.

Blending Influences Together

Over time, opinions about what makes kids tick have swung in a wide arc. During some periods, experts have proclaimed that genes largely determine how kids turn out; at other times, scientists have pictured kids as blank slates upon which almost anything could be written. Today, most child psychologists believe that biological, psychological, cultural, social, and chance circumstances interact to create the unique characteristics of each child, and that the degree to which each of those factors influences a particular child can never been known with any degree of certainty.

You may want to think of kids as being like different types of plants. Right now, for example, we're (once again) trying to grow some tomatoes in our backyard, which is in a Southwestern desert. As you know, tomatoes need lots of water, protection from rabbits and excessive wind, fertilizer, and sun. We've got the sun part covered; the rest is a challenge. When we do manage to harvest a fine, plump homegrown tomato, nothing tastes better. Some kids are like our tomato plants; they need lots of specialized attention and care.

Other kids are more like the ubiquitous tumbleweeds in our region. Tumbleweeds don't need fertilizer; they can grow with little water; rabbits don't bother them much; and the wind merely helps them spread their seeds. It's not that soil, rain, wind, and sunshine don't matter, but tumbleweeds can thrive under a wide range of conditions. Kids with an easy temperament (refer to "Investigating the link between genes and temperament," earlier in this chapter) are rather like tumbleweeds. They do well with relatively little care and a variety of parenting styles. They can survive many hardships and challenges.

Whether a particular child is more like a tomato plant or a tumbleweed is largely a genetically determined issue, but all the other factors discussed in this chapter (parenting, culture, luck, nutrition, and so on) affect how things turn out after that. Given that multiple factors interact to influence child development, what does that mean in terms of caring for children? In other words, who is responsible for how a child turns out — good, bad, or in between? Many clients have asked us that question over the years. They've wondered whether they take the blame for failure or credit for success.

To find the answer to that question, just review the contents of this chapter! Consider the multiple influences that converge to direct kids' development. You can't possibly isolate one factor as being predominant over others. Yet that's what many parents try to do when they blame the second-grade teacher, a grandfather, the neighborhood, or even their own parenting for a difficult child.

Teachers, parents, and caregivers usually do the best they can. Even if they do everything to absolute perfection, though, they still can't claim all the credit or all the blame. Just remember to "water" the kids in your care — and good luck!

Chapter 3

Goals of Growing Up

. . . .

In This Chapter

▶ Looking at love and affection

▶ Exploring patience

▶ Calming down

▶ Seeing the self

▶ Getting ahead

. . . .

*I*f you're reading this book, it's likely that you're already a grownup (or close to it). Take a minute right now and ask yourself what the people who helped rear you did to help you along the way. You probably got enough to eat as a kid. Furthermore, you probably had a roof over your head, clothes to wear, and basic medical care. Ideally, you also got a little bit more, like love and attention, education, and support.

Most new parents, when asked what they hope for their child's future, say something like "We want our child to be happy and successful." How do parents and all the others involved in a child's life help a child achieve the goals of happiness and success?

In this chapter, we discuss four tasks or goals of growing up — tasks that, when successfully accomplished, result in an overall sense of satisfaction and well-being. These four tasks are

✔ Discovering how to relate to others

✔ Mastering self-control

✔ Acquiring balanced views of oneself

✔ Finding meaning through accomplishments and education

Although we discuss these tasks separately, please realize that they are intricately interconnected. Thus, problems mastering tasks in one area tend to spill over into other areas.

Attaching to Others

Adults who have partners overwhelmingly report enjoying both better health and greater happiness than those who do not have a committed relationship. Humans are social beings, and we do better overall with good connections and social support, at least some of which often comes from marriage or committed partners. Networks of friends and the general community also contribute to happiness.

The ability to form these attachments begins in infancy. Early on, children show different ways of relating to other people. Some kids are comfortable relating with their peers; others are anxious and withdrawn; some are angry and avoidant; still others show chaotic ways of relating. These ways of relating — often referred to as *attachment patterns* or *relationship styles* — are caused by a mix of genes and the environment (nature and nurture).

Relationship styles are relatively stable from early childhood through adulthood, although they can change. An inhibited, shy 4-year-old is likely to remain somewhat shy throughout his life, and an outgoing, fearless 2-year-old probably will show a propensity to take risks and be an extrovert later in life, but neither of these outcomes is a given. Experiences, therapy, a relationship (whether good or bad), learning, and parenting style may also affect what happens to relationship styles.

Looking at loving attachments

Finding out how to have a loving, intimate relationship begins early in life. Babies naturally turn to their primary caregiver for nurturance, support, and a sense of safety. When the baby's needs are met effectively, the bond between parent and child usually develops smoothly. This close bond sets the stage for relating well to others over time.

On the other hand, attachment between baby and parent sometimes goes awry, due to health problems (such as unexpected separations due to prolonged hospitalization of mother or baby), genetic influences (such as temperament styles), or parenting styles that don't fit the child very well. Children with disturbed attachment styles may struggle with peers and other relationships later in life. They may have trouble trusting others, feel fearful in new relationships, avoid other kids, or act aggressively with little or no provocation.

In the first few months of life, babies need to feel safe and secure. As a caregiver, you can foster development of secure attachment by attending to their needs promptly and sensitively. It's almost impossible to spoil a baby.

Finding friendships

By the age of 3 or 4, children start forming friendships with one another. Making friends with other kids contributes a lot to a child's ultimate sense of well being and happiness. Children establish friendships most readily when they've had a secure, loving bond with their parents or other close caregivers first.

Children with good friends have fewer mental-health problems. Friendships teach kids how to trust, give them perspective on how they stack up in the world, teach them how to obtain help when they need it, and much more. Friends also teach the skills needed for later, intimate relationships.

Try to help toddlers and preschoolers find friends. Facilitate play dates, visits to the park, preschool, and other opportunities for interacting with kids their own age. Start early. Be active and involved in these early relationships. Kids need instruction about how to be nice. It's good to be explicit with kids at this age — to tell them "Be gentle," "Take turns with your toys," and "Stop whining," for example.

Getting along with others skillfully

Much of life involves interacting with people. Those who know how to get along with store clerks, teachers, neighbors, and (later) bosses thrive. All such relationships require a set of *social skills* — skills needed for relating with people — that must be mastered as a child. Although this type of social relationship may be more superficial than friendships, intimate relationships, or family bonds, mastering the skills needed for these connections makes life easier and helps a person get what he or she needs.

Kids first find out about social skills by observing, modeling, and receiving direct instructions from their parents. If things go well, kids usually master basic skills like saying "please" and "thank you" in their first couple of years of life. Shy, withdrawn kids may have a harder time learning social skills than easygoing, extraverted kids do, but all children can benefit from acquiring these abilities. See Chapters 5, 6, 9, and 13 for more information about how and when children develop social skills and what goes wrong when they experience problems relating to others.

Teach children basic social skills such as politeness. Don't let kids interrupt, and tell them why they shouldn't. Let them know when they are doing good things socially, and correct them when they don't. Give them specific feedback, such as "I liked it when you shared your toy with Bobbie" or "When I'm on the telephone and you're talking to me, I can't hear what the other person is saying; please don't do that."

Controlling Impulses and Emotions

Babies arrive in this world with virtually no ability to regulate their impulses and emotions. If they're hungry, they cry. If they feel pain, they cry. They cry when they're tired and cry when they're wet. They don't ponder these responses; neither do they delay them. But why should they? It's not like they can do much to help themselves out of their distressing predicaments. Babies depend completely on their caregivers to meet their needs and alleviate their distress.

Even during the first few months of life, however, babies can sometimes be distracted for a few moments while they're waiting to be fed, and they can figure out how to soothe themselves when they're upset by sucking on a pacifier or thumb. These early forms of self-regulation are more likely to progress when babies get their basic needs met.

The twin abilities of postponing gratification and controlling the expression of emotions are pillars for later adjustment and happiness. Parents, teachers, and members of the community can either thwart or foster the development of these abilities. As children mature, they have more opportunities to improve self-control. They discover how to calm themselves down when they feel frustrated. They come to understand that delaying their initial impulses often pays off for them.

In the next section, we explore how learning to delay gratification and regulate emotional expression provide a sound foundation for children's well-being and happiness.

Taming the need for instant gratification

Much of what leads to trouble for both kids and adults involves difficulty in putting off short-term pleasure for longer-term gains. What kid will turn down candy just because it may later cause cavities or extra pounds? How many adolescents have succumbed to peer pressure and consumed alcohol, tobacco, or drugs? The short-term fear of rejection, perhaps combined with the pleasure of indulging, too often wins out over good sense and awareness of long-term consequences such as addiction or trouble with the law.

Hundreds of studies of children from a variety of cultures and backgrounds have demonstrated convincingly that kids who figure out how to resist temptations, tolerate frustration, and delay gratification do far better in the long run. These studies (many of which followed children for a decade or more) have shown that preschoolers who already possess the skills of tolerating frustration and delaying gratification later in life become better students, have more friends, get along better with others, score higher on the Scholastic Aptitude Test, earn more money, have fewer psychological problems, maintain a healthier body weight, and report greater happiness than kids without this ability.

It's difficult to think of any other psychological competency that has this power to predict success, achievement, and well-being. What's especially fascinating about this research is that this ability can be measured as early as the age of 4 or 5, and its influence perseveres into adulthood. You may be able to train kids to delay gratification as they get older, but we recommend getting started early.

To teach kids how to delay gratification, make them delay gratification. Consistently instruct kids by saying things like the following:

- ✔ "First, eat your vegetables; then you can have dessert."
- ✔ "We have to clean up before we can watch that movie."
- ✔ "After you do your homework, you can go outside."
- ✔ "I know you want that toy, but I don't have extra money this week. We'll have to save for it."

Think of teaching self-control as being like developing muscles. The more times you practice lifting weights, the stronger you get. Give kids lots of opportunities to learn self-control. They may not like it in the short run, but they will profit enormously over time.

Calming emotions

Newborns have the capacity to show contentment and distress — and that's about it. By the second year of life, they both feel and communicate the full range of emotions, including curiosity, happiness, distress, anger, fear, sadness, disgust, and surprise.

An important task of childhood is learning how to bring emotions under reasonable control. Children who cannot manage their emotions are likely to experience problems with teachers, parents, and other kids. They get dirty looks from waiters at restaurants when they melt down. Their parents feel annoyed and embarrassed by their behavior. Overly emotional kids are less popular with other kids and teachers, so they receive lots of negative feedback, which only adds to their negative emotions.

Teaching kids how to manage their emotions should start early — as soon as they're able to understand and follow directions, which usually happens by or before the second birthday. The following general principles are consistent across age groups:

✔ Validate or empathize with the emotion itself. You might tell the child, "I see that you're upset," "He must have hurt your feelings," or even "Your knee must really hurt after that fall."

✔ If a child is clearly physically or emotionally hurt, always take a few minutes to comfort and soothe him. Just be careful not to fall for trivial, manipulative attempts to obtain comfort that are based on little or no real injury

✔ Give the child an alternative response. You might suggest that she take a few deep breaths or count slowly from 1 to 20.

✔ If the child doesn't calm down quickly, remove him from the situation for a time-out. You can give legitimate, physical hurts a little longer, but even those injuries shouldn't be used as an excuse for prolonged crying and whining. (See Chapter 8 for more information about time-outs.)

✔ Model calm yourself by not getting angry or upset.

✔ Never, ever give into tantrums!

✔ Talk in a calm, gentle voice (although you can be firm if need be).

✔ Reward or praise successes when a child manages to calm herself down more quickly than usual.

✔ After the incident, when the child is perfectly calm, discuss the situation, and offer ways to cope better in the future.

Developing a Self-View

Through the first year of life, infants develop an awareness of themselves as being separate from the rest of the world. They slowly acquire knowledge about themselves: their likes and dislikes, their skills, and how their bodies work. As they develop further, they begin to evaluate themselves, which results in what's called *self-esteem* or *self-worth*.

Self-esteem involves three aspects:

✔ **Awareness:** Children become aware that they have some quality, such as being a child who walks, runs, swims, sings, or talks; someone who has brown eyes, red hair, a twin brother, a wagon, and a bright blue shirt; or someone who knows how to read.

✔ **Evaluation:** Children ask themselves various questions ("Is my blue shirt beautiful or ugly? Do I run fast or slowly? Am I a good reader or a bad one?") to evaluate their awareness. These evaluations or appraisals can be positive, negative, or in between.

✔ **Emotional reaction to the evaluation:** Children react to their evaluations by asking further questions (such as "How do I *feel* about being a fast or slow runner, a good or bad reader, or owning a bright blue shirt? Is being a fast runner important to me? Does having a blue shirt make me feel great or embarrassed?"). The emotional part of self-esteem is the most critical part, and it's also where trouble brews.

Looking at healthy versus unhealthy self-esteem

Most parents and teachers believe that children should feel good about themselves — in other words, have positive self-esteem. Well, we believe that too — to a point. Positive self-esteem, if overemphasized, can actually cause harm. Are we saying that children should have low self-esteem? Absolutely not. Low self-esteem has been associated with depression and all sorts of problems. Overly positive self-views, however, can get in the way of being healthy and happy just as much as overly negative self-views do.

In the following sections, we look at two types of unhealthy self-esteem and one type of healthy self-esteem.

Curbing overly positive self-esteem

Yes, kids can think too highly of themselves. Generally speaking, kids who think highly of themselves are thought of highly by their peers, but that's not always the case. Kids who think they belong at the very top of the totem pole aren't always viewed favorably by other kids, and numerous research studies have demonstrated that when so-called high self-esteem inflates too much, a host of problems start emerging. Children with the very highest levels of self-esteem tend to be more aggressive, violent, and demeaning of others. They're also hypervigilant and overly sensitive to criticism. Thus, they seem to lose flexibility in responding to various events in the world. Criticism, failure, or frustration send them into a tailspin.

If you've read one or more of the hundreds of books written on the importance of promoting positive self-esteem in kids, you may be surprised that it's possible to take the concept too far. But kids who score the highest on self-esteem measures would likely endorse statements similar to the following:

✔ "I rarely, if ever, feel poorly about myself."

✔ "I think I am better than other kids."

✔ "I almost always feel positively about myself."

✔ "Other kids look up to me."

When you look this list of items over, a phrase other than *high self-esteem* may come to mind — something like *narcissism,* perhaps. In fact, narcissism is used to describe those who feel excessive admiration or love for themselves. When self-esteem levels go too high, they morph into narcissism, which psychologists generally agree represents a type of emotional dysfunction — not a desirable trait.

In the story that follows, Logan, a child with overly positive self-esteem, resorts to violence when his self-views are challenged.

> **Logan,** who is 10 years old, looks in the mirror and brushes his hand through his newly highlighted hair. After he begged his mom for weeks, she finally took him to her hairstylist. Logan's mother has trouble saying no. She tries hard to make up for the fact that Logan's father is out of the picture by not setting limits, giving the child anything he wants, and telling him how special he is no matter what he does.
>
> Logan can't wait to get to school. He's already picked out his clothes and shoes. He's hoping to be able to spend some time on the playground before classes start, bragging and showing off his hot new look. He believes that the whole school will be jealous of him.
>
> When Logan arrives at school, one of the fifth-graders notices his hair. "Everyone look at Logan!" he yells. "Logan's turned into a girl!"
>
> A few kids notice and laugh. Logan's face turns bright red. He runs over to the other boy and shoves him, screaming obscenities. The fifth-grader, who is about a foot taller than Logan, shoves him back, laughing. Full of rage, Logan keeps charging at the older boy. A teacher finally pulls him off.
>
> Later, in the school office, Logan is suspended for fighting. His mother must leave work again to pick him up from school. She doesn't understand why Logan gets into so many fights. She does everything she can for him.

You can minimize the risk that kids will develop overly positive self-esteem by not giving them baseless praise for trivial efforts, not giving into their every whim and fancy, and by setting reasonable limits even if they protest.

Encouraging healthy self-esteem

Babies begin to build ideas about themselves by having experiences with other people and by finding out what they can accomplish on their own. If a 6-month-old boy has been reaching for a colorful toy and finally rolls and scoots over to get it, he likely feels pretty powerful. He wanted something, and *through his own efforts*, he was able to get it. Good job!

If, on the other hand, the same boy is whining and crying because the toy is out of reach, and an adult hands it to him, that boy will have missed an opportunity to feel competent and to develop healthy self-esteem. A useful alternative may be for the adult to push the toy a bit closer so it takes a little work, but not out of reach.

Babies and toddlers pretty much consider their needs and wants to be the most important needs and wants in the world. That's perfectly normal. School-age kids with healthy self-esteem, however, start to understand that they may not be the center of the universe. If they're guided by caring adults and experiences, they begin to see that they may excel in some things but not in all things and that effort often means as much as accomplishment. Kids with healthy self-esteem value their talents and positive qualities but are able to accept their weaknesses and foibles. They see themselves as human beings, neither inherently better nor worse than others.

Mia's story illustrates how someone with a disability can still develop healthy self-esteem.

> The teacher hands **Mia** last week's spelling test with "65%" written in red across the top. "Darn," Mia says, "and I studied all week for that test. Oh, well, at least I got more than half right, and I'll probably get 100 percent on my math test." Mia's teacher smiles and tells her that she's proud of her attitude and effort.
>
> Mia has dyslexia, a reading disorder that also includes problems with spelling. Her parents and teachers have explained to her that her disability will make it tougher for her to spell as well as other kids in her class, but she still needs to study for tests.
>
> Mia keeps working on spelling and, with extra help and practice, has shown considerable improvement. Her self-esteem is balanced. She understands that like everyone else, she has both strengths and weaknesses.

Adults can help children maintain healthy self-esteem by praising efforts, not results. Don't worry too much about getting the words right; just try to reserve praise for *meaningful* attempts to achieve a goal.

Healthy children learn that they are important, but so are other things. This understanding may be aided by exposing children to spirituality, morality, environmental concerns, or social causes. Helping children see that they're part of a bigger universe adds meaning to their lives and keeps their self-esteem at a healthy level.

Avoiding deflated self-esteem

Low self-esteem is bad for kids. Children who view themselves poorly tend to achieve somewhat less in school. They're more prone to depression and anxiety. They're rejected by their peers more often than their classmates with healthy self-esteem. They feel inadequate, and that sense of inadequacy is too often reinforced by others who give them negative feedback. They're unable to respond to the varying demands of the world in a flexible manner. They focus on and magnify their weaknesses and negative traits while being unable to accept that they also have strengths.

In the following example, Evan's low self-esteem is largely due to lack of parental involvement.

> **Evan,** who is 6 years old, yearns for attention. He has an older sister and a younger sister. His parents spend most of their time working, watching videos, or yelling at the kids to behave. Evan has come to believe — with pretty good reason — that the only time he gets attention is when he's in trouble. He comes to believe that he's less deserving than other kids and that his parents love his sisters more than they love him. He feels empty and deprived.
>
> Today, the family is grocery shopping. As usual, the girls are whining and complaining about getting cookies or candy. Evan trails behind the others, head down, looking at the lower shelves. He notices a brightly colored pack of gum at eye level. Suddenly, he grabs the gum and puts it in his pocket. He smiles, feeling a bit better. No one has noticed.

Evan is on an early path to finding a negative self-image. He desperately tries to fill the void with excitement. Children who shoplift or steal at young ages often suffer from low self-esteem.

You can help kids avoid developing low self-esteem by paying appropriate attention to them. In addition, it's good to give them tasks that are challenging yet within their reach. When they fail, it's important not to criticize harshly, but to praise their efforts as well as provide corrective feedback. Finally, it helps if their caregivers also have healthy self-esteem. If you have problems with low self-esteem, work on it with a mental-health professional, and you'll do a better job of helping kids do the same.

Exploring the real problem: Self-absorption

When self-esteem gets out of balance, whether it's too low or too high, kids focus excessively on themselves. They worry about having to maintain their inflated self-views in the face of criticism, or they dwell on every single mistake. In both cases, they ruminate about themselves. Psychologists refer to rumination about the self as *self-absorption,* and literature strongly suggests that self-absorption contributes significantly to all types of emotional dysfunction.

When kids focus on helping others, they become less self-absorbed. Consider encouraging children whom you care about to volunteer in their communities.

Enhancing Education

People often think of education as beginning with school, but education begins with the first experiences and continues for a lifetime. The best education gives children the ability to adapt to their world, benefit from experience, and live satisfying and meaningful lives. Two forces within children enhance education: intelligence and motivation.

Experts disagree on how much intelligence and motivation are influenced by genetics versus experiences and the environment. Although differences in opinion remain, most professionals agree that both of these variables likely have a genetic component that sets the range, but the child's environment determines where in the range he or she ends up.

Investigating intelligence

Intelligence is complicated, although most people think of intelligence as being something that kids are born with, that can be measured with precision, and that is always beneficial.

Intelligence involves a surprisingly wide range of abilities, including but not limited to the following:

- ✔ Ability to process information rapidly
- ✔ Ability to set goals
- ✔ Abstract reasoning
- ✔ Athletic ability
- ✔ Creativity
- ✔ Common sense
- ✔ Empathy
- ✔ Foresight

- ✔ Flexibility in responding to varying demands
- ✔ Frustration tolerance
- ✔ Impulse control
- ✔ Learning facts and information
- ✔ Logic
- ✔ Mathematical ability
- ✔ Mechanical ability (visual and spatial)
- ✔ Musical ability
- ✔ Skill in communication
- ✔ Skill in relating to other people

Standard intelligence tests measure only a slice of these abilities and don't assess things like musical talent, athletic skill, creativity, and advanced social skills.

Although genetics appear to strongly influence the slice of intelligence measured by intelligence quotient (IQ) tests (as well as other types of intelligence), the environment and experiences can also affect the abilities measured by such tests as well as those that aren't measured.

A child with a very high IQ is not assured of achieving success or happiness, and vice versa. Those with relatively low IQs sometimes achieve both in abundance. Intelligence without mastery of impulses, social skills, motivation, and healthy self-esteem isn't likely to result in happiness, well-being, or even success. (For details on how the goals of growing up work together, see the final section of this chapter, "Inspecting Goal Interactions.")

Mastering motivation

Motivation refers to the extent to which children are able to focus their energies and attention on sustaining certain actions and behaviors to achieve goals. Highly motivated kids persist longer than other kids do and tend to accomplish more, even though they aren't necessarily more intelligent or talented.

If you wonder how to go about getting kids to be motivated, try the following tips:

✔ Teach children that ability and intelligence are traits that aren't entirely chiseled in granite — that persistence and effort will increase their actual abilities.

✔ Praise children for making a good effort rather than for having achieved a successful outcome. Thus, if a child scores well on a test, it's a good idea to say something like "You worked really hard on your studies; that's why you did so well. Good job!"

Avoid praise focused on a child's innate abilities, such as "Great job on that test; you're the smartest kid in the class!" That kind of praise makes kids believe that any failure means that they can't do better, so why try?

Inspecting Goal Interactions

The four goals of childhood — developing secure attachments, acquiring healthy self-esteem, mastering impulses, and enhancing education — all interact. Thus, if kids develop secure attachments with others, they're likely to find it easier to tolerate frustration, because they can lean on their friends for support. If they can tolerate frustration, they will find it easier to focus on studies and pursue their goals relentlessly even when they encounter obstacles. Furthermore, achievements accomplished through hard work and perseverance, lead to healthy self-esteem.

There's no guarantee, however, that a child who meets or exceeds expectations on one or two of these goals won't struggle with one or two of the others. Thus, in Chapters 5, 6, and 7, we discuss what to expect and how to maximize children's abilities to reach these four goals through each major developmental period. By focusing on these goals, parents, teachers, and child-care workers will be able to maximize the chances that children will get where they need to go and have happy, fulfilling lives.

Part II
Watching Kids Grow

The 5th Wave   By Rich Tennant

In this part . . .

We discuss the astonishing changes that occur between conception and the first year of life. We warn prospective parents about avoiding dangerous toxins and show them how to prepare for a healthy pregnancy.

Next, we toddle through preschool, discussing how the growing child learns to communicate and gain foundational skills necessary for later independence. Then we leap into the school years, when kids start making friends and learning self-control. Finally, we lay out the unique challenges of the teenage years, including rebellion, sexuality, and more. Scary stuff.

With the information in this part, readers can be aware of what normal looks like and be on the lookout for trouble. Throughout these chapters we give practical tips on how caregivers can help kids smoothly achieve developmental milestones.

Chapter 4

Pregnancy, Delivery, and the First Year

In This Chapter

▶ Taking a glance at pregnancy

▶ Explaining delivery

▶ Looking at newborns

▶ Seeing what babies can do

Most of the 134 million babies born each year enter the world screaming. The path from a single cell to a human being capable of communicating distress — loudly — is a miraculous process. You may wonder why we include information about prepregnancy, pregnancy, and delivery in a book on child psychology and development. We do so because what happens during this time greatly affects the physical condition of the baby, and anything that affects the physical health of the baby has a great effect on later psychological, emotional, and physical development.

In this chapter, we take you on an incredible journey beginning with the single cell, moving on to the first scream and concluding with the first words at about a year old. We describe normal prenatal development and discuss some of the risks that can negatively affect the developing baby. We spend a few moments looking at delivery and the amazing abilities of newborns. Then we travel through the first year of life, describing developmental milestones and the process of attachment.

Preparing for Pregnancy

If you're a woman who's considering becoming pregnant, you have a few issues to consider *before* attempting to conceive:

- ✔ **Overall health:** First and foremost, you need to assess your overall health. Every day, you should take a multiple vitamin that includes folic acid, because folic acid reduces the risk of miscarriage and helps ensure the proper development of the fetus's brain and spinal cord.

- ✔ **Immunizations:** You need to bring your immunizations up to date, especially those for rubella (sometimes known as German measles), because rubella can cause lots of problems in fetuses, including blindness, deafness, and brain damage.

- ✔ **Substance use:** Refrain from using illegal drugs, smoking, and drinking.

- ✔ **Weight:** If your weight is an issue, try to bring it under control, because excessive thinness or obesity can increase the risk of a problematic pregnancy.

- ✔ **Use of medicines:** Review your prescription and over-the-counter medications carefully with your doctor, as some could cause problems during pregnancy.

- ✔ **Sexually transmitted diseases:** Finally, know whether you have any sexually transmitted diseases, as these can be passed on to the fetus or cause other problems during pregnancy or birth. If you have not been tested for STDs, talk to your doctor about your risks, ideally before you become pregnant.

Zipping from Zygote to Birth

Conception involves the joining of sperm from a male with an egg from a female, forming what's called the *zygote.* When fertilization occurs, the single cell rapidly divides into two distinct masses. The inner cells become the baby, and the outermost cells form the *placenta,* a protective shell surrounding the developing baby. This first stage, which lasts about two weeks, is called the *germinal phase* of pregnancy.

The biggest challenge during the germinal phase is implantation. The growing group of cells needs to attach to the inner lining of the woman's uterus. Surprisingly, an estimated 60 percent of all conceptions never result in successful attachment of the zygote to the uterine wall, ending the pregnancy — often before the woman is aware that she was pregnant.

The time from conception to birth is called *gestation.* Normal pregnancies last about 38 weeks. Because most women don't know the exact day of conception, however, doctors use the first day of the last menstrual cycle as a way to calculate gestational age. For most women, the last menstrual period is actually about 14 days before conception. To address this discrepancy, doctors describe the length of pregnancy as 40 weeks. Our discussion about the development of the embryo and the fetus refers to gestational age as measured from conception.

Seeing normal development in the womb

After successful implantation, the business of growing a baby moves forward quickly. Starting in the third week after conception, the mass of cells, now called an *embryo,* begins to differentiate further.

Between the third and eighth weeks, the embryo forms all the structures that will support an independent living baby, including these three layers:

- ✔ **Ectoderm:** The systems that will come into contact with the outside world such as skin, hair, parts of the eyes, the ears, and the nervous system.
- ✔ **Endoderm:** The digestive system, respiratory system, and glandular system.
- ✔ **Mesoderm:** The muscles, bones, circulatory system, and sex organs.

The time from three weeks to eight weeks is critically important for the normal development of the embryo. It's especially important for pregnant women to live healthy lives and avoid possible toxins during this time. See the later section "Avoiding harmful exposure" for more information.

The embryo becomes a *fetus* nine weeks after conception, and the mother's body begins to show signs of pregnancy. By the end of the third month, the sexual organs of the fetus emerge. The mother detects movements of the fetus by the fourth or fifth month. At the same time, the fetus begins to demonstrate sensitivity to lights and sounds from the external environment. During the last couple of months, the fetus prepares to live apart from the mother's body.

Advances in medical care of premature babies have lowered the stage at which a newborn may be able to survive on its own, also known as the *age of viability.* With state-of-the-art medical care, babies as young as 22 weeks and a little over 1 pound in weight have been known to survive. Before 22 weeks, even with intensive care, most fetuses don't survive. Premature babies that do survive are at risk for cerebral palsy, learning disorders, and other anomalies. (See Chapter 11 for more information about premature babies.)

The last three months of pregnancy are especially important. During this time, every single day that the baby remains in the womb enhances its health and ability to survive.

Checking out the baby

Until relatively recently, pregnant women had no idea what gender the baby was, whether it was healthy, or whether there was more than one baby. In fact, when Laura (one of the authors of this book) became pregnant for the first time more than 30 years ago, she was concerned about her rapid weight gain. At 6 months, her physician sent her to a local hospital for what was then a relatively uncommon test reserved for special circumstances: an ultrasound. This test bounces high-frequency sound waves off the fetus to form an image of the baby — or, in Laura's case, *two* babies.

Today, ultrasound is the most commonly used test in an obstetrics office. It's used to check growth, gender, the amount of amniotic fluid, and the condition of the placenta, as well as to diagnose multiple pregnancy. Ultrasound is considered to be relatively safe and has replaced the use of X-rays.

Here are a few other screenings that may be done during pregnancy:

- ✔ **Blood-chemistry tests:** These tests measure changes in the mother's blood chemistry and (through the umbilical cord) the fetus's blood. They can indicate infections, monitor diabetes, and sometimes detect genetic disorders.

- ✔ **Amniocentesis:** Another test, called amniocentesis, involves withdrawing a small amount of amniotic fluid. This test, usually given after 16 weeks of pregnancy, can help detect genetic, biochemical, and nervous-system disorders. It involves a slight risk of fetal injury, infection, or spontaneous abortion, so the test isn't carried out routinely for healthy mothers.

- ✔ **Chorionic villus sampling (CVS):** This test analyzes cells from the placenta to check for genetic problems. This test can be done earlier than amniocentesis (about 10 weeks) and carries similar risks.

Watching out for danger signs

Unfortunately, things can go wrong during pregnancy, preventing the fetus from making it to full term or causing health problems for mother or baby. Some of the most common concerns include preterm labor, gestational diabetes, and pre-eclampsia. The following sections tell you more.

Preterm labor

Preterm labor occurs when the mother experiences contractions and cervical dilation before 37 weeks of pregnancy. The *cervix* is the lower portion of the uterus that closes to keep the fetus in the uterus until birth; it dilates or widens to allow the baby to be born.

Women are at especially high risk for preterm labor if they smoke; have high blood pressure, gum disease, infections, or diabetes; are obese; are carrying multiple fetuses; suffer from stress; or abuse drugs or alcohol.

Preterm labor can be caused by a host of other medical risk factors, which is why mothers-to-be need excellent prenatal care. Signs of preterm labor include cramping, a gush of fluid from the uterus, backache, pelvic pressure, bleeding, and other discharges. Any of these signs should be reported to a doctor immediately.

Preventive measures for preterm labor include

- ✔ Keeping hydrated
- ✔ Avoiding smoking, alcohol, and nonprescription drugs
- ✔ Keeping regular doctor's appointments
- ✔ Managing high blood pressure
- ✔ Checking and managing diabetes
- ✔ Taking care of teeth
- ✔ Limiting caffeine

If a woman experiences preterm labor, she should be evaluated by a physician. Treatments include bed rest; hydration; medications to stop the labor; and in some cases, *cerclage,* which is one or more stitches sewn into the cervix to prevent it from dilating.

Babies born too early may develop normally. However, they are at greater risks for having physical problems associated with prematurity (see Chapter 11) as well as problems with learning (see Chapter 12).

Gestational diabetes

Gestational diabetes occurs when a woman who did not have diabetes before pregnancy develops insulin resistance, which causes a rise in blood-sugar levels. Gestational diabetes usually occurs after the 20th week of pregnancy and goes away following birth.

The increased blood-sugar levels associated with gestational diabetes pose a risk to both infant and mother. The condition also increases the risk of preeclampsia (see the next section).

Babies born to women with this disorder are often overweight due to excess sugar levels. Sometimes, they are born with low blood sugar or jaundice. Overweight babies are more difficult to deliver and are at greater risk for developing diabetes later in life.

Ectopic pregnancy

Ectopic pregnancy occurs when the fertilized egg implants itself outside the mother's uterus. The signs of an ectopic pregnancy include abdominal pain (usually sharp, stabbing sensations), vaginal bleeding, low blood pressure, dizziness or fainting, and back pain. Ectopic pregnancy occurs in about 2 percent of all pregnancies.

Ectopic pregnancy can threaten the life of the mother and almost always requires surgical or medical intervention. A physician should review any of its symptoms immediately.

A woman's risk factors for gestational diabetes include

✔ Obesity

✔ Age (older than 25)

✔ Family history

Treatment for gestational diabetes includes diet, exercise, and monitoring of blood-sugar levels. Sometimes, medications are also used.

Pre-eclampsia

Pre-eclampsia is characterized by high blood pressure, excess protein in the urine, headaches, blurred vision, abdominal pain, nausea, dizziness, swelling, and decreased urine output. This condition affects 5 percent to 10 percent of all pregnancies and can range from mild to severe.

Complications of pre-eclampsia include decreased blood flow to the placenta, separation of the placenta from the wall of the uterus, elevated liver enzymes, seizures, and cardiovascular damage.

Women are at especially high risk for pre-eclampsia if they

✔ Have a personal or family history of the disorder

✔ Are pregnant for the first time or by a different man than previously

✔ Are carrying two or more babies

✔ Have diabetes

✔ Are obese

✔ Are younger than 20 or older than 40

✔ Have a history of asthma, high blood pressure, migraines, kidney disease, or lupus

✔ Became pregnant many years after a previous pregnancy

Pre-eclampsia is a serious medical condition. Failure to treat it can cause serious consequences for the mother or the baby, including death. Having to deliver a baby before term also increases the risks associated with prematurity. The only effective cure for pre-eclampsia is delivery of the baby. Medications can manage symptoms, and close medical monitoring sometimes allows the pregnancy to proceed long enough for the baby to be born safely.

Limited data suggests that Vitamin D insufficiency may contribute to the development of pre-eclampsia. Taking a Vitamin D supplement may help, but women should always consult a physician before taking any supplements during pregnancy.

Research has shown that pre-eclampsia is more common in women who haven't been with their partners for a long time. Some studies suggest that the reason lies in the reaction of the woman's body to the man's semen. Apparently, repeated exposure to a particular man's semen through sex usually leads to the woman's body becoming desensitized (a reduced immunological reaction) to the effects of the semen. Researchers also believe that this desensitization may occur more readily in women who engage in frequent oral sex and swallow their partners' semen — strange, but apparently true.

Avoiding harmful exposures

At one time, it was widely thought that embryos and fetuses lived in a highly protective environment (in the amniotic fluid surrounded by the placenta), largely shielded from the effects of exposure to chemicals, environmental hazards, drugs, and other harmful agents. Since the 1930s, it's been known that X-rays can have harmful effects on a developing baby, and every decade since has led to discoveries about other agents that can cause similar problems. These external agents are known as *teratogens:* forces, events, or substances not found in nature that can harm the developing embryo or fetus.

The drug thalidomide managed to shatter the belief about fetal imperviousness to external agents in the 1960s. This drug was developed as a mild sedative and was often taken for morning sickness. Tragically, this medication resulted in numerous babies being born with malformed limbs, some of which failed to develop at all.

From the late 1940s through the early 1960s, another unexpected discovery was that diethylstilbestrol (DES) given to prevent miscarriages was actually a teratogen with delayed effects. The daughters of women who were prescribed DES experienced numerous health problems, both upon birth and decades later. These problems included increased risk of vaginal, cervical, and breast cancers; vaginal abnormalities; and problems with pregnancy. In addition, the sons of women who took DES experienced genital-tract abnormalities.

We now know that teratogens cause more infant deaths than any other single cause and account for more than 20 percent of all infant deaths. How much a teratogen affects the fetus depends on the following principles:

- ✔ The genetic makeup of the developing baby affects how, to what degree, and in what ways a particular teratogen will influence development.

- ✔ As the dosage of any particular teratogen increases, its effects on the fetus or embryo usually increase as well.

- ✔ The age at which an embryo or fetus is exposed to a teratogen can greatly affect the nature and severity of the teratogen's effects.

- ✔ Different teratogens can cause malformations, behavioral disorders, death, impaired growth, or cognitive deficits.

- ✔ Teratogens may affect the baby through different routes, such as the mother's bloodstream (through the placenta) or radiation passing through the mother's body.

The range of known teratogens has increased dramatically over the past half century or more. Table 4-1 lists some of the most commonly known teratogens.

Be aware that the list of teratogens in Table 4-1 is not all-inclusive, because new teratogens are being discovered all the time. As a general rule of thumb, women who are planning to become pregnant should consult their physicians and avoid taking any medications that aren't clearly needed for their health. Furthermore, they should avoid exposure to chemicals, paints, and other agents of all types unless absolutely necessary and after a physician has given them the all-clear.

Table 4-1	Common Teratogens
Teratogen	*Possible Effects on Embryo and Fetus*
Legal Substances	
Alcohol	Cognitive impairment, heart problems, facial malformations.
Caffeine	Premature birth, lower birth rate, miscarriage. The data on caffeine are somewhat confusing and mixed, so high consumption (over three cups per day) is generally discouraged.
Tobacco	Retarded growth, prematurity, deformities, increased infant mortality.
Prescription and Over-the-Counter Medications	
Aspirin, ibuprofen	Bleeding, miscarriage, possible cardiovascular problems. These effects are more likely to occur when the medicines are taken in large quantities.
Diethylstilbestrol (DES)	Vaginal abnormalities, vaginal and cervical cancer in females; genital-tract abnormalities in males. This medication is no longer prescribed for pregnant women. It has rarely been prescribed for breast and prostate cancer.
Phenytoin	Retarded growth, facial malformations, heart defects.
Retinoic acid (Retin-A)	Mental retardation, various deformities and malformations, impaired kidney function, neural-tube defects, psychological problems.
Tetracycline	Stained teeth, problems with bone growth.
Thalidomide	Deformed limbs, damage to internal organs, death.
Trimethadione	Growth retardation, developmental delays, irregular teeth, low-set ears, V-shaped eyebrows.
Environmental Agents	
Arsenic	Miscarriage, stillbirth.
Lead	Mental retardation, miscarriage, anemia.
Mercury	Unpredictable mutations, mental retardation, motor problems.
Polychlorinated biphenyls (PCBs)	Retarded growth.
Pesticides	Various cancers, reproductive problems.
Radiation	Impaired physical growth, mental retardation, childhood leukemia, cancers later in life, miscarriage.
Infectious Diseases	
AIDS	Impaired immune function, malformations of various types.
Cytomegalovirus (a common type of herpes virus)	Hearing loss, mental retardation, vision and hearing loss, dental problems.
Rubella	Mental retardation, vision and hearing problems, heart abnormalities, death.
Syphilis	Mental retardation, developmental delays, seizures, death, blindness, deafness.
Toxoplasmosis (a common parasite found in cat feces or soil)	Mental retardation, pneumonia, seizures, hydrocephalus, cerebral palsy.
Varicella virus (chicken pox)	Scarring of the skin, blindness, seizures, mental retardation, low birth weight.

Table 4-1 doesn't include illegal drugs such as heroin, methadone, cocaine, crack, LSD, marijuana, and Ecstasy. Most experts believe that such drugs have a range of teratogenic effects. One problem with knowing exactly how toxic these drugs are to the embryo and fetus is that it's difficult to separate out the fact that those who use such drugs also tend to smoke and consume alcohol more than other mothers do. They also tend to live in more impoverished neighborhoods and have less-than-ideal diets. Nonetheless, consumption of such drugs during pregnancy is widely considered to be a terrible idea (not that it's ever a good one).

So yes, we realize that the list of teratogens is scary, especially when you realize that they could represent hundreds of chemicals, pollutants, and pathogens of all sorts. At the same time, please realize that most pregnancies work out well after they've made it past the first few weeks. Most kids are born reasonably healthy. If you're pregnant or considering becoming pregnant, do what you can to avoid teratogens, but don't become obsessed about these concerns, which can increase your stress levels while doing little to decrease your risk. (Also, we hate to tell you this, but stress itself is a teratogen!)

Discussing Delivery

At a certain point in pregnancy — about 38 weeks after conception — the baby's brain says, "I'm ready to come out." Hormones are released into the mother's bloodstream to alert the muscles in the uterus to start *contracting* — tightening and starting the process of pushing the baby down the birth canal.

Most babies have already changed positions so that their heads are low in the mother's uterus. Labor starts when the mother's contractions become strong and regular (about 5 to 10 minutes apart), and the cervix begins to *dilate,* or open. As labor progresses, contractions become closer together and last longer. The cervix opens to about 4 inches (10 centimeters) to allow the baby's head to pass through safely.

When everything works out right

First-time moms can expect to labor between 12 and 16 hours. Each child after the first usually takes less time. Labor can vary widely, though, from a few hours to a few days.

When the cervix is completely open, the baby is ready to be born. At this time, the mother is usually urged to push the baby out by using the muscles in her abdominal wall and diaphragm. The baby advances through the birth canal (some proceed quickly, and others take their time). When its scalp appears to the outside world, the baby is said to have *crowned.*

After the baby emerges from the mother, the umbilical cord is cut, and any mucus in the baby's throat is removed. The placenta is expelled a few minutes later, during the final contractions. If baby and mother suffer no complications, the baby is usually weighed, wrapped up, and given to the mother to hold. Love begins.

Encountering complications

Pain is considered to be a normal part of childbirth — not a complication. Depending on circumstances, some women choose to go through childbirth without assistance from pain medications. Those who choose so-called *natural childbirth* often take classes on breathing and relaxation to prepare for the delivery.

Mothers who take classes to prepare for childbirth usually experience less pain, have more knowledge about the birth process, and feel more confident about going through delivery.

Many mothers, whether they have taken classes or not, choose to take medications during their labor or delivery. This choice should not be viewed as weakness. Medications are generally considered to be safe and aren't thought to have long-term effects on the baby. Mothers and their medical team may choose to use pain relievers or pain blockers.

An epidural block, performed by a physician or nurse anesthetist, reduces or eliminates all sensation from the mother's breasts down to her feet. The mother can't get out of bed but is awake, alert, and able to participate in the birthing process. This technique involves a slight risk to the mother of elevated blood pressure or headaches; when given in large doses, it may interfere with labor and delivery.

Caesarean sections

A baby may have to be removed through an incision in the mother's abdomen and uterus — a procedure called a *Caesarean section*. These surgical procedures have become increasingly common. Today, 20 percent to 30 percent of all births in industrialized countries are performed by Caesarean section. In sterile hospital settings, the vast majority of these operations are performed without complications, but like all surgical procedures, they involve some risk.

A medical provider may consider a Caesarean section when

- The mother has an infection that could be passed on to the baby.
- The baby's heart rate drops or changes rapidly.
- The umbilical cord is wrapped around the baby's neck.

- ✔ The baby's head isn't in the birth canal.
- ✔ The placenta has detached from the uterine wall, and the mother is bleeding.
- ✔ The mother's cervix hasn't opened sufficiently.

Multiple births

When a woman is carrying more than one baby, greater risks are involved. The biggest risk is prematurity (see Chapter 11). Other problems include inefficient labor, increased maternal bleeding, difficult positioning of the babies, and decreased oxygen to the babies due to crowding. A physician should monitor a multiple pregnancy closely.

Maternal depression

Pregnancy, labor, and delivery take a lot of effort and energy, so huge hormonal shifts happen during delivery and after birth. Most mothers feel exhausted and suffer a bit of what's called the baby blues — or mild, temporary depressive symptoms. Lacking energy and feeling sad is perfectly normal, because the new mother's body needs to readjust, refresh, and relax. Many cultures support this normal reaction by having the mother rest during the first weeks after delivery while relatives take care of her, the home, and the baby.

More than 10 percent of mothers don't snap back, however, and develop a more serious condition called *postpartum depression.* This depression, if untreated, can interrupt the bonding process between mother and child. Babies whose mothers remain depressed may suffer lags in development, irritability, and behavior problems.

If a new mother seems to be unable to care for her baby or herself, or has thoughts about hurting herself or her baby, her doctor should evaluate her condition. Postpartum depression can be treated successfully through psychotherapy or medication.

Rating babies when they're born

Immediately after birth, a baby is thrust into the world without any experience in breathing, staying warm, eating, digesting, or eliminating. One minute after birth, the baby is evaluated on five measures of health: heartbeat, effort of respiration, muscle tone, color, and reflex. These signs of health are rated and tallied to form the *Apgar score.* The rating is repeated five minutes after birth and sometimes again later, if there's some sign of distress. The Apgar score ranges from 0 to 10, with 0 meaning lifeless and not breathing independently, 8 meaning that the baby is doing well, and 10 meaning that there are no problems at all.

Very few babies ring the Apgar bell at 10 when they're born. In fact, almost no babies born in Denver, Colorado; Albuquerque, New Mexico; or Mexico City obtain perfect Apgar scores. Why? Babies born at high altitudes almost always have blue hands and feet due to the lower levels of oxygen in the air.

Everyone gets cranked up about his or her baby's Apgar score, but a score of 8 or higher really means that there's no cause for concern. Even lower scores don't predict later development very well; they just mean that the baby needs close monitoring for a while.

Always have hope and faith! When co-author Laura's twins were born at 27 weeks of gestation, the firstborn had an Apgar score of 2, and the secondborn had an Apgar score of 0. The infants were put on respirators and airlifted to another hospital that had a neonatal intensive-care unit. Laura was told that they had little chance of survival. Now, 30 years later, both babies are registered nurses — and mothers themselves.

Watching Babies Grow

The first year of life is a time in which enormous changes occur. The newborn baby is equipped with the ability to hear, see, smell, taste, and touch. Soon after birth, the baby can recognize and be soothed and comforted by a familiar person.

Tracking temperament

Look through the window of a newborn nursery for a few minutes, and you'll see some babies sleeping contently, others moving around grimacing, some staring quietly, others thrashing, and a few red-faced and crying.

Babies are born with innate temperamental styles (see Chapter 2 for more on genetic influences and temperament). Some babies are easygoing from Day One. They cry only when they're uncomfortable; when they're fed, changed, picked up, wrapped, or unwrapped, they quickly calm down. These babies fall asleep easily and adjust to new situations. Other babies are difficult to soothe, may startle easily, get upset by changes in routines, and are fussy for no apparent reason. A third group of babies are hesitant and unsure but eventually warm up. Finally, some babies are combinations of all these temperaments and can't really be categorized.

Although temperament may be largely genetic, the way people respond to children can alter or modify their genetic predisposition. How a parent and child match up in temperament is called *goodness of fit.* If an easygoing child has easygoing parents, for example, the child will likely maintain an easygoing temperament. A child with a difficult temperament, on the other hand, may be made worse or better depending on goodness of fit.

Following are a few cases that illustrate how genetic temperaments may change or remain the same over time:

> **Jacob** arrives in the world with a difficult temperament. He screams for about three hours every afternoon and wakes four times a night, according to his stressed-out mother. She worries that she must be a terrible mom for not knowing how to calm him down. Her own frustration seems to make Jacob even more irritable.

> **Charlotte** comes into the world easily and has an easy temperament. She doesn't cry very often and is easily comforted. Her mother worries about everything, however, from how much her baby is eating to how fast she develops. As she gets older, Charlotte's easygoing temperament becomes tinged with anxiety.

> **Ella** has a difficult temperament, and her first few months are filled with crying. She has been timid and jumpy from the beginning. Her parents give her lots of attention and care and remain calm when she's fussy. Her difficult temperament becomes less so by the end of her first year.

Rocking and rolling

Newborn babies appear to be rather helpless; they can't voluntarily raise their heads, grasp objects, or even scoot across the floor. They're born with many reflexes that help keep them alive, however.

The first set of reflexes helps keep oxygen available to support life. These reflexes include breathing, sneezing, hiccupping, and moving legs and arms when the baby is covered with something that could block air. Other reflexes such as sucking and *rooting* (turning the mouth toward an object that has brushed the baby's cheeks) help keep newborns nourished. Swallowing allows milk to be consumed, and spitting up occurs when tummies are too full. A newborn cries to tell the world that something isn't right. Other survival reflexes include shivering when cold and staying still when too hot.

Deliberate motor skills (as opposed to reflexes) occur when babies purposefully move parts of their bodies. These movements help babies explore and learn about their world. During the first year, normal babies' motor skills grow very rapidly. Two branches of skills develop: gross motor skills, which involve big muscles or muscle groups; and fine motor skills, which involve lips, tongues, toes, and fingers.

A normal baby achieves the following gross and fine motor achievements during the first year:

- ✔ Holds up head
- ✔ Rolls over
- ✔ Reaches for objects
- ✔ Sits up without help
- ✔ Grasps objects
- ✔ Manipulates objects
- ✔ Crawls (some babies never crawl but scoot instead)
- ✔ Stands with help or holding on
- ✔ Walks with help

All babies are individuals, and they have different timetables for development. If your baby or one that you care for isn't developing as you expect, don't panic, but talk the situation over with the baby's medical provider. (See the Appendix for more information about developmental milestones.)

Learning like lightning

During the first year of life, the infant learns by experiences. The experience of sucking on a nipple — an early reflex — provides relief from the discomfort of hunger. The experience of sucking on a pacifier or a thumb provides a different kind of satisfaction — comfort, but no reduction in hunger. Soon, the baby can differentiate between the two experiences. Sucking on something that gives nourishment also involves swallowing, whereas sucking on a thumb or pacifier does not.

The infant quickly learns by association and develops a primitive understanding of cause and effect. Crying a certain way will bring a caregiver. Smiling will make someone else smile. Saying "Ma-ma-ma-ma" causes Mom to get much more excited than saying "Ga-ga-ga-ga" does. A rattle makes a great noise; the dog loves to lick; when spoons fall on the floor, someone picks them up.

Babies start to learn that objects exist even when they can't be seen or heard, beginning with the primary caregiver, who appears and disappears throughout the day. By about 8 months of age, a secure baby (see the next section) understands and believes that the caretaker will return. This is also the beginning of the baby's awareness that he or she isn't the same entity as the caregiver.

This new awareness has its cost. A friendly baby can be amused by most friendly faces. Have you ever smiled at a baby across the room in a store or restaurant? Before about 9 months, human smiles or unexpected silliness can get babies to laugh. Sometime around 9 months, however, most babies experience a fear of unknown faces. (For some infants, that fear is barely noticeable; for others, it can be quite dramatic.) This development, called *stranger anxiety,* is perfectly normal; it indicates that the baby is maturing and learning.

Additional learning that babies generally demonstrate by the end of the first year include making gestures to communicate, playing peekaboo, saying a few words such as "Mama" and "Dada," and understanding simple commands like "Bring me your bottle" and "No." They can communicate wants verbally in one-word sentences like "juice." See the Appendix for more details about when different cognitive skills develop.

Becoming attached

Psychologists disagree about numerous issues, but they generally agree that humans are social creatures and that how they relate to one another has a great deal to do with their ultimate happiness and sense of well-being. Furthermore, they agree that the emotional bonds that form between infants and their caregivers establishes the foundation for how a child will get along with other kids. Connections with peers ultimately help determine how easily later intimate relationships become established.

These emotional bonds are generally described as infants' or children's *attachment style* (the way they relate to their caregivers). Various theories have been proposed to explain why and how attachment styles evolve, but a combination of genes, learning, modeling, and parenting styles no doubt contribute to the process.

Those styles begin to appear in the first year of life. (Somewhat similar patterns are evident clear through adulthood, however.) In a general sense, during the first couple of months of life, infants respond to all people in almost the same manner. From 2 to 7 months, they show signs of recognizing people they've seen frequently. Finally, from 7 months to 1 year and beyond, they begin demonstrating protest on separation from caregivers, fear of strangers, and some signs of intentional communication.

More specific attachment styles appear by the time children reach 12 to perhaps 24 months of age. Researchers, beginning with developmental psychologist Mary Ainsworth and colleagues, conducted a large series of studies in which infants engaged in various interactions with their mothers as well as strangers. They also studied what happened when the mothers and the strangers left for a little while and then returned. Based on these studies, the researchers determined that children can usually be classified in one of the following four attachment styles:

- ✔ **Secure attachment:** Most infants demonstrate this attachment style, which is characterized by using the mother or another primary caregiver, as a safe, secure base that allows them to explore their environment with comfort. If they're briefly separated from their mothers, they may be distressed, but they're easily soothed upon the mothers' return. Babies may form a secure attachment to multiple caregivers.

- ✔ **Avoidant attachment (insecure):** These infants don't show as much distress if they're separated from their mothers. When a mother returns, however, the baby avoids contact with her and ignores her attempts to communicate.

- ✔ **Ambivalent resistant attachment (insecure):** If these infants are separated from their mothers, they become very upset and distressed, and they're not easily soothed and comforted by the mothers' return. They may cry and show signs of anger toward their mothers.

- ✔ **Disorganized attachment (insecure):** These infants demonstrate disorganized, inconsistent patterns of behavior when they're separated from and reunited with their mothers. They can look fearful, odd, dazed, and/or disoriented. They may freeze or start rocking in a repetitive manner.

Assessing an infant or child's attachment style is a bit complicated. You can feel free to make your own informal assessment of your child, but don't take it too seriously without consulting a professional.

Researchers have designed other schemes for categorizing attachment styles, but we stick with these four categories throughout this book.

Sudden infant death syndrome (SIDS)

Most new parents check on their sleeping babies from time to time, marveling at the miracle of life. But for about 2,300 parents in the United States each year and many more around the world, the unthinkable happens: Their babies aren't sleeping but are dead. The leading cause of death for babies between 1 month and 1 year old is sudden infant death syndrome (SIDS).

At this time, no one really knows what causes this devastating event. Scientists suspect that a baby with some predisposing risk factor sleeps on his tummy or in an area with soft bedding or toys and stops breathing.

The risk factors that increase the likelihood of SIDS include

- Sleeping on the tummy instead of the back

- Being born prematurely or with low birth weight

- Sleeping in a soft bed or a bed with comforters, blankets, or soft toys

- Being exposed to smoke (the more people in the household who smoke, the greater the risk)

- Being overheated

- Getting a respiratory infection

- Being exposed to drugs or smoke prenatally

- Having a teenage mother

The rate of SIDS deaths in the United States has gone down by more than 40 percent since the Back-to-Sleep campaign began in the 1990s. Most experts believe that the decrease can be attributed to the campaign to teach parents and caregivers to put babies to sleep on their backs. For parents, child-care workers, and others who take care of babies, here are some things to do to decrease the chances of SIDS:

- Always put infants down to sleep on their backs.

- Keep babies away from smoke.

- Never put a baby down on a squishy, soft mattress or with other soft items that might cause suffocation.

- Make sure that the baby gets good medical care before and after birth.

- Don't let the baby get too warm, and keep the room that he or she sleeps in well ventilated.

- Encourage breastfeeding.

- Limit exposure to people with infections.

Chapter 5

Tackling the Toddler Years (Ages 1–4)

∙∙∙

In This Chapter

▶ Starting to walk

▶ Getting along with other kids

▶ Feeling proud

▶ Figuring out the world

∙∙∙

*O*ne day, which for most children occurs around their first birthday, a magical event happens: the first wobbly, independent step. The step represents the beginning of a time of explosive development. During the next three or four years, kids go from precariously staggering around the house to running and jumping. Their vocabularies of 2 or 3 words at age 1 grow to as many as 10,000 words by age 4.

In this chapter, we describe normal development during the preschool years. We take a look at the major tasks of childhood during this fun and challenging time: attaching to others, having empathy, developing a self-view, controlling emotions, delaying gratification, and acquiring new skills.

Watching Attachment Evolve from Parents to Others

In the first year of life, human babies are completely dependent on adults to take care of their basic needs. With hard work by the caregivers and a little luck, those needs are met during the first year. The right genes don't hurt either (see Chapter 2). If all goes well, these babies begin venturing out and exploring the world. The changes in the relationship between caregivers and toddlers can be unexpected, annoying, and (with the proper attitude) lots of fun.

Wandering away from Mom

Almost all parents and caregivers report strong feelings of love for their babies. Humans are biologically programmed to respond with comfort and care when a baby cries. Although parents can get tired and crabby after sleepless nights or frustrated by a baby who can't seem to be comforted, most of the time, their love for their infants is strong and uncomplicated.

That unconditional acceptance and love can be challenged, however, after toddlers start to exert independence and explore the world away from their mothers. They may notice that toilet paper can be unrolled, for example, and to see what happens, they pull it throughout the house. They come to real-ize that tipping things over creates interesting sounds, sights, and reactions from Mom or Dad. They discover that pulling the dog's tail makes him yelp and that ice cream tastes better than green beans.

Even for those who love babies fully, completely, and without judgment, a time of reckoning comes. Suddenly, a sweet innocent baby is a toddler who knows how to push buttons, quickly picking up the tricks of the trade that will work on her particular adult caregivers. She masters a repertoire of temper tantrums — whining, begging, crying, or asking the same question over and over — while continually flexing her newly formed muscle of inde-pendence. Such exploration away from caregivers and pushing of buttons sets the stage for independence and relationships with others. These actions as a whole demonstrate the unfolding attachment process.

Demanding, frustrating preschoolers do best when they feel securely attached and loved. The adults who care for them need to combine discipline with love. Here are a few ideas:

- ✔ Don't take a child's misbehavior personally.
- ✔ When saying no, remain firm and emotionally neutral (which we know is easier said than done).
- ✔ Understand that the toddler or preschooler is testing the limits.
- ✔ Find time to give hugs and kisses.
- ✔ Play with, read to, and engage your preschooler in positive activities every day.

Many young children become attached to a blanket, stuffed animal, or other toy. These comfort objects become temporary mother substitutes of sorts. This habit is totally normal and gives preschoolers ways to soothe them-selves. Although we know of a few kids who take their stuffed animals to col-lege, comfort objects usually are discarded or forgotten well before weddings and graduations roll around, so caregivers should relax and let children enjoy these items.

Interacting with others

For preschoolers, play is the best way to learn. Very young children usually play with toys or objects by themselves or near other children. As they get older, they may watch and imitate other children, and interact with them a little. Sometime before school age, most children learn to play together, share, take turns, and have some structure in their activities.

Sharing with others

Sharing is a fundamental social skill that enhances kids' abilities to get along with one another as well as form good friendships. At age 1 or 2, kids don't share; in fact, one of their favorite words in the world is "Mine!" Sharing doesn't come naturally. Rather, this skill (like most skills) must be taught over a period of years.

Here are a few tips for teaching kids to share appropriately:

- ✔ **Begin teaching taking turns and sharing when your child reaches about 2½ or 3 years of age.** Don't expect a whole lot right away; sharing gets easier as the child matures.

- ✔ **Model sharing.** Take any chance you can to demonstrate yourself sharing with another, older child or even with an adult.

- ✔ **Explain why sharing is important.** Keep the explanation simple, and don't expect the child to understand the concept right away. Repetition helps.

- ✔ **Take a disputed toy away.** If kids start to squabble over a toy, it's best to take it away. Don't try to sort out who was "right," because both children probably contributed to the dispute in one way or another.

- ✔ **Explain what sharing and not sharing do.** Tell toddlers that sharing means others will probably share with them and that when they don't share, others won't either. Expect to repeat this instruction.

- ✔ **Contain your own emotions.** Even though selfishness is obnoxious, it's perfectly normal at this age, so try to model calm and avoid yelling at a child who takes something from a playmate.

Talking together

Preschool children are quite self-centered. Basically, they want to feel good and have fun. That's perfectly natural. But as their worlds expand beyond the family, showing interest in other people becomes important.

A critical social skill that remains helpful throughout life is the ability to converse. This skill can be taught and encouraged in very young children. Parents and caregivers can model the behavior and coach young children in the art of conversation.

Here's an actual dinner-table conversation between 3-year-old Alaina and her 2½-year-old cousin Carter:

> *Alaina:* "Carter, what did you do at school today?"
>
> *Carter:* "I played with friends."
>
> *Alaina* (loudly): "You played with friends?"
>
> *Carter:* "At my school."
>
> *Alaina:* "What's your friend's name?"
>
> *Carter* (no longer understanding Alaina): "Carter!"
>
> Everyone at the table laughed.

Alaina demonstrated advanced social skills for a 3-year-old. Obviously, her mother had coached her on asking questions — an invaluable skill for making friends.

Playing rough

One kind of play activity that often makes adults nervous is known as *rough-and-tumble play*. Chasing, catching, and falling down characterizes this type of play. Kids love to run around in circles, screaming. Rough-and-tumble play actually encourages skills like turn-taking, self-control, and coordination.

Monitor children during play activities. Sometimes things get out of control, and an adult needs to step in.

Rough-and-tumble play also occurs in many animal species. Our dogs like to roughhouse in the backyard, chasing, growling, biting, and running in figure eights. Every once in a while, we hear a squeak, and then the play stops. But the dogs don't seem to be hurt, and they go back at it the next day — just like kids.

Understanding others' points of view

Perspective-taking, or putting oneself in another's shoes, begins when children understand that other people have feelings and thoughts that are independent of and different from theirs. This process starts late in the first year of life and continues, for most children, beyond the preschool years. Self-awareness and awareness of others form the foundation of perspective-taking.

A critical part of perspective-taking comes when children begin to be aware of other people's emotion, which fascinate preschoolers. They stare unabashedly at a child who's crying, are riveted by an angry exchange, and smile when others are laughing. In the normally developing child, this natural curiosity eventually leads to empathy. Children who have developmental delays, especially autism (see Chapter 13), struggle greatly with this aspect of development.

You can see early empathy in young children. They may offer an unhappy child a blanket to hold, kiss or hug another child who's hurt, or become upset when a friend or family member is upset.

You can help preschoolers develop empathy by talking about and labeling the feelings of those around them.

Looking in the Mirror: Self-Views

If you hold a baby in front of a mirror before his first birthday, he'll likely quiet down, look at his reflection, and possibly coo at himself. Closer to his second birthday, the boy will not only be interested in the mirror, but also will clearly recognize the reflection as himself. Not too long after self-awareness come self-evaluation and self-esteem. Most toddlers and preschoolers don't suffer much from low self-esteem or poor views about themselves, but from school age forward, this issue becomes much more important and potentially problematic. During this stage, self-views begin to emerge and they continue to affect children throughout the rest of their lives — whether for better or worse.

Acquiring competence

During the preschool years, children develop an amazing number of skills. Most learn to walk, run, jump, play, talk, listen, and independently use the toilet. How well they achieve these developmental milestones and the reactions of the adults around them help determine whether they feel competent or inept. Young children develop healthy self-esteem by acquiring skills.

To help toddlers develop feelings of competence, give them tasks that are achievable. When a task is too difficult, the child is likely to give up or become negative.

Feeling guilty

Most 2- and 3-year-olds don't feel guilty about anything they do. That's perfectly normal, and we don't recommend that those who take care of young children spend much time making them feel guilty. At the same time, negative feedback is sometimes necessary and appropriate. It's perfectly okay to tell a young child "No hitting; be gentle" or "When you scream in the restaurant, other people get upset; please speak softly."

When providing negative feedback to a child, be sure to criticize the unwanted action, not the child. Tell her why the behavior was unacceptable. Say something like "When you grabbed your sister's toy, she was sad. Please don't take toys without asking."

Most preschoolers behave because an adult has told them that bad behavior has consequences, not because they have much of a conscience. Therefore, they need frequent reminders about how their actions affect other people. Feeling guilty about doing something that hurts someone else is an early sign of moral development.

Exerting Early Control

In Chapters 3 and 4, we note that infants up to age 1 have rather limited self-control. Sure, they can settle themselves down by sucking their thumbs, and sometimes, you can soothe them with rocking, swaddling, soft music, and distraction. But the infants don't know how to calm themselves consciously.

Some parents believe that responding consistently and promptly to a baby's distress will increase the baby's crying and whining over time. In fact, studies show that responding consistently to babies' needs helps them see the world as being more predictable, and they're more readily soothed as a result.

From ages 1 to 4, little tykes need to learn early skills such as curbing their impulses, thinking before they act, behaving reasonably at mealtimes, understanding limits, and deciding which emotions to express and when to show them. As we state in Chapter 3, controlling impulses and delaying gratification may be the most important skills any child ever learns. Many experts contend that such emotional and behavioral regulation may be more predictive of later success than scores on intelligence tests.

At the same time, many parents struggle to buy into the idea that self-control is absolutely critical, so they may hesitate to set appropriate limits for their kids. Some parents were brought up in an excessively harsh manner and want to be sure that their kids don't suffer the same fate; other parents never have figured out adequate self-control themselves and find it easier to give in to their kids' demands to deal with the frustration of telling them no. Toddlerhood offers abundant opportunities for practicing limit-setting and teaching self-control.

The following sections discuss five areas related to these critical skills that teachers, parents, and child-care workers need to understand to foster optimal child development.

Fortunately, you can teach kids self-control at virtually any age after their first year or so, but it's a lot easier to do so early rather than late. In other words, tackling an out-of-control teenager is about a hundredfold more difficult than working with a kid in the throes of the "terrible twos."

Going from no to yes

Sometime between the ages of 1 and 3 or so, most kids learn something rather magical: They can actually say no to their parents! Also, they may start to do the opposite of what people ask them to do. They throw temper tantrums and intentionally drop food on the floor. They hit other kids. Cute? Well, not really.

Realize, however, that kids are defiant, mischievous, and disruptive because doing these things is normal, natural, and necessary for learning. Preschoolers are starting to understand that they have some degree of autonomy and independence. They don't have the language skills to get their needs met easily, so they discover that being oppositional sometimes does the trick.

If you're a caregiver for a child in this age range, use this realization —defiant behavior is normal — to keep your own frustration and anger in check.

Here are our suggestions for helping children inhibit oppositional behavior:

- ✔ **Model calm behavior, no matter how upset you feel.** Realize that you can be firm without being angry and upset (at least on the outside!). Save yelling for emergencies only. If you yell all the time, yelling loses meaning and fails to grab kids' attention.

- ✔ **Establish regular routines.** Children do better when their worlds are reasonably predictable. Have set times for sleep, naps, and meals. Some deviations will happen, of course, but try to stick with the regimen when you can.

- ✔ **Childproof the house or classroom.** Put caps on unused electrical plugs; lock up dangerous chemicals, medications, and substances; put breakables out of reach; and put locks on cabinets and windows. Childproofing isn't just about keeping your kid safe; it also helps decrease the number of times you feel compelled to say "No" and "Don't touch!" These words work better when they're said less frequently.

- ✔ **Give kids only a couple of choices.** Don't ask what they want for lunch or offer six choices. You could say, "Do you want macaroni and cheese or peanut butter and jelly?" If they say "Neither," make the choice yourself.

- ✔ **Distract and redirect kids before things get out of hand.** When you see a child starting to get frustrated, suggest an alternative activity such as coloring.

- ✔ **Never, ever cave into temper tantrums.** You're bound to cave sometimes, but keep those times to a bare minimum. When you cave in to tantrums, you might as well tell your kids that you *like* it when they misbehave! (For more information, see the nearby sidebar "Terrible tantrums.")

- ✔ **When children whine, tell them that you can't understand them.** Whining is just like having a tantrum. If you give in, whining will increase. Tell children to use clear words expressed in a normal tone to ask for something, and tell them that you'll never say yes when they whine.

- ✔ **Use a time-out, or take away a toy or a privilege.** The idea is to remove kids from where they want to be or to take away something they want. We recommend that time-outs for children this age last about 2 to 5 minutes after the child calms down. This approach to setting limits on behavior is probably more effective than punishing or spanking kids. Make sure that any time-out area is safe and secure. (See Chapter 8 for additional details about using time-outs and withdrawal of privileges or taking away a favorite toy for a while.)

- ✔ **Praise successes.** Any time kids do what you ask them, let them know that you're pleased. Make a goal of spending considerably more time being positive with your kids than being negative with them.

When you set consistent limits and say no to kids appropriately without undue harshness or anger, they slowly learn to control and limit their own behavior. One of the first indications of such control occurs in toddlers who start to misbehave and then say, "No! No!" They're modeling what they've seen and are starting to internalize the process.

If you're an educator, caregiver, or parent, and you find yourself unable to contain your anger with kids, please consider getting professional help. Excessive harshness, whether it's emotional or physical in nature, can cause lasting harm to children.

Going from terrible to terrific eating

Parents around the world worry a lot about their kids. All too often, they worry about their kids' eating: what they eat, how much they eat, and how they act at the dinner table. We're not entirely sure why parents focus much on this issue. Perhaps it's out of concern for toddlers' nutritional needs and health; possibly it's due to the emphasis placed on food by the culture in general or by food manufacturers' advertising. (Mind you, worrying about how much a child eats when poverty leads to food scarcity is a different issue and completely appropriate.)

Terrible tantrums

Every parent since the beginning of time has wondered what to do about temper tantrums, which kids learn to throw early and often. There's a reason for the phrase "the terrible twos": Kids around that age are notorious for throwing such fits. The power of tantrums to bring an adult parent to his knees is a sight to behold.

The cause of many tantrums actually lies in how parents respond to them early on. Here's an example:

Jill asks for a cookie at the grocery store. Her father says, "No." Jill asks again and gets the same response. Jill asks a little louder, and Dad says, "No, not now." Jill whines, "Please, Daddy. I want a cookie now!" Dad holds the line and says, "I said

no!" in a louder voice. Jill starts to cry. Dad doesn't respond. Then she throws herself on the floor, wailing so loudly that other shoppers take notice. Dad, now feeling horribly embarrassed, says, "OK, but just this once!" Obviously, Jill won this battle. She'll be far more likely to resort to this tactic in the future because she's learned that it works.

The best way to respond to temper tantrums is to hold firm, no matter how difficult that may be to do. We encourage parents and caregivers to get down at the child's level, make eye contact, and tell him to stop. If this doesn't work, a swift exit from the scene may be in order, even if it's inconvenient. Calling a time-out is another strategy (see Chapter 8).

In any event, you can see food dramas played out on the stage of almost any family-oriented restaurant every day of the week. Once, we were seated next to a couple of parents who were urging their 3-year-old boy to eat "a little more" of his pancakes. The mother repeated the phrase "Take another bite" (or some derivative of the phrase) 27 times, and the father chimed in another 4 times. Yes, we were so fascinated that we counted! The parents' anger escalated, and their toddler tossed his bacon on the floor. We figured that we were watching the beginnings of trouble with picky eating, down the road.

If you find yourself worrying about a child's eating, consider the following issues and suggestions:

- ✔ Eating is as natural as breathing. Normally, you don't need to encourage either function.

- ✔ Anxiety, tension, and worry in adults causes worry in kids, which makes them less interested in eating.

- ✔ Any behavior that you pay a lot of attention to is likely to increase in frequency. Therefore, constantly cajoling a child to eat encourages pickiness and refusal to eat. Besides, a little pickiness and moderate drops in appetite are rather common in 2- and 3-year-old kids.

- ✔ If a child deliberately plays with food or throws it on the floor, calmly remove it. Don't engage in a power struggle. If the child continues misbehaving, announce that mealtime is over.

✔ If a child fails to eat at one meal, she's very likely to eat more at the next. Hunger usually kicks in quite effectively.

✔ Many toddlers fill up on juice or unhealthy snacks between meals. If you want them to eat better at mealtimes, watch what they eat between meals. Be sure their snacks are healthy and modest.

✔ In most cases, kids eat what they need.

✔ See a doctor if a child gains or loses significant weight for no obvious reason. The doctor regularly monitors weight at well-child checks, but if you have concerns, check in sooner.

✔ Be prepared for the fact that some meals won't go well. You may have to get up and leave a restaurant and/or remove the child until he calms down. Parents who can deal with these frustrations calmly early will enjoy the benefits of a well-behaved child in the years to come.

✔ Parents should "model" good eating and avoid over emphasis on either eating or weight concerns.

Increasing kids' attention

Focused attention is a skill that children need for just about everything. Kids who can maintain attention on teachers learn to read more readily. Kids who have the ability to focus are able to plan and to think through the consequences of their actions; in other words, they can think before they act. Interestingly, they also appear to have fewer negative emotions. Parents can do much to help their kids improve their attention skills.

We believe that teaching kids to increase their ability to focus and concentrate is a very good idea, and the process doesn't have to be painful. Here are a few suggestions:

✔ **Work on puzzles with your child.** Puzzles require lots of focused attention on finding pieces of just the right shapes and colors. (Be sure to note the suggested age ranges on the package.)

✔ **Practice having children who have started to talk repeat what you say.** Say "Dog, cat, mouse," for example, and then have the child repeat the words. Younger kids sometimes learn to repeat sounds like "ba, ga, da." Kids learn to listen and develop memory with this game.

✔ **Engage your child's attention whenever possible.** Study the soap bubbles in the tub with your child, and point out how to make them pop. Ask your child to show you all the green cans on the store shelf. Whatever it is, call a child's attention to it.

✔ **Read to kids.** Point to the pictures in the book as you read. Although kids may start out showing little interest in books, they usually gain interest quickly and start bringing you books to read to them.

✔ **Sing simple songs together.** Singing helps improve both memory and attentional focus.

✔ **Don't have the TV set on in the background.** Programs with structured educational themes and stories may actually help a little after the age of 3, but blaring newscasts, programs with lots of violence, and game shows that lie beyond kids' grasp probably do more harm than good. In general, limit overall TV watching.

✔ **Make sure that kids get adequate sleep and naps.** It's a lot easier to pay attention when you've had enough rest.

Calming down

Emotional dysregulation is said to occur when kids' emotions are too intense, too easily triggered, and swing from extremes. Well, emotional dysregulation pretty well defines the emotions of most toddlers. Just around the time they start walking, toddlers suddenly become emotional wrecks. Anything can seem to set them off into a wailing, defiant mess.

From about the age of 2 on, kids start — with lots of help — to regulate or moderate their emotions. They also learn when it's best to express their feelings and when it's best to inhibit them. To be successful, young children need an adult to model and describe ways of calming down. If you're a child's caregiver, and you start to feel upset about something, you can say something like this: "I'm getting upset right now. I think I'll take a few deep breaths and slowly count out loud from 1 to 10."

When toddlers are frightened, uneasy, or frustrated, all they know is that they feel bad. They may be unable to express what's going on, so their reactions are limited. A 2-year-old boy won't be able to say that he's crabby because he didn't have a nap. A 3-year-old can't tell you that she's feeling jealous of her new baby brother. A 5-year-old is unlikely to be aware that she's worried about how she'll meet the challenges of kindergarten.

Help children identify and understand feelings by labeling them. Discuss both positive and negative emotions with young kids. Talk about how a youngster probably feels happy and excited about going to a friend's birthday party, or how he feels sad or angry when the new baby cries and wakes him up.

It's great when adults can own up to their own feelings, too. Tell a child that you're feeling crabby, and that's why you need him to be quiet, or say that you're feeling surprised and happy that she drew you a picture.

When young children feel totally out of control, they may respond better to touch than to words. A place to settle down in a trusted adult's arms may be the best way to help a child calm down. Kids and adults generally don't listen very well when they're in the midst of a meltdown. Wait for a calmer time to talk about what happened.

Some toddlers can be overly sensitive to touch. If a child starts arching his back, squirming to get away, or going limp, respect those messages, and limit physical contact. If the child is out of control, hold the child loosely so that he doesn't hurt himself or others.

Tolerating frustration

Life presents a never-ending series of frustrations for kids and adults alike. See Chapter 3 for a general description of frustration tolerance and delay of gratification, which are essential skills.

Toddlers need to develop these skills, because those who don't have them are likely to do the following:

- Blame other kids for things they shouldn't
- Make excuses for their misdeeds
- Have trouble inhibiting their anger and aggression
- Fail to share with other children
- Have more difficulty paying attention in school and, thus, achieve less

Some of the earliest research on frustration tolerance and delay of gratification involved a rather simple game played with 4-year-olds. Experimenters offered kids a single marshmallow if they wanted one right away, but they were also told that the experimenter was going to leave the room, and if they could wait until he returned, they could have two marshmallows.

They were also given the option of ringing a bell early, and the experimenter would come back in and let them have a single marshmallow. In other ways, holding off on immediate gratification paid off. Kids who could inhibit their immediate desires were found to do much better down the road in terms of school, achievement, and getting along with other children.

Preschool ages — ages about 2 to 5 — are ideal times to start teaching kids how to tolerate the inevitable frustrations that they will confront throughout their lives. Here are some of our suggestions for doing so:

✔ **Model patience whenever possible.** Suppose that you're putting together a bicycle with training wheels, and you're not mechanically minded. Try saying things such as this: "I have a hard time with things like this. I just need to go slow and steady. Eventually, I'll get it together, and if not, I can ask someone for help." When you succeed at part of the task, consider saying, "Wow, that was great. It really helped me stick with it."

✔ **Praise kids when they stick with something a little longer than usual.** Don't overdo praise for trivial accomplishments, however. And be sure to specifically point out what you're praising.

✔ **Talk slowly.** In general, slow your pace a little on tasks, and describe what you're doing to kids.

✔ **Teach kids skills for distracting themselves.** When you're waiting in line, for example, tell your child to sing a favorite song softly over and over or to count the number of people in line.

✔ **Teach kids to transform the thing they want so much into something else.** If they're waiting for birthday cake, tell them to imagine that the cake in front of them is made of plastic.

✔ **Teach kids that delays pay.** Over and over again, tell them they can have what they want if they first do something that they don't especially want to do. This rule — first, you do this, and then you can have that — is called *Grandma's rule.* You can say, "First, you pick up your toys, and then we can go outside." Don't give in. A variant of this rule is to offer the opportunity to get more of what they want if they wait a while first.

✔ **Don't jump in to help your child with a task too soon.** Let kids struggle a little while first. Even then, ask whether they want help before you start providing it. Otherwise, you impart the message that you don't think they're capable of doing things themselves.

✔ **Act; don't yak.** In other words, don't lecture, criticize, and admonish kids for being impatient. Criticism will only make things worse. Reprimands don't teach kids anything.

Mastering the World

Preschoolers learn best by directly experiencing the world around them, and the best experiences are often everyday events. Imagine taking a toddler to the grocery store, and think about all the things you can teach. You can talk about safety and car seats, and about why kids need to hold an adult's hand in the parking lot (teaching little and big). You can discuss healthy fruits and vegetables, naming the colors and counting them. You can remind the child not to touch everything in the store and tell her that if she's well behaved, she can have a sucker (self-control).

Toilet-training toddlers

In the early days of psychology, Sigmund Freud (1856–1939) and others placed a great deal of importance on toilet training. Freud purported that toilet training constituted one of the most important challenges of the so-called anal stage of development, which usually begins after a child's first birthday. He suggested that if anything goes wrong during this stage, the child will likely grow up to be *anal retentive,* which is characterized by excessive neatness and compulsive perfectionism, or *anal expulsive,* which is characterized by carelessness, defiance, and disorganization.

Research has largely failed to validate Freud's concerns. Nevertheless, toilet training is still considered to be a major task of toddlerhood. Parents, teachers, and child-care workers alike fret over when and how to toilet-train a child. We have a few general tips and guidelines for you regarding toilet training (but realize that there are no absolute hard-and-fast rules):

✔ **Wait until the child develops awareness that his diapers have become wet or soiled.** That stage usually occurs somewhere around the second birthday, although this time frame varies a lot from child to child.

✔ **Make sure that the child can follow simple commands.** These commands can be as simple as "Bring me the ball."

✔ **Wait for the child to show interest and aptitude.** The child should show at least some interest in sitting on the toilet and should also be capable of pulling her own pants up and down.

✔ **Be sure that the child has a reasonable degree of predictable regularity.** Most kids start having bowel movements at fairly regular times such as after dinner or after a bath.

✔ **Focus on the positive.** When parents decide to proceed with toilet training, they need to focus on being positive. Nothing is more important than maintaining a positive attitude. Criticisms and harsh words impede the process.

For loads of information and details about how to proceed, see www.healthy children.org and search for *toilet training.* The American Academy of Pediatrics developed this Web site for parents and their children.

In visits to local stores, preschoolers can learn how to identify colors; count; recognize letters; and develop memory, language, and social skills. Parents, teachers, and other caregivers can enrich the lives of little ones by noticing and continually commenting on the environment. You can find opportunities for teaching all around you.

Using words and following directions

Babies and toddlers use words quite creatively. A 1-year-old may use the word *dog* to mean every animal that has four legs. As the child matures, words become more specific. Following are general guidelines for language development during the preschool years:

✔ **A 1-year-old**

- Has a vocabulary of a few words that have meaning.

- Chatters or babbles, using sounds that seem to have no real meaning.

- Can follow simple directions, such as "Bring me your bottle."

- Enjoys verbal play.

- Knows what is meant by common names such as Mama, Dada, or his own name.

✔ Points and makes noises to indicate interest in something (such as juice or a cookie).

✔ **A 1½-year-old**

- Can name many familiar objects.

- Likes to repeat sounds or phrases.

- Begins to combine words to make sentences, such as "Mama go" or "Up Dada."

- Understands "No."

- Can follow simple directions that include prepositions such as *in, on,* and *under.*

✔ **A 2-year-old**

✔ Has a vocabulary of more than 100 words.

- Starts to use words like *me, I,* and *mine.*

- May talk in a loud voice or strained pitch.

- Can make caregivers understand most of what he is saying.

- Knows what to do when she is asked to point to body parts like eyes and ears.

✔ **A 3-year-old**

- Puts three words together into sentences that contain nouns and verbs.

- Can use past tense and plurals.

- Has a vocabulary of close to 1,000 words.

- Asks questions, especially "Why?"

- Can make others understand most of what she says.

- Begins to relate stories to other people.

- Knows his own name, age, and gender.

✔ **A 4-year-old**

- Uses language in make-believe play.
- Begins to know colors.
- Can repeat up to four numbers said slowly.
- Talks about her own activities.
- Understands concepts like bigger, smaller, slower, and longer.
- Can follow directions about objects that are not in his direct line of vision, such as "Please get the ball from the playroom."
- Can make most people understand what she says.

Different children develop language at quite different speeds. If a child doesn't seem to be progressing at the same rate as others, discuss your concerns with a health-care professional.

Knowing how things work

A preschooler is like a little scientist, learning through experimentation and trial and error. Those who care for these little ones can expand their knowledge by allowing them to participate in daily activities.

Kids at this age love to be involved and helpful in almost any household chore and other everyday activities. Here are a few ideas:

✔ **Cooking:** Plan simple meals that involve gathering and talking about ingredients, mixing, cooking, and eating. Children can learn when certain ingredients are combined, they change form. (Flour mixed with eggs can turn into pizza crust, for example.) They can learn about categorization by classifying kinds of foods. They can learn counting and measurement. Kids of all ages love to cook. Just be sure to keep them away from sharp knives and hot surfaces.

✔ **Doing laundry:** Preschoolers love to sort clothes by dark and light, which gives them more experience in categorizing. Throw in a bit of information about the colors of the clothes for more learning. Kids learn what temperature means by putting their hands in cold water or feeling the warm towels coming out of the dryer.

✔ **Playing with sand and water:** Put a toddler or preschooler in a sand box with a few pieces of plastic food storage containers and you have a physics lab in progress. The child learns about gravity and mass by pouring, dumping, and an occasional throw. Add water and the learning and entertainment value skyrocket.

✔ **Feeding and caring for animals:** Most kids love animals and get a kick out of feeding them — and not always dog or cat food. Our dogs have gotten a bit pudgy lately because our four young grandchildren feed them fruit snacks, cereal, macaroni and cheese, and birthday cake (among other goodies). At times, we think that a good portion of the dogs' nourishment comes from licking the children's sticky hands and faces.

Another part of dog care that preschoolers love is picking up poop. Let's face it — poop is a pretty hot topic among the toddler set. Going around with a pooper scooper (well supervised, of course) is a coveted activity around our house. It's interesting that older children dread this chore.

Teetering, Toddling, and Stacking Blocks

Playing and exploring take lots of motor coordination, both gross (large muscles) and fine (small muscles). A toddler barely toddles, but by the time she's almost ready for kindergarten, she'll be a skillful runner, jumper, climber, and hopper. This section tells you some of the achievements that your 4-year-old is likely to accomplish.

By 4 years old, preschoolers should be able to do the following:

✔ Throw, kick, and sometimes catch big balls

✔ Balance on one foot for a few seconds

✔ Dress themselves in clothes that have no buttons or ties

✔ Eat without spilling too much, and use spoons and forks

✔ Hold a cup and drink from it without spilling

✔ Build towers of about eight blocks

✔ Pedal a tricycle

✔ Hold a crayon or marker between the first two fingers and thumb

✔ Make lines and circles with markers or crayons

✔ Turn pages in a book

✔ Use scissors under supervision

✔ Walk up and down stairs without help

✔ Play with modeling clay

✔ Wash and dry hands

✔ Brush teeth with supervision

✔ Use the potty

Not all children achieve these physical goals on time. There are many reasons for variations, some of which are related to the growth and development of an individual child. Many children, however, don't achieve these motor skills on time because they haven't had sufficient encouragement or opportunities to practice.

Parents, teachers, and caregivers should be aware of normal development and allow children to experience spills, falls, messes, and failures along the way of learning new skills. Letting kids drink out of a sippy cup until they go to school, for example, prevents spills at the cost of failing to teach skills.

Chapter 6

The Middle Childhood Years (Ages 5 – 12)

*F*alling between the fast-paced first few years and the angst of adolescence, middle childhood is often a time of relative stability. Children of these ages tend to be healthy (with fewer colds and cases of the flu), and their body growth slows down a bit compared with the previous years. Much of the focus during this developmental period is on acquiring basic skills. For many children, emotional and behavioral turmoil is not quite as pronounced as it was during toddlerhood or will be in the adolescent years that lie ahead. When children develop additional skills of thinking, behaving, and relating, they're more prepared for the somewhat-greater autonomy of adolescence and young adulthood.

The influence of the family and primary caregivers on children is still powerful, but the pressure of the peer group starts to grow, and children begin to venture outside the home for approval. They wrestle with identity during these years, developing increased self-awareness and self-judgment. Finally, during the middle childhood years, children face the tasks of learning to read, write, and perform arithmetic.

In this chapter, we discuss how children in the middle childhood years develop friendships, discover their own unique identities, work on improving self-control, and get through the daily challenges of school.

Getting Stronger, Bigger, and Faster

Children who have access to adequate nourishment go through incredible physical changes during the middle childhood years. No longer top-heavy toddlers with disproportionately large heads, by age 5 most children have body proportions similar to those of adults. They grow about 2 or 3 inches in height every year and gain 5 to 7 pounds.

It's no wonder that many children in this age group complain of *growing pains,* which occur in more than a quarter of all children, usually in the legs. Kids with growing pains typically respond well to massages or heating pads, but a physician should be consulted if these pains are intense or chronic.

Kids grow at different rates through middle childhood. Some have growth spurts early; others, much later. Girls often tower over boys for a while; then boys catch up and surpass girls closer to adolescence.

During these years of rapid growth, children also master running, skipping, and bike riding. They improve in both strength and stamina. Their fine motor skills leap from drawing crude circles and squares to creating legible hand-writing. In addition, most kids learn to tie shoes, use scissors, and handle small tools skillfully. Children of these ages benefit from having access to a variety of experiences that allow them to practice and master these skills.

The following list represents some useful ways you can help kids acquire this mastery:

- ✔ Children should be involved in regular physical education and opportunities to play with other children.

- ✔ Kids of this age can improve their fine motor skills with regular hand-writing practice, as well as with creative opportunities to use crayons, paints, clay, and other media.

- ✔ Organized sports, introduced when a child shows interest and ability, can help improve social and physical development. Sometimes, individual sports (such as martial arts, swimming, and gymnastics) are better choices than team sports for children who are particularly shy or lagging in motor development.

  Parents and coaches must be responsible for maintaining a safe and healthy environment. Also, adults should be good role models, encouraging not only physical fitness, but also good sportsmanship.

- ✔ Middle childhood is a great time to expose children to music. Their fine motor and cognitive skills benefit from learning to play an instrument.

Precocious puberty

During the middle childhood years, children experience steady growth and early signs of puberty. Although normal variations occur, most girls begin to grow breast buds around 10 years old, and sparse, lightly pigmented pubic hair starts to appear between the ages of 11 and 13. Girls start their periods around the age of 12 and are fully mature by the age of 15. Boys generally start puberty about 2 years after girls, with pubic hair appearing around the age of 12 and full sexual maturity occurring at about age 15.

There are increasing worries that puberty is starting earlier than before, however. One study which appeared in the journal *Pediatrics* in April 1997 sampled 17,000 girls in the United States and found that 8 percent of Caucasian girls and 25 percent of African American girls had precocious puberty. Some experts recommend that puberty should be considered to be early only when it occurs before the age of 7 in Caucasian girls and 6 in African American girls. This finding was partially replicated in a newer study, which appeared in the journal *Pediatrics* in September 2010. Using a smaller sample, the authors found that Caucasian girls were entering puberty precociously at a slightly higher rate than previously.

Few studies have been conducted on early puberty in boys, probably because the results of precocious development in boys are less obvious. Some research in Denmark found that the age of puberty in boys is decreasing, however.

Causes of precocious puberty are unknown, but improved nutrition appears to be one factor. So does obesity, which is now a common childhood problem. Genetics play a role as well. Animal studies have connected exposure to chemicals such as pesticides that increase hormone levels with early puberty.

If a child develops precocious puberty, a physician should be consulted. Sometimes, an underlying physical cause may require treatment. Also, both physical and psychological problems may result from early development of sexual characteristics. Girls especially seem to be at risk for developing stress and body-image problems, and may start engaging in self-destructive adult behaviors such as smoking and drinking. Boys sometimes benefit from early maturity but are also at risk for teasing and taunts by their classmates.

Making Friends

Although children remain dependent on their families for love, support, and guidance throughout the middle childhood years, their interests expand beyond the family. Learning how to make and keep friends depends on social competence and skills that continue to progress throughout the middle childhood years.

Ambivalence about ambidextrousness

About 1 of every 100 kids is ambidextrous — equally skilled with his right and left hand. This trait sounds rather desirable and could come in handy for lots of tasks. In baseball, for example, an ambidextrous player can bat from either side of the plate or perhaps even pitch right- or left-handed. Sounds rather nifty, doesn't it?

On the other hand, researchers in Finland reported in 2010 that at ages 7 and 8, ambidextrous kids may be at risk of developing problems with reading, math, and writing in their teenage years. They also show a greater likelihood of having attention deficit disorder (ADD; see Chapter 12) than kids who have clear-cut hand dominance. This finding doesn't mean that ambidextrous kids *will* experience learning problems or ADD — only that they're at higher risk for these difficulties than other kids are. The increased risk probably has something to do with the way information is processed by the two hemispheres of the brain.

At the same time, most experts do not endorse the idea of imposing or forcing handedness among those who are either left handed or ambidextrous. No one really knows for certain what the effects of doing so would be. We guess you could say that experts are ambivalent about ambidextrousness.

When preschoolers play together, their intentions are simple: They want to have fun. They pay little attention to who their playmates are or to whether those other kids are judging them. This stance changes rapidly during the middle childhood years. Suddenly, playmates' opinions matter. Children start comparing one another on accomplishments and failures.

Research shows that from an early age, children judge one another. Ask most kindergarteners which kids in their class get in the most trouble, for example, and they're likely to give you a couple of names. Ask some third-graders which kids are the "smart kids," and they'll tell you the best students in the class (who are also the ones that the teacher calls on most often). Ask fifth-graders who are the bullies and who are the victims, and they consistently name the same kids.

School-age children also have opinions on which kids they'd like to be friends with. Many studies ask kids to name the classmates they would most like to have as friends and which ones they would *not* like to have as friends, and the results have been pretty consistent over the years and in different settings. Children during the middle childhood years like kids who are cooperative, reliable, and kind. They don't like children who are aggressive or children who are timid and withdrawn.

Engaging socially

Children who are popular and have many friends tend to be well-adjusted through adolescence and adulthood. Therefore, caregivers and teachers should encourage children to learn the skills that will help them become accepted by other children. Children choose other children to be their friends if they view them as having these traits:

- ✔ **Cooperative:** Cooperative children listen to directions, take turns, play by the rules, don't use aggression to get their way, work well with others, and willingly sacrifice for the good of their group. They ask questions of others and have a good grasp of the give-and-take of conversation.

- ✔ **Reliable:** Children who are considered to be reliable do what they say they will do. If they say they will play with a particular person, they follow through, even if someone more appealing shows up. In a group project, they pull their fair share. They tell the truth and don't disclose secrets. These children seem to be secure and authentic.

- ✔ **Kind:** Kind children show empathy. They do nice things for other people, animals, and the world around them. They are polite and show respect for other people. They don't take advantage of weakness in other kids and refrain from mean teasing.

Children figure out how to cooperate, show compassion, and become reliable by modeling those around them. In the past, if parents, caregivers, and teachers valued and modeled these qualities, children acquired them. Unfortunately, adults must now compete with media heroes who don't always support those qualities. When famous sports players, movie stars, animated characters, or other celebrities model narcissism, cruelty, or lack of control, children can be swayed to emulate those negative qualities.

Concerned parents, caregivers, and teachers should be aware that negative role models can influence the children they care about. It's a good idea to limit viewing of violent or aggressive multimedia. Because it's darn near impossible to keep kids away from all negative influences, however, it's important for caregivers to talk about values and the consequences of immoral behavior.

Helping shy kids

Shy kids feel anxious and inhibited around other kids, especially in new situations. Because socializing with other children becomes so important during the middle childhood years, shyness stands out as an issue at this time. The vast majority of kids feel some shyness once in a while. Some children feel uncomfortably shy and have difficulty participating in social activities. A minority of children experience shyness to a debilitating degree. (See Chapter 14 for information about social anxiety disorder, which describes these kids.) This section discusses children who exhibit an uncomfortable but not serious case of shyness.

Kids with debilitating shyness become frozen when meeting other kids. They hold back from almost all social interactions, including games, sports, and play. They almost never speak up in class and appear to be anxious. Sometimes, they even become phobic about going to school at all. We recommend consulting a mental-health professional and/or a child's school counselor in such cases.

It's important to realize that a little dose of shyness may be a good thing. Shy kids rarely break rules or engage in aggressive behavior. Also, moderate shyness often improves over time. Uncomfortably shy kids tend to miss out on many potentially fun activities, however.

Shyness is thought to be caused by a combination of temperament (see Chapters 2 and 4 for information about how genes and temperament lead to shyness), difficult experiences with parents, and teasing and criticism from other kids.

When encountering kids who have a bit of problematic shyness, parents, teachers, and caregivers can help. Specifically, they can do the following things:

- **Express empathy about kids' anxiety.** Caregivers can explain that they understand self-consciousness or worry about meeting new kids. They can tell them whether they've had similar feelings in the past.

- **Nudge them a little.** Make suggestions or set goals with them, such as saying hi to one new kid each day, asking the teacher a specific question, or telling another kid that they like his shoes.

- **Teach them to help others.** Have them help out on a penny-collection fund drive or participate in a class project collecting baskets for overseas soldiers.

- **Suggest that they go out for a team sport.** They don't have to be advanced athletically, but playing for a team puts them in contact with other kids. On the other hand, don't have them go out for a sport if their skills in that area aren't at least reasonably consistent with those of their peers.

- **Encourage them to join a club.** Sometimes kids clubs that rally around common interests, hobbies, or activities like coin collecting, astronomy, or model planes may be less stressful than expecting kids to approach others on their own.

- **Prime them to interact.** Make a few specific suggestions for shy kids to greet other kids, even just by waving hello.

- **Enlist help at school.** Teachers can help by putting shy kids in important leadership roles.

Running into bullies and enemies

Unfortunately, kids sometimes fail to get along with one another. In fact, close to two thirds of all kids in the third grade report that they have experienced one or more relationships with another child whom they describe as an enemy.

Because relationships filled with antipathy are so common, should parents, teachers, and child-care workers be concerned about them? Probably. Research suggests that kids who have more hate-filled relationships than their peers do experience worse overall adjustment, lower achievement in school, and an increased incidence of addiction in ensuing years.

Children who have many enemies often lack good friends. Parents and teachers who notice these unhappy kids need to help them improve their social skills and develop healthy friendships. For ideas, see the preceding section, "Helping shy kids." Consulting a school counselor or a child mental-health professional is also a good idea.

Bullying is another serious interpersonal problem that increases between the ages of 5 and 12. Overall youth violence appears to have peaked in the mid-1990s and is showing signs of dropping, but bullying at school remains a serious concern for teachers, parents, and children alike. According to the U.S. National Center for Education Statistics, more than 40 percent of sixth-graders reported having been bullied at some time during the 2007 school year. More than 14 percent of these kids reported being physically injured (cuts, bruises, and so on) by the bullying.

The effects of bullying, particularly when repeated and systematic, aren't limited to physical injuries. Children who have been bullied often experience fear, anxiety, and/or depression. Sometimes, their concentration and achievement are also affected. They may withdraw or isolate themselves. Some of these problems may endure into adulthood.

Even the bullies themselves are at risk for problems down the road, although their problems look a little different from those of their victims. Bullies tend to run into problems with the law and frequently are convicted for criminal behavior. Also, they typically fail to develop good relationships.

You may wonder who is at risk for being a bully or a victim. The risk factors are quite different for each role, although they both have poor problem-solving skills. Bullies tend to have the following characteristics:

- ✔ They show supreme confidence and high, if not inflated, self-esteem. Yet many people incorrectly believe that bullies have low self-esteem.
- ✔ They are impulsive and have low frustration tolerance.

- They don't perform well in school.
- They have little empathy for their victims.
- They have poor problem-solving skills.
- They abuse substances more often than their peers do.
- They make friends fairly easily — but as you can imagine, those friends are often the wrong ones.
- They're stronger and larger than their peers.
- They strike out in anger with little provocation.

On the other hand, victims of bullies tend to have the following traits:

- They're insecure and have low self-esteem.
- They're overly sensitive, quiet, and cautious.
- They have poor problem-solving skills.
- They have poor social skills and don't make friends easily.
- They're relatively isolated.
- They suffer from depression and/or anxiety.

If you're a teacher, parent, caregiver, or just someone who cares about kids, and you see a child who shows signs of being a bully or a victim of bullying, you should take action, because the long-term consequences for both bullies and victims are not good. See Chapters 9 and 10 for information about what you can do to intervene.

Knowing who matters: Family or friends

Experts used to agree that what children become depends almost exclusively on their genes and their parents. Parents and families were assigned primary responsibility for determining how kids turn out. Thus, if a child turned to drugs, the culprit was genes, bad parenting, or both. Similarly, if a child achieved great success, the parents and/or good genes deserved the credit.

Today, that consensus has pretty much fallen apart. Although controversy reigns with respect to which factors matter and to what degree, many experts now contend that peers and neighborhoods have far more influence on child development than was previously recognized. The reason is rather obvious. Just look at who kids most want to please. More often than not, it's their peers more than their parents. Kids learn the language and accents of their friends and shun their parents' ways of speaking. Kids turn to drugs or study hard for their exams due to the influence of their friends as much as anything else.

We're not ready to declare parenting a nonissue; in fact, we think that parenting matters a lot. We do believe that parents need to examine their kids' friends closely, however, and they should consider moving if they reside in questionable neighborhoods (assuming that such a move is economically possible).

Developing Self-Esteem

In the first few years of elementary school, children begin to compare themselves and their achievements with other children. Their sense of self-worth or self-esteem sometimes gets a bit unstable. Preschoolers are pretty self-centered and don't notice what other kids are doing, but that self-centeredness changes when they enter school and kids start comparing themselves to everyone else.

A first-grade girl who reads pretty well sees that another boy can jump rope longer than she can, and she thinks that this contrast means that she's no longer the perfect child she thought she was. That kid who can jump rope, on the other hand, may compare his brown eyes with those of a blue-eyed classmate and feel less attractive.

As kids grow, their self-views become more focused on what they value. The girl who doesn't jump rope very well is satisfied that she can throw a ball across the gym, and the brown-eyed boy realizes that eye color isn't so important. Therefore, for most kids, self-esteem remains pretty stable until adolescence.

Balanced self-esteem during the middle childhood years is developed when children are given opportunities to achieve goals and praised for their efforts. Teachers and parents have to provide tasks that are challenging but achievable with effort and practice. Beginning readers, for example, should be provided books that contain some words that they don't know yet, but not so many that they can't follow what's going on. Also, the focus of praise needs to be on the effort that the child expends, not on the actual results obtained.

Research shows that praising efforts promotes persistence, and persistent children achieve more than those who give up easily.

As you see in Chapter 7, self-esteem explodes as an important issue in adolescence, but the middle childhood years form the foundation for lasting self-views. At this age, self-esteem can be greatly influenced by peers, so a child who is unpopular in school may suffer from a low self-view.

Parents, teachers, and other caregivers should pay attention to a child who worries about not being popular, providing opportunities to improve social skills (see "Making Friends," earlier in this chapter) and opportunities for success in various endeavors such as athletics, academics, or simply pursuing special interests and hobbies.

Some teachers, parents, and coaches believe that all kids need praise just for breathing. But the Dodo's verdict in *Alice in Wonderland* — "Everybody has won, and all must have prizes" — is counterproductive to developing truly healthy self-esteem.

Discovering Self-Control

Generally speaking, kids manage to get through the "terrible twos" and the preschool years reasonably intact. As they enter the middle childhood years, most of them have acquired at least rudimentary self-control. They can wait their turn during games; they're able to persist with schoolwork; they can eat their vegetables before demanding desert. At least, that's the theory.

Some kids, however, continue to show signs of being oppositional and have difficulty tolerating frustration as they enter the middle childhood years. If a child you care about shows signs of defiance that seem to be problematic, consult a mental-health professional.

This section is about developing optimal levels of self-control, focus, and morality, as well as the ability to regulate emotions, in normally developing kids.

Tolerating the tough times

In Chapters 3 and 5, we note the crucial importance of frustration tolerance as a fundamental life skill that children need to acquire to develop into psychologically healthy adults. Ideally, they begin acquiring this skill before starting school, but it's important to foster frustration tolerance from age 5 to 12 as well. Many of the principles of teaching this skill to preschoolers also apply to teaching kids in this age group.

Here are a few ideas for promoting frustration tolerance in middle childhood:

  ✔ **Model calm tolerance of frustration yourself.** Many adults haven't acquired advanced frustration-tolerance skills themselves. If that description applies to you, work on it! Consider getting professional help as well. When you're frustrated, tell kids that you feel that way, but also tell them how you're going to deal with your frustration (such as take a break from a task; tell yourself to go slow and easy; take a few slow, deep breaths; or count slowly from 1 to 20).

✔ **Reward them for delaying gratification.** Give them lots of opportunities for earning larger rewards if they put off immediate gratification.

✔ **Teach them the value of savings.** Piggy banks are great for kids ages 5 to 10. Later, you can set up bank savings accounts and show them how the amount grows. Put a little of their gift money (such as birthday cash) into these accounts, and have them add some of their earnings from chores or things they do for others.

✔ **Apply consequences when they get frustrated and blow their cool.** If children whine, throw a tantrum, or misbehave when they don't get what they want, be sure to give them a time-out (see Chapter 8) or some similar consequence that fits the crime. Thus, if they throw a tantrum in a store about not getting to buy a toy, put one of their favored toys away for a few days when you return home. Be sure to explain why you're doing so.

✔ **Give reasons, but don't reason with them!** When you discipline a child, it's very helpful to explain _once_ why you're doing so. Don't get into a dialogue in the hope of eliciting a child's agreement with what you've done, however. Doing so will only reinforce the disruptive behavior that started the ball rolling downhill.

✔ **Have lots of positive times with them.** Kids in middle childhood have an easier time tolerating frustration if their frustrating times are sand-wiched between lots of good times. Remember to play with your kids, take them to fun activities, and let them know when they're doing great. Kids love to please, and you need to give them approval whenever you see them coping well.

Staying focused

Acquiring the skills necessary for successful living requires focus and atten-tion, and life has many distractions. Children who are able to pay attention and persist in goal-directed behaviors have distinct advantages over those children who can't seem to stick with their tasks or who flit from one thing to another. Children who have problems paying attention miss out on many learning opportunities. Some children have severe problems in this area and are diagnosed with an attention deficit disorder (see Chapter 12). Focus, however, is a skill that you can develop and improve by making changes in the growing child's environment.

During the middle childhood years, children benefit from the following strate-gies, whether or not they have problems with focus:

✔ **Limit TV and video games.** The average child in the United States watches television four hours a day and spends an additional two hours on the computer. Kids need to be active and actively engaged, however, and TV and computer activities have been found to relate to decreased ability to pay attention.

✔ **Play board games or card games with children to improve attention.** When children are required to count cards, wait for turns, and think about strategies, their attention improves.

✔ **Read books out loud, and encourage independent reading.** Make sure that reading together is a pleasant experience. If your child has trouble reading independently, be sure to talk to a professional about getting her an evaluation (see Chapters 12 and 18). If you wait too long, it will be more difficult to intervene.

✔ **Help children become more organized.** Keep school assignments in folders, decrease clutter, and help them learn about the benefits of to-do lists and calendars.

Acquiring morality

You can find a variety of detailed technical theories about how morality develops. Suffice it to say that children make major leaps in their understanding of morality during the middle childhood years. At around the age of 5, they're pretty much limited to knowing that a few actions will get them in trouble and a few others will not. Rewards and punishments govern most of their behavior at this time, and they don't have much of what could be called a developed conscience.

As middle childhood progresses, kids learn to make flexible judgments about what's right and wrong. They adopt standards and rules about how to behave as their consciences develop. They display altruistic behavior and empathy for others. Furthermore, they can even begin to see when moral standards conflict and can make active choices about what to do. They begin to understand what actions are virtuous and righteous, and take actions that conform to these standards rather than do what will profit themselves most in the short run. They feel guilty when they fail to do what's right. At least, that's the case if all goes well.

Interestingly, a fair measure of self-control probably is necessary for a child to be able to act in a moral fashion. A 10-year-old who finds a $5 bill in a grocery-store aisle, for example, may need some real self-control not to pocket the cash. Having self-control alone isn't sufficient to make a person moral, however. A cold, calculating criminal can have considerable self-control yet be highly immoral.

If by the middle childhood years, a child appears to be failing to develop a strong sense of right and wrong, and doesn't show remorse for transgressing basic rules, a consultation with a mental-health professional may be in order. See Chapter 15 for more information about how to deal with children who consistently demonstrate problems with appropriate behavior and morality.

Parents, teachers, and caregivers can do some things to facilitate the development of moral behavior in middle childhood, including the following:

- ✔ **Help kids see the consequences of their actions.** If a child declares his intention to commit a hurtful action (or just appears to be ready to do so), ask him what's likely to happen if he does. Also ask him how his action would likely make the other child feel.

- ✔ **Model empathy.** It's a good idea to express empathetic views of other people out loud and in front of kids of all ages.

- ✔ **Encourage kids to apologize.** Apologizing helps kids internalize the idea that their behavior affects others. If done correctly, apologizing instills a modest, healthy amount of guilt for inappropriate behavior.

- ✔ **Model altruism.** Do things for your neighbors, and perhaps have kids help out and participate. Explain that picking up your neighbor's newspaper when she's out of town is simply a nice thing to do. Explain that not only will others be more likely to help you when you help them, but also, it's just the right thing to do.

- ✔ **Set consistent limits, but with warmth rather than anger.** Harsh, punitive parenting makes kids want to rebel, and they're more likely to fail to incorporate the moral lesson involved with consequences.

- ✔ **Explain the reasons for right and wrong behavior.** However, you need to keep those explanations very short and avoid endless lecturing. Lectures go in one ear and out the other.

Regulating feelings

Throughout the middle childhood years, learning to control emotions in an adaptive way continues to be a critical task. *Emotional regulation* refers to being able to display emotions appropriately. It's perfectly normal to cry when hurt, to become angry when frustrated, or to be afraid when facing something dangerous, but some children seem to be more easily emotionally aroused than most of their peers, and that can be a problem. Children who don't improve self-regulation during these middle childhood years are more likely to develop emotional problems, social problems, and academic problems as teens.

Children who have difficulty in this area tend to have the following traits:

- ✔ They cry easily and loudly.
- ✔ They get angry about small events.
- ✔ They seem to be sad, apathetic, distressed, or irritable.
- ✔ They're overly fearful.
- ✔ They act withdrawn from the world.
- ✔ They get overwhelmed easily.

Multiple research studies indicate that both early experiences and genetics predict how well a given child will develop control. Later experiences, however (including family life, the presence of a caring adult in the school or community, and psychotherapy), can improve emotional functioning in children. Children who have difficulty controlling their emotions will benefit from the following:

- ✔ **Warm caring from adults:** Acknowledging and accepting children's feelings often calms them down. Remind children that it's always okay to have a feeling, but there may be better ways of expressing it.
- ✔ **Consistent discipline without physical punishment:** For the most part, spanking or physically disciplining children don't work as well as other forms of discipline. Research indicates that children who are disciplined harshly have more difficulties with emotional regulation than children who haven't experienced routine spankings.

Achieving Success

Words provide the vehicle for young children to enter the world of imagination and magically bring forth pictures in their minds. Words make it possible for children to think about people, objects, or events without having to rely on direct experience. This ability, called *representational thought,* allows children to see the present at the same time that they recall the past and imagine the future. Thus, language becomes a powerful tool in the acquisition of knowledge.

Children in the middle childhood age group start sorting their world into logical categories, and they soon learn that there are multiple ways to sort. When we told our 4-year-old granddaughter, Lauren, that we were her mother's parents, she laughed and said, "No way!" To a 4-year-old child, a person can be in only one category, and for each of us, that would be grandparent. Now that she's almost 6, Lauren knows that people can have different relationships. We can be parents and grandparents at the same time. She can be granddaughter, daughter, and sister.

The abilities to use representational thought and categorize are necessary for the mastery of many academic goals. States, cities, countries, and continents are all geographical entities, for example, and dogs, cats, monkeys, and people are all mammals. In addition, the alphabet has 26 letters that represent sounds, and to read and write, children put the letters or sounds together to make words. In mathematics, numbers represent certain quantities that can be added, subtracted, divided, or multiplied. Kids in middle childhood must understand these concepts to learn how to read, write, and perform mathematics.

Managing motivation

Most children arrive at school eager, enthusiastic, and ready to learn. Maintaining motivation throughout the middle childhood years is a challenging task for educators, parents, and students. Face it — as entertaining as some classrooms, teachers, books, and lesson plans can be, large amounts of learning require drill and practice, and to master huge amounts of basic skills, students must persist with patience.

Why do some children keep on keeping on while others give up? Like most questions in child psychology, this one has no simple or straightforward answer. Table 6-1 depicts issues that can either increase motivation in kids or decrease it.

Table 6-1	Looking at Motivation
Motivator	*Demotivator*
Good nutrition	Hunger or poor nutrition
Adequate sleep	Poor sleep habits
Parents' or caregivers' interest in and support of education	Parents' or caregivers' lack of involvement in or concern about education
Peers with high motivation	Peers with low motivation
Adequate resources in schools	Insufficient supplies and poor teacher training
Interventions designed to address children's strengths and weaknesses	Failure to recognize learning challenges and deficits
Enthusiastic teachers	Teachers with low expectations or burnout
Rewards for making good efforts	A lack of rewards or rewards given haphazardly
Opportunities for creative learning	Overreliance on mechanistic workbook assignments
Emphasis on warmth and acceptance by teachers and parents	Overuse of criticism and judgment by teachers and parents

If a child in this age group shows poor motivation, look at the basics first. Make sure that the child is healthy and well nourished and that he or she is getting enough sleep. Parents can improve motivation in their kids by attending school events, showing interest in what their kids do, and closely monitoring their homework. They can consult their kids' teachers as well as the school counselor if need be. Poor motivation shouldn't be ignored. Chapters 8 and 9 provide specific ideas for addressing this problem.

Assessing readiness for school

One debate that many parents and teachers want resolved is when kids are ready to enter school. States vary somewhat in terms of the age at which they accept kids into kindergarten, although they often admit children who reach the age of 5 on or before September 1. Whatever the cutoff date is, many parents struggle about whether to start kids who turn 5 in the couple of months before the cutoff date, because the kids would be the youngest in the class.

Although research on this issue has been somewhat contradictory, there is evidence that kids who enter kindergarten 9 to 12 months older than their peers may start with a slight academic edge that actually manages to endure over the years. As a result, some experts have even called for putting kindergarten-age children in three age groups based on similar age and maturity. No one knows for certain whether such groupings would help level the playing field, however.

We can't say that a child who just turned 5 before starting kindergarten is at a major disadvantage, so we will refrain from making a strong recommendation that parents hold such kids back for another year. If a child lacks certain skills or maturity levels, however, especially if he or she is barely over the cutoff entry date, delaying school entry may make a great deal of sense.

Here are a few of the skills that are desirable for kids to acquire before starting school:

- **Opening nonchildproof containers and boxes:** It helps if kids can open a box of crayons or lunch-box items without assistance.
- **Basic counting:** A child going to kindergarten for the first time ideally should be able to count to 10. Practice counting items with your child at home, at stores, and elsewhere.
- **Knowing and recognizing at least some letters:** Practice recognizing and sounding letters with kids.

- ✔ **Knowing their phone number and address:** Not all [...] before starting school, but it's a good one to work o[...]

- ✔ **Sticking with a task or activity for 10 or 15 minutes** [...] skill gradually.

- ✔ **Feeding themselves:** Kids entering school should be [...] and forks and to drink out of regular cups without as[...]

- ✔ **Getting along with other kids:** Kids at this age should be able to engage in cooperative play reasonably well.

- ✔ **Following directions that have several parts:** Practice asking kids to bring you items and then do something else.

- ✔ **Having basic motor skills:** Kids in this age group generally need to be able to hold pencils and crayons, climb stairs, open doors, and use scissors under supervision.

Please realize that if a child merely lacks one or two of these skills, it may not be a major problem. If you have any doubts or see other problematic concerns in terms of emotional, behavioral, learning, trauma, or autism (see Part IV for details on picking up some difficulties early), you should call the child's pediatrician for information about Child Find, a nationwide program designed to spot early developmental problems and intervene as necessary. For more information and specifics about a particular state, go to: http://www. nichcy.org/Pages/Home.aspx

Reading, writing, and doing arithmetic

The elementary-school years offer children the foundational skills necessary for developing into literate adults. Children learn to read, write, and calculate in the primary grades — usually, grades 1 through 5. Mastering these skills and learning a little about science and history take up most of the primary-school curriculum.

Most kids start kindergarten unable to read more than a few words. They may be able to count to 10 but can't add and subtract. At best, their writing is limited to their name or a couple of letters or words.

By fifth grade, children's skills in the following areas have made quantum leaps:

- ✔ **Reading:** Students should be able to analyze the plot of a story. They also should be able to compare and contrast characters and events, and to recognize whether a story is being told in first or third person. Fifth-graders typically can understand the author's intention (such as to entertain, inform, or persuade) and can use other resources — such as dictionaries, thesauruses, and Web sites — to help them decode written work.

✔ **Writing:** Students should be able to write legibly and use writing to communicate. In their writing, they should be able to use and understand nouns, verbs, adverbs, and adjectives, and they should be able to write sentences that have subject/verb agreement. They should be able to recognize errors, capitalize correctly, and use punctuation properly.

✔ **Arithmetic:** Students' mathematical skills should include the ability to read and write numbers from negative to positive, including fractions and decimals. They should be able to divide whole numbers by one- or two-digit whole numbers. Ideally, they're capable of adding and subtracting fractions as well as decimals. They should have mastered the ability to compare numbers as being less than, greater than, and equal to. In addition, fifth-graders should be able to use mathematics to solve real-world problems.

Chapter 7

Traversing the Teen Years (Ages 13–18)

Adolescence is a time of transition that lies between childhood and adulthood. It may surprise you to learn that this transition period is a concept that has emerged in the past century or two. Before that, kids reaching puberty were pretty much thought of as little adults and put to work. As the Industrial Revolution began in the 18th and 19th centuries, large numbers of menial sweatshop jobs were created and filled, many by children.

Society, rather appropriately, became appalled by the effects of forcing children to toil in these jobs for long hours. Child-labor laws were enacted, and kids were kept in school longer. Voilà! Adolescence was created by a modern, enlightened society. Unfortunately, adolescence isn't always an easy transition.

This period of development often comes along with large amounts of free, at least semiautonomous time, which creates a distressingly large number of opportunities for adolescents to be seduced into destructive, self-indulging, aggressive, and/or antisocial behaviors. In fact, many psychological disorders first show up during the teen years, and most of these disorders have only increased in frequency in the past half century or so. Nevertheless, the majority of kids manage to complete adolescence relatively intact, as do their parents and teachers.

In this chapter, we provide an overview of the teenage years. We describe the way relationships and friendships evolve. We discuss how adolescents' rapidly changing bodies and biological rhythms create challenges. For many adolescents, this period of development is marked by experimentation with drugs, sex, and risky behaviors. Teens commonly become highly self-absorbed and concerned with their images. They also make significant progress intellectually during these years. Getting through adolescence in one piece sometimes feels like a remarkable achievement.

Shifting Attachments

The attachments children form with their mothers, fathers, or other close caregivers usually lasts a lifetime. Evolutionary theory suggests, however, that one purpose of life is to reproduce. The young must leave their nests, fly away, and form families of their own. To have the courage to leave home, teens begin to form close attachments to others their age. In the early teen years, these attachments tend to be of the same sex; later, teens hang out in mixed groups; and in the final adolescent years, they often focus on dyadic sexual relationships (whether homosexual, bisexual, or heterosexual in nature).

The importance of forming good relationships throughout life has been demonstrated in numerous studies. People who manage to obtain good social support networks in their lives tend to be happier, achieve more, cope with stress better, have greater satisfaction with their lives, have healthier immune systems, and enjoy better overall health than those with less effective social networks. Adolescence is a time in which critical skills of relating with others develop.

Conflicting loyalties

Some teens transition seamlessly from childhood to adulthood. At some point, however, most adolescents question the values and morals of their families. These questions may take the form of late-night musings with friends, soul-searching poetry, or risky actions that surprise and shock their parents.

The tug-of-war between the teen's family of origin and the culture of friends is a normal part of growing up. Teens need to say no and question authority to figure out the directions of their own independent lives. This time of questioning leads adolescents to paths that may look very similar to those of their parents, very different, or a mix of their own direction combined with that of their parents. Issues like religion, careers, values, work ethics, and sexuality are considered and debated during adolescence.

Fostering friends

In Chapter 6, we note that friends grow in importance during middle childhood: the school-age years, 5 to 12. The importance of these relationships grows even further during adolescence. As young teens exit middle childhood, their quest for autonomy increases, and friendships help them achieve the skills they'll need to get along in life as adults. Thus, most teenagers spend more time with their peers than they do with their parents or other adults.

How well or poorly these relationships go has a major effect on teenagers that can endure for a lifetime. Teens who feel rejected, disconnected, and/or alienated tend to have greater risk for the following events compared with other kids:

- ✔ High levels of anxiety
- ✔ Bouts of depression
- ✔ Risky behavior
- ✔ Substance abuse
- ✔ Feelings of loneliness
- ✔ Failure in school

To avoid feelings of disconnection, kids try to find groups with which they can identify and obtain some sort of acceptance. Some groups are considered to be more desirable than others, of course. Terms for various groups of teens change all the time but include the *brains* (smart in schoolwork), *jocks* (athletes), *Goths* (wear black and have pale skin), *preppies* (dress conservatively and are teachers' pets), *populars* (everyone wants to be their friends), *geeks or nerds* (usually very smart but socially awkward), *emos* (very emotional), and *artsy* (into arts and/or drama). You can probably guess for the most part which groups are considered to be desirable versus "not so much." Unfortunately for parents and teachers, teens frequently prefer to be *populars* or *jocks* rather than *brains.*

Understanding types of peer influence

How do peer groups and friendships influence adolescents? Through a variety of mechanisms. The types of influence include the following:

- ✔ **Modeling:** Peer groups model expected behavior. Chapter 2 reviews the fact that modeling or observational learning is one of the three major ways that children learn from their experiences in the world.

- ✔ **Reinforcement:** Reinforcement is a type of operant conditioning (see Chapter 2) in which kids reward one another (often through praise or increased status) for the actions that they take.

- ✔ **Threats of rejection, harm, or exclusion:** Unfortunately, peer groups also influence their members through intimidation, threats of rejection, threats of physical harm, and exclusion. Because humans are fundamentally social creatures, threats of exclusion are usually perceived as being quite serious and can lead to depression. See Chapter 15 for more information about gangs, which often rely on these methods of influence.

- ✔ **Teaching one another:** Peer groups and friends teach one another directly. These relationships help adolescents develop their identities, understand social norms and mores, and appreciate the role of empathy and emotional support more deeply than they did in friendships at earlier ages.

Noting how parents and teachers can help

If friendships and peer groups are so critical to navigating adolescence successfully, you may wonder how parents and teachers can facilitate healthy relationships. Here are some ways you can help:

- ✔ **Promote secure parent/child attachment.** Numerous studies show that the quality of the relationship between adolescents and their parents spills over into the quality of relationships with peer groups and friends. It also appears that the relative importance of the father's relationship with his offspring grows during the children's adolescences.

- ✔ **Provide reasonable supervision.** Perhaps it goes without saying, but the children of parents who have a pretty good idea of what their kids are doing, with whom, when, and where usually have healthier peer groups than otherwise.

- ✔ **Talk with teenagers about their peers and friendships.** It's important not to pry, but let teens know you're interested and willing to provide advice when they report difficulties with their friends.

- ✔ **Give suggestions on how to deal with conflict.** Teach adolescents that the best solutions usually involve compromise rather than viewing conflict as black-and-white.

- ✔ **Talk with teens about putting themselves in other people's shoes.** Ask teens to try out other people's perspectives and viewpoints on difficult issues.

- ✔ **Teach teens the value of volunteering and helping others.** Consider finding ways that teens could tutor other adolescents or volunteer in their community.

- ✔ **Encourage participation in team sports or clubs.** If teens have very little athletic talent, perhaps they could be encouraged to join clubs with kids who have similar interests (collecting, debating, and so on).

✔ **Emphasize goals involving cooperation.** Reviews of large numbers of studies of adolescents have demonstrated that goals that are set up to emphasize cooperation more than competition and/or individuality have a double benefit. Cooperation seems to improve the quality of students' friendships, as well as how much they learn and achieve in school. Cooperative goals involve teaching teens to share information and help one another, whereas competitive goals emphasize win/lose situations in an atmosphere of distrust, and individualistic goals involve an emphasis on the individual with little regard for others.

Social networking among friends

Teens communicate via texting and short communiqués of all sorts on an ever-growing number of social-networking sites: Bebo, Facebook, MySpace, Twitter, Gather, Habbo, and many more. Is this a good thing or not?

Frankly, we don't know, but many experts believe we should find out. Teens frequently send dozens, if not hundreds, of brief messages each day through these e-connections and spend as long as eight hours every day on one type of electronic device or another. Therefore, it seems that someone ought to determine the effects of this change in the way adolescents communicate and spend their time.

It's quite possible that diminished real-world, face-to-face time may mute the ability of teens to understand and use subtle social cues, interpret body language, and communicate their own emotions in nuanced yet crucial ways. These subtle skills are typically learned during the teenage years and may be much more difficult to acquire later. Also, interest in close, intimate relationships could suffer from overreliance on texting. After all, Facebook isn't exactly a site replete with in-depth conversations.

On the other hand, e-communication could have an important upside. Kids who are extremely shy or lacking in social skills may actually find this form of communication to be an easier first step in venturing out. And adolescents who suffer from more serious forms of social deficits, such as a disorder on the autism spectrum (see Chapter 13 for more information), may find that the clarity of written symbols greatly enhances their otherwise-seriously-impaired abilities to decipher subtle emotions. Teenagers like these may be able to connect with others their own age in ways they simply couldn't do otherwise.

Therefore, research is clearly needed to determine whether all this texting and e-communicating exerts more harmful or beneficial affects on teenagers. In the meantime, parents and teachers should set rules and limitations on the use of phones, computers, and other devices. Until experts and parents know more, common sense should prevail. We do know that having dinner together as a family uninterrupted is a good idea and if students are sitting in class, listening to the teacher is a better strategy than texting. Furthermore, keeping conversations going between teens and parents can allow parents to do something if they hear that abuse or cyber bullying is going on.

Changing Bodies

Adolescence, like infancy, involves rapid physical transformations. Many of those physical changes are the result of changing mixtures of *hormones* (chemical substances in the body that affect growth, emotions, and behaviors). These hormonal surges begin the process of puberty. *Puberty* refers to the time period that starts and completes the process of leaving childhood and becoming a sexually mature adult.

Increasing hormones

Before the physical signs of puberty are obvious, a signal originating in the brain tells the growing body to increase the production of hormones that lead to the growth and development of a sexually mature adult. The primary hormones involved are estrogen in females and testosterone in males. These hormones trigger the development of primary and secondary sex characteristics. The primary sex characteristics are those structures and functions that are needed for reproduction, such as changes in the uterus in females and changes in the penis and testicles in males. Body-hair growth under the arms and in the pubic area is an example of a secondary sex characteristic.

Hormones are often blamed for moodiness and risky behaviors in teens, and there is indeed some truth to that hypothesis. In males, increasing levels of testosterone can be associated with anger and aggression. In females, changes in hormone levels before menstruation are linked to moodiness. Science has not been able to explain, however, why high levels or fluctuations of hormones in some teens (and adults) really don't have much effect on either behavior or mood, whereas for others, slight changes or elevations seem to trigger rage, giddiness, or grief.

The influence of hormones on adolescent moods and behaviors appears to be an interaction of biology, psychology, and culture. In terms of biology, good nutrition is linked with earlier puberty, especially in girls. Increased psychological stress, such as when teens live in crowded urban areas, is also linked to early puberty.

Culture may dictate how adolescents express their newfound interest in sexuality. In some cultures, for example, it's taboo for unmarried adolescents to have any physical contact; other cultures support early sexual relations and marriage. The vast majority of teens adheres to their cultures' expectations, so don't blame all early sexual behavior on raging hormones.

Changing body clocks

Getting out of bed in the morning can be tough for anyone, but it's especially tough for teenagers. That's because teens experience changes in their *circadian rhythms* — the biological clocks that regulate sleep and wake cycles. Over the past 20 years or so, loads of researchers have discovered what parents and teachers have always known: Teens have trouble falling asleep at night (before 11 p.m. or so), and getting up early. Therefore, teenagers, who generally need more than eight hours of sleep a night, just don't get enough sleep. As a result, they arrive at school with minds dulled by sleep deprivation. Sleepiness results in poor concentration, poor memory, irritability, and even impaired driving.

Unfortunately, teens' school schedules usually collide with these biological facts. High school start times often begin well before the teenage brain is in gear for optimum learning. Scientists and politicians have often called for later start times for teens, but few school districts have changed their schedules, citing transportation issues, concerns about fitting extracurricular activities into the day, and finances as reasons.

Yet experiments have shown that respecting the biological clocks of teen students by delaying the start of the school day can result in huge improvements for schools and students. Giving teenagers a bit more sleep in the morning is associated with improved attendance, fewer visits to the nurse, less tardiness, and even higher grades. Making the change seems like a no-brainer.

Resisting Temptations

By the end of adolescence, teenagers gain instant admittance to a world of opportunities, responsibilities, privileges, roles, and options. These possibilities involve joy, risks, sadness, losses, and gains. The world of those leaving adolescence behind changes dramatically, as they now can do the following things:

- ✔ Drive a vehicle
- ✔ Vote
- ✔ Enter into binding contracts
- ✔ Serve on a jury
- ✔ Get married

- Engage in sexual activity with consenting adults
- Join the military
- Be criminally charged as an adult
- Gamble legally
- Enter college

A few of these new responsibilities and rights don't occur exactly on everyone's 18th birthday, but they're rolled out for most people around that time in life. Obviously, readiness for all these new duties doesn't happen on a single day, such as an 18th birthday.

Taking on these tasks responsibly requires adolescents to learn a lot about how to control their impulses, manage their emotions, and control rebellious behaviors.

Ideally, the task of learning self-control begins in the preschool years, continues during the school years, and completes by the end of adolescence. Teachers, parents, and child-care providers all need to realize that the early-adolescent years may represent their last chance of giving kids solid footing and a good start into adulthood. If a child is demonstrating serious deficiencies in self-control during early adolescence, a referral to a mental-health professional may be in order. Chapter 15 provides specific examples of such serious signs.

Constraining impulses

Experts are rather fond of pointing out that the adolescent brain isn't fully developed, and there's truth in that assertion. The brain doesn't complete its developmental processes until a person's early 20s. The frontal lobes are the final areas of the brain to develop, and they're responsible for many vital functions, such as these:

- Planning
- Judgment
- Self-control
- Reasoning
- Problem-solving
- Executive functions (integrating and managing incoming information)

Thus, without fully developed frontal lobes, teenagers tend to be more impulsive in a wide range of areas than mature adults are. They take more risks; they react to stress more strongly; they fall prey to peer pressures; they often act aggressively; and they frequently focus on short-term rewards while ignoring longer-term negative consequences.

The problem with controlling impulses is made even worse by the common belief among adolescents that they're literally *invincible* — immune to harm or defeat and simply impervious to any dangers in driving, having sex, taking drugs, or skydiving.

Just because adolescents don't have completely developed brains and tend to be more impulsive than adults doesn't mean that they're incapable of making reasonable decisions or that they don't hold some culpability for their actions. After all, many adolescents don't consistently violate reasonable social norms.

You can facilitate the acquisition of impulse control during the adolescent years. Here are a few things you can do:

- ✔ **Instruct teenagers how to think about future consequences.** You can ask questions such as "What would likely happen if you actually did that?"

- ✔ **Teach skills involved with patience.** Most adults know that they can use distraction or remind themselves about the benefits of waiting patiently. You can model using wait time productively by making plans for later that week. Voice the planning process out loud.

- ✔ **Teach active problem-solving skills.** These skills include brainstorming lots of solutions, evaluating the likely outcomes of each solution, rehearsing the chosen solution, trying out the solution, and evaluating the results.

- ✔ **Take every opportunity you can to talk about the value of impulse control.** Also, model this behavior whenever possible.

- ✔ **Pay attention when a teenager manages to make good choices and control his impulses.** Let him know that you noticed!

Riding emotional roller coasters

Emotional regulation goes hand in hand with impulse control, and the two concepts are indeed quite similar. *Emotional regulation* refers to the ability to moderate, adjust, or control emotions, whereas *impulse control* refers more to actions a person may take when feeling strong emotions. Thus, a particular teenager may feel extreme anxiety or even rage without having a way of moderating those feelings, yet not act out improperly. As you can imagine, however, the ability to moderate emotions makes controlling impulses a whole lot easier to do.

Studies have shown that adolescents can learn to regulate their emotions. Even teenagers who aren't showing serious signs of emotional problems can benefit from strategies for managing their emotions. See Chapter 14 for more information about emotional disorders and Chapter 17 for therapies that work.

Here are a few suggestions for helping teens acquire the ability to regulate their own emotions:

✔ **Teach them to label their emotions.** Many teens don't know what they're feeling. If you're a teacher, parent, or caregiver, you probably have a pretty good idea what emotions a child may be feeling. Suggest a few possibilities (anxious, sad, distraught, upset, angry, and so on). Knowing emotions is a good first step toward emotional regulation for any adolescent.

✔ **Provide them with a few skills for tolerating strong emotions.** Here are a few examples:

  • Exercising (such as running or weightlifting)

  • Slow, deep breathing

  • Distraction (such as slowly counting backward from 100)

  • Listening to favorite music

  • Taking a long hot bath or a soak in a hot tub

  • Writing about the feelings

✔ **Teach them to repeat some coping phrase that they find useful.** Examples include "All bad feelings pass with time," "I've lived through this before, and I can again," and "Feelings are just feelings; they can't hurt me."

These skills are great ones to teach almost any teen, but you shouldn't force teens to practice these techniques if they're not interested. If you know an adolescent who is exhibiting serious difficulties in coping with life (see Part IV for the various forms that these problems can take), please consider a referral to a mental-health professional and/or the family doctor, who can evaluate the situation and make a referral if one is indicated.

Rebelling: The good and the bad

Adolescents are notorious for being oppositional, if not outright rebellious. Teenagers relish in the defiance and turmoil that they create. Parents and teachers find this behavior quite frustrating, but they need to realize that there's a good reason for this rebelliousness.

Specifically, a major task adolescents face is to discover that they can function independently from their parents. To achieve that independence, most teens engage in at least a few obnoxious, rebellious behaviors. Adolescents wear clothes that their parents don't like, listen to music that their folks can barely stand, spend money foolishly, act as rudely as they can get away with, and sometimes experiment with drugs and sex. With a little luck, they manage to stay within the rules just enough to avoid any lasting, harmful effects from all their rebelliousness. As often as not, teens learn a lot about their abilities, values, and desires for the future through these trials and tribulations.

One of our colleagues once suggested that the cure for such adolescent rebellion would be to have teens all freeze-dried (like instant coffee) at the age of 12 and undo the process when they hit 18. We have a feeling that as great an idea as it sounds like, it probably just won't work! Instead, we do have a few suggestions that may make the process a little easier for teachers, parents, and caregivers:

- ✔ Resist the temptation to micromanage teen behavior. Let go of the little stuff, and try to realize that much teen oppositionality is little stuff.

- ✔ Don't criticize anything that you don't have to criticize.

- ✔ When teens are in bad moods, let them know you're available to talk, but respect their need for space and privacy.

- ✔ Don't snoop into every private detail, even though technologies now exist that make such snooping easier than ever. You may find out things that you'd have no idea what to do about, and you could seriously rupture your relationship with your child if you do.

- ✔ Set household rules, limits, curfews, and expectations only for important things, but have clear consequences for violations. When a violation occurs, follow through on the consequence, but don't lecture. Teens very well understand what they've done to deserve the consequence.

- ✔ When they ask you for advice, feel free to talk, but see whether you can get them to come up with a good answer by asking questions rather than directly telling them what to do.

If teens engage in excessive oppositional behavior or lawbreaking, consider a referral to a mental-health professional.

Exploring Identity: Who I Am

"Mirror, mirror, on the wall, who am I?" "What will I become?" "What is the purpose of my life?" These are the types of questions that most adolescents grapple with. At the same time that they're thinking about the meaning of life, they're studying the tiny red speck on their forehead, desperately hoping that it won't become a cursed pimple.

Thoughts of nuclear disaster, world famine, and environmental catastrophe compete with the terror of deciding what shirt to wear to the meetup group. Adolescence is a time in which the search for identity roils and sometimes resolves; at other times, resolution doesn't occur until adulthood. An adolescent wrestles with issues like these:

- Will I finish high school?
- Will I continue to college?
- Where can I go to college?
- What will I become?
- Am I a good person?
- Which group of friends will I associate with?
- What will be my religion?
- Am I attractive?
- Will I have a religion?
- What are my politics?
- Am I comfortable with my body?
- How close will I be to my family?
- What is my sexual orientation?

Not all these questions are answered during adolescence, but the teen years are when kids start pondering them. The following sections review various aspects of self-views and identity what most teens grapple with.

Focusing on me

Adolescence is a time of extreme self-consciousness. Young children love it when people pay attention to them, but adolescents have a different perspective: They both believe and fear that people are *always* looking at them. So when they walk into a room, most teens believe that they're the center of the universe and that all the other members of the human race are thinking about and judging them. They think that for the most part, they can't possibly be as smart, pretty, or popular as they should be.

This painful fear of being judged probably accounts for why self-esteem commonly drops during the early teen years. Low self-esteem often accompanies depression, anxiety, and other problems. Perhaps that's why many parents, educators, and child-care workers worry a lot about instilling high self-esteem in kids.

On the other hand, generations born after the mid-1960s have consistently thought better of themselves than did those in earlier generations. In 2006, Dr. Jean Twenge and colleagues looked at more than 16,000 college students and found that their scores on a measure of *narcissism* (excessively high self-esteem) have risen steadily over the past several decades. Two-thirds of the students in 2006 had scores that were indicative of excessive narcissism. Check out Dr. Twenge's book, *Generation Me* (Simon & Schuster), for more details.

Narcissistic people generally have problems with the following:

- ✔ Forming and maintaining good relationships
- ✔ Telling the truth
- ✔ Avoiding violence and aggression
- ✔ Controlling their impulses
- ✔ Expressing emotional warmth

Arguably, teachers and parents should worry a little less about instilling high self-esteem in kids. No one thinks that it's a good idea for kids to think poorly of themselves (low self-esteem), but the consequences of inflated self-esteem are mostly negative. Besides, self-esteem usually pops right back up again by middle and late adolescence (ages 15 to 18).

As in middle childhood (ages 5 to 12), healthy self-esteem is balanced and based on accomplishments, not meaningless praise for everything kids do. Teenagers do best when adults reward hard work and effort. Research has shown consistently that too much focus on the self (also known as self-absorption) tends to underlie many types of emotional disorders.

Body image: Looking in the mirror all the time

Body image refers to how people characterize and feel about the way they look. Teens go through dramatic changes in appearance in a short time and are often overly concerned with body image. Unfortunately, most adolescents aren't thrilled with what they see. They find themselves saying things like:

> "I'm too fat! I have an ugly nose. My ears stick out. My head is too big. Just look at my feet, they're huge. I hate my hair! I'm too skinny."

Teens are influenced by singers, actors, models, and other celebrities they see in the media. Those people aren't representative of what most people look like, however. It's no wonder that girls usually want to be thinner, and that's why the teen years are usually when eating problems begin. (See

Chapter 14 for more information on eating disorders.) Boys usually want to be stronger-looking or taller than they really are.

Signs of an unhealthy body image include

- Frequent complaints about how a teen compares with others
- Excessive concern about weight
- Excessive requests for reassurance about appearance
- Purging after eating
- Excessive dieting
- Compulsive exercising
- Requests for plastic surgery for inconsequential, perceived defects
- Illegal steroid use
- Excessive purchase of expensive supplements

If these signs seem to be especially extreme or persist for months, parents or teachers should consider a referral to a mental-health professional and/or the child's physician. See Chapter 14 for more information about eating disorders (which often stem from body-image concerns), and see Chapter 17 for effective treatments.

Parents and teachers should model healthy body images by not making derogatory comments about their own bodies or other people's — whether they're overweight or not. It's okay to discuss health, wellness, and nutrition from time to time, but it's best not to dwell upon issues like weight and appearance.

Developing sexuality and sexual identity

During childhood, kids learn about gender. At that age, gender simply means dividing people into groups of boys or males or girls or females. Depending on the social world children live in, those gender roles are pretty clear. The awareness of gender during adolescence grows, and there are many more questions to be asked and answered about sexuality. First, look at some terms that are commonly confused by parents and their kids:

- **Gender identity:** What people believe about whether they are inwardly male or female. A person's gender identity can match his or her external biological gender, or it may be different.
- **Gender role:** The way a person acts (primarily male or female). These behaviors are highly determined by culture.

- ✔ **Heterosexual:** A person who is attracted to and sexually aroused primarily by someone of the opposite sex, also known as heterosexual orientation.

- ✔ **Homosexual:** A person who is primarily attracted to and sexually aroused by someone of the same sex. Like heterosexuality, homosexuality is another kind of orientation. Homosexual men are usually called gays. Homosexual women are usually called lesbians.

- ✔ **Bisexual:** Someone who is attracted to and sexually aroused by both sexes. Bisexuality is also a form of sexual orientation.

- ✔ **Transgender:** A person who feels like he should be a she or she should be a he. This has nothing to do with behavior — only with feelings. Transgender people can be heterosexual, homosexual, or bisexual. Some transgender people eventually undergo surgery to make their external selves match their internal experience.

- ✔ **Transvestite:** A person who dresses and acts like the opposite sex. Transvestites can be heterosexual, homosexual, or bisexual.

Adolescents experiment with sexuality, gender roles, and gender identity. Teachers and parents should be open to the possibility that a teen who announces that he or she is straight or gay may actually have a change in mind a few months later.

Many years ago, psychologists thought that homosexuality among males was caused by overbearing mothers and passive fathers bringing up wimpy little boys. Obviously, science has progressed from that arcane idea. Like everything else, sexuality (both gender and identity) is affected by an interaction of genetic influences, hormones secreted during prenatal development, hormones secreted during puberty, and social and cultural influences. Clearly, most young people appear to have distinct preferences in the way they express themselves sexually and whom they are attracted to. The process sometimes begins before adolescence but often is not finalized until the end of the teen years or even somewhat later.

Parents should try to take an open, nonjudgmental stance in talking with teenagers about sexual identity issues. If they find their own emotions too difficult to handle or if their teen exhibits high distress about the issue, it's a good idea to consider a referral to a mental-health professional.

An especially controversial issue is whether sexual orientation can be changed. This controversy has been especially interesting, given some of the unexpected, well-publicized sexual exploits of public figures. We don't know the answer. Most social scientists who are interested in sexuality believe that people couldn't change their orientation easily even if they were provided medical or psychological interventions.

Resolving identity issues

To answer questions about identity, teenagers spend great amounts of time thinking about and looking at themselves. Their search for identity can lead them through many episodes of experimentation. At the end of the teen years, most teens end up with one of the following types of resolutions to their identity (which could still change in later years):

- **Clear commitment:** These teens figure out who they are and want to become. They seem to be stable and well adjusted.

- **Rebellious:** Rebels without a cause, these teenagers really aren't committed to anything except being against everything that their parents, culture, or society supports.

- **Unstable:** Sometimes rebellious, at other times committed, but usually confused, these adolescents don't know what to do and may shift from one extreme to another.

- **Deferred:** Some of these teens try to hold off on choosing an identity. They're often dependent, apathetic, and stuck. Making a decision to do nothing, of course, is really making a decision.

- **Narrow choice:** These teens get caught up in a specific group, such as a gang, a cult, or a religion (usually fundamentalist).

The best result is that a teenager reach a clear commitment to an identity by the end of adolescence.

For those still in one of the other categories, talking to a mental-health professional, a trusted relative or family friend, or a spiritual counselor may help resolve the problem. Sometimes parents aren't the best choice if the anguished teen is struggling to find his own, independent place in the world.

Advancing in Thinking

Teenagers think — a lot. Their brains are wired to regard their world as though it revolved around them. Psychologists refer to this way of thinking as *egocentric*. Gradually, however, the self-conscious, self-absorbed adolescent mind expands to include the world at large. As teenagers move toward adulthood, so do their abilities to think logically and morally and to make plans.

Increasing logical thinking

The adolescent mind is capable of solving problems through sophisticated processes. Unlike the concrete-thinking children of middle-childhood years, teens can imagine and strategize solutions to complex problems. Think of the brain as being an efficient computer. Information comes in and gets crunched, and solutions come out. To solve problems, teens must be able to do the following:

- ✔ **Use selective, focused attention:** That means paying attention to what is important. Think about how many teens can listen to music while doing homework.

- ✔ **Have adequate short-term memory:** That means being able to hold on to bits of information in memory, such as strings of numbers, letters, or words.

- ✔ **Have working memory:** Working memory involves holding information in the mind and manipulating it. Think of solving short word problems or thinking through a set of instructions.

- ✔ **Have long-term memory:** Long-term memory includes factual information learned from direct experiences at home, at school, and in the neighborhood.

- ✔ **Use advanced reasoning:** Teenagers start to use hypothetical thought; they can solve novel problems using what they already know. *Deductive reasoning* (sometimes called *top-down reasoning*) involves starting with a general principle and applying that principle to a specific instance. All humans need water to survive, for example, and if Sherry is human, she needs water to survive.

  Inductive (or *bottom-up*) *reasoning* starts with examples and forms a general principle or conclusion. In that case, a teen would notice that all living humans drink water and then conclude that water is necessary for life.

- ✔ **Use metacognition:** *Metacognition* is "knowing about knowing." In other words, adolescents develop the ability to understand something about their own mental processes. Unlike younger children, teenagers generally understand that someone who apparently is inactive may actually be deep in thought, for example. They can also appreciate the fact that their own ability to think varies due to boredom, fatigue, or distractions.

Although teenagers' ability to reason and think abstractly grows exponentially as they approach adulthood, they're often hampered in using these advanced skills due to problems with handling their volatile emotions. They will be able to use advanced ways of thinking and problem-solving consistently only as they learn to regulate or moderate their emotions (see "Riding emotional roller coasters," earlier in this chapter).

Moving ahead morally

Young children have primitive ideas about morality. They mostly do what they're told to receive rewards and avoid punishment. As they mature, children typically understand more about norms, expectations, and values of society as a whole. They begin to see the value of helping others and may understand that laws and rules are not capricious, but benefit society as a whole.

As they advance through adolescence, some — though not all — teens develop more advanced ideas about morality. They come to understand human rights and principles of fairness. Sometimes, they demonstrate advanced moral principles through concrete, altruistic actions that have no obvious benefit to themselves but that enhance the lives of others.

Keep conversations open with teens. They need to express their views about morality, which represents their attempt to experiment with ideas and concepts. Teens challenge their parents, teachers, and others in authority. Although they have advanced thinking skills, they often have overly rigid ideas about morality and fairness. Their actions frequently fail to correspond with the high moral standards they express due to their emotional impulsivity. Alternatively, they may express obnoxious ideas about morality that they don't act on. The bottom line for adults is to understand this experimentation and to keep their cool. Excessive harshness and criticism just encourages rebellion.

Setting long-term goals

Teenagers and impulsive behaviors seem to go hand in hand. Yet normally developing teens begin to understand that what they do today may affect their future. *Begin* is something of an overstatement, because lots of teens don't consider future consequences. For that matter, lots of adults never seem to master that skill either.

So although teenagers are able to understand that their actions have consequences, because of their impulsivity, hormones, or moods, they may not act in accordance with their thoughts. Parents and teachers need to be understanding but not necessarily forgiving of this tendency. Learning to be able to set future goals and do things necessary to achieve those goals is another important lesson that should be practiced in adolescence. Here are a few examples of how to support teens who are learning how to set long-term goals:

- ✔ **Alaina,** a 13-year-old, hasn't been allowed to have her ears pierced. Her mother tells her that she can earn extra spending money by doing extra chores. When she saves enough money to pay for ear piercing, she will be allowed to have her ears pierced.

✔ **Carter,** age 15, looks forward to starting driver's education next year. In preparation, his father tells him that he must maintain a 3.5 grade-point average the year before he drives and keep that average to have his father pay for discounted automobile insurance. Otherwise, Carter must pay for the insurance himself.

✔ On the first day of school, **Mr. Roberts** tells his 10th-grade class that those who get good grades on their quizzes in the first half of the semester will not be required to take the midterm exam.

Part III
Growing Great Kids

The 5th Wave   By Rich Tennant

"You belong to a Dungeons and Dragons group, you're a committed Goth, and you're failing Medieval History?!"

In this part . . .

We tell you what families can do to foster attachment, control misbehavior, and enhance child development. We also take a look at how parents can improve their attitudes in dealing with their kids. Then we turn to schools, telling parents how to evaluate the various educational options that are available.

Finally, we discuss the role of communities in supporting children and families. Communities vary in terms of how child-friendly they are. We tell you what to look for and give a few suggestions about work you can do to improve your community.

Chapter 8

Creating Functional Families

*P*arents have been parenting for a real long time. Throughout most of history, people had kids and just reared them. Your great-grandparents didn't have shelves of books telling them when to feed their babies, how to discipline them, or where to send them to school. For the most part, parents loved their kids, and their kids grew up.

We believe that most parents understand the essentials of good parenting without having to get a lot of expert help. Parents know that they should generally be kind yet firm with their kids. They know that they shouldn't spoil or deprive their kids. They know that they need to love their children but also encourage independence.

So in this chapter, we don't spend a lot of time telling parents what they already know. Instead, we concentrate on giving some practical information and tips to help parents or caregivers do what they already know how to do — a bit better and perhaps with more confidence. For even more advice, review Chapters 3 through 7 for tips on promoting the core goals of childhood (securing solid attachment, developing healthy self-views, controlling impulses, and enhancing achievement).

We also appreciate how difficult it can be to rear a child in these challenging times and that some children present special challenges, so with that in mind, we encourage parents and families to be kind to themselves. We all do the best we can do.

Promoting Parental Attachments

The real goal of parenting is to rear a child who eventually leaves. That's a really tough job. Throughout childhood — and really, throughout life — the opposing branches of dependence and independence bend back and forth. Bonding is established during positive interactions between child and caregiver. These early experiences of closeness make the later tasks of education and discipline go more smoothly.

Bonding early

Babies enter the world fully equipped for bonding. They seek out human contact and quickly learn how to keep the contact coming. Caregivers can give infants what they need by holding, feeding, and caring for them. Bonding and attachment gets a bit tougher for some caregivers, however, as the child gets older and starts venturing off.

Bonding and forming an attachment with a child takes time, but it doesn't take extraordinary planning or financial resources. Children love attention, and if you spend time doing what they want to do, they will reward you with love. Sit down with a little one and color, play board games, play card games, or go for a walk outside. Read stories and books. Have a child read a book to you. Go to a park.

If you're a parent or caregiver who must spend lots of time away from home, make special efforts to stay connected with your children. Kids love to get messages and mail (yes, even the electronic kind). They benefit from knowing that others are thinking about them.

Increasing independence

When the child has fully attached to a caregiver, the pushing away begins almost immediately. Children learn independence by becoming masters of everyday matters. Children who walk well navigate easily away from their primary caregivers. Children who talk well make connections with others. Children whose families provide them opportunities to be successful in their worlds gain self-confidence and appropriate self-esteem.

At the same time, some children, because of special challenges, aren't able to walk smoothly or talk well. They may have trouble with achieving self-confidence and success. In those instances, caregivers need to set goals at a level consistent with the child's abilities and make sure that the child is given the opportunity to interact with others in a safe place. The goals of independence must be in harmony with the child's abilities, and those individual abilities can be celebrated and supported at almost any level (please refer to Part V).

Examining Parenting Styles

Four major types of parenting styles have been identified in numerous studies conducted across the world. Each of these styles tends to influence children in particular ways. Those influences vary somewhat from culture to culture, however, in terms of what they look like as well as the effects they have on kids. Most of the early research emphasized European American families, so we first focus on how these parenting styles play out for them. Then we note a few of the ways that some of these styles may vary elsewhere in the world.

In this section we talk about "parenting," but many people in a child's life can do the parenting. Kids are raised by parents, extended family, neighbors, and teachers.

Being authoritarian/dictatorial

The *authoritarian/dictatorial* parenting style is characterized by a lack of warmth and affection combined with high expectations and standards for children's behavior. These parents tend to be somewhat harsh and resort to punitive discipline. They don't tend to demonstrate a lot of concern for hearing their children's viewpoints. Such parents demand instant obedience without discussion.

Kids of parents who use the authoritarian/dictatorial parenting style tend to have more anxiety than other kids, and their self-esteem trends toward the low end. Their ability to tolerate frustration isn't particularly good. Sometimes, they respond with anger; at other times, they develop depression.

Actually, we've added the word *dictatorial* to the more commonly used term *authoritarian* to help you distinguish this style from the similar word *authoritative* (which we cover in a later section in this chapter). Sometimes, we even mix those two terms up, so please don't think we're being condescending!

Allowing permissiveness

Parents who have a *permissive* parenting style are usually very warm and accepting of their children, expressing affection for them frequently. At the same time, they don't set many rules and aren't particularly demanding of their kids. They don't set high expectations. They listen to their kids' viewpoints but don't see themselves as being largely responsible for determining how their kids turn out.

Children raised by permissive parents tend to be disobedient. They also have very low ability to tolerate frustration, have poor self-control, and are relatively unhappy, especially compared with kids reared by parents who use an authoritative style (see the following section). They're often immature and somewhat dependent, and they may remain in their parents' home into their young-adulthood years.

Giving the gift of authoritativeness

Parents who typically use an *authoritative* parenting style express affection and warmth readily, much like permissive parents do. They usually express interest in listening to their kids, but unlike permissive parents, they set high standards and limits on misbehavior. Their discipline style is firm but not harsh. They rarely, if ever, resort to force, although they make their expectations clear and deliver unpleasant consequences for misbehavior as they believe it's called for.

In general, children raised by authoritative parents have the best outcomes. They achieve well in school; they have friends and good self-control. They're happy and mature. These kids are usually well behaved, and they actually listen to their parents (well, much of the time, anyway). They're not especially drawn to risky behaviors, and they rarely join gangs or express anger in inappropriate ways.

Detaching by unplugging or being uninvolved

Parents who use an *uninvolved* parenting style are relatively detached from their kids. They neither express warmth and affection readily nor set high expectations for behavior. They tend to be withdrawn from their kids and the entire parenting process.

Perhaps it's not surprising that children with uninvolved parents often have the worst outcomes compared with children of the other types of parents discussed in this section. These kids run a high risk of delinquency, substance abuse, and deviant behavior. They have poor self-control and aren't especially adept socially. They often exhibit an array of mental, learning, behavioral, and emotional problems (see Part IV).

Making sense of the four parenting styles

Perhaps you're thinking that we've just laid out exactly the type of parenting style that you should use and that you should feel horribly guilty if you don't match the "right" one. Well, hold the phone. First of all, the impact of parenting style on how kids turn out isn't all that precise. Some kids clearly do just fine with uninvolved parents or with those who are permissive or authoritarian/dictatorial, and some kids don't do very well with parents who use the "ideal" parenting style of authoritative.

How can that be the case, you may ask? Well, as we discuss in Chapter 2, many factors influence the way that children ultimately turn out. Genes, temperament, the environment, culture, and peers all enter into the mix. Parenting style makes a difference, but it's far from the only influence. Furthermore, some parents don't match any of the parenting styles perfectly. Thus, you could be a parent who is generally authoritative, but you occasionally blow up and come off as rather harsh and authoritarian/dictatorial.

Also, some studies suggest that the influence of parenting style may vary somewhat from one culture to another. Thus, in some African American cultures as well as certain Asian cultures, a somewhat harsher, authoritarian/dictatorial style doesn't appear to exert as much (if any) damage on kids as it does on kids in European American cultures. Sometimes, kids in those cultures appear to get the message that a harsher parenting style represents part of how they know that their parents care about them. In all cultures, of course, we believe that kids wouldn't do well with authoritarian/dictatorial parents if the parents were over the top and overtly abusive.

Yes, parenting matters. In general, we believe that children do best when their parents usually parent in a way that reflects an authoritative style (warm and accepting, yet with firm discipline), although a little variation probably doesn't matter a great deal and depends a little bit on the specific culture a child is reared in. Know that no one is perfect and that kids turn out the way they do for many, many reasons other than the quality of one's parenting.

Becoming the Parent You Want to Be

The last time we checked, our local bookstore had a 5-foot-tall shelf that ran more than 25 linear feet, brimming with nothing but books on how to parent. These books advise readers on how to handle every single problematic behavior that any child anywhere in the world has ever engaged in (well, almost, anyway)! One pretty good one is *The Big Book of Parenting Solutions:*

101 Answers to Your Everyday Challenges and Wildest Worries, by Michele Borba, EdD (Jossey-Bass). It contains some very nice, straightforward advice about lots of things your kid might do.

At the same time, we think that most parents or others involved in raising kids can do a darn good job if they simply follow a few basic parenting principles that can be applied to all sorts of specific situations. When they understand these general maxims, they need to spend a little time focusing on any beliefs they hold that could get in the way of implementing good parenting intentions. That's what we provide you next: four critical principles of parenting followed by information on recognizing problematic emotional issues and beliefs about parenting.

Considering four parenting principles to remember

That's right; just four. No doubt we could give you a list of 40 parenting principles, but no one would remember a list that long. Besides, these four rules can take you further than you may think. Working hard on doing these things right will make you a better parent than attempting to know the "right" thing to do at every moment.

Active listening and validation

Kids need to be listened to. They need to feel validated even when they're wrong. Hmm — you may think that this principle is a direct path toward caving into kids' outrageous demands (and kids' demands can get very outrageous sometimes!).

But that's not what we're saying at all. You can actively listen to kids and let them know that you fully understand what they're feeling without giving in to them. Here are a few specific ways you can carry out this important parenting principle:

1. **Validate at least part of what they say.**

    Even if your kids say, "I hate you!" or "You're the meanest mother in the entire world; you never let me do anything that other kids do," you can always respond with "I understand that you're upset" or "I can see how you might feel that way" or "You probably feel pretty upset right now." It's really tempting for parents to get angry when their kids say things that are obviously untrue. You can reduce the heat a bit, however, by trying to find something to validate or agree with.

2. **Ask about their feelings.**

    It's important for kids to know that you value and care about what they feel, even if it seems that they're feeling upset or angry about something of little or no consequence. Thus, you can ask questions like "So how do you feel about that?", "Are you upset with me right now?", and "Are you feeling sad about what your friend told you?"

3. **Probe further.**

Even when your kids are upset with you, it can be useful to ask them more about what's bothering them. Consider saying things like, "Tell me more about what's bothering you," "Help me understand what you're feeling," or "What do you think caused your friend to do that?"

Again, active listening doesn't mean you need to "agree" with what your kids may have to say. Neither does it mean you can't set limits. In fact, it's not a good idea to let active listening go on and on. When kids are upset, however, they expect you to react with upset and/or anger. Doing so is a weak response and communicates that they "got to you."

Strong parents remain calm and listen; then they decide what to do next. Sometimes, that means giving kids a consequence that they don't want; at other times, it means empathizing with their plight when you fully understand what's going on.

Conditional reinforcement and unconditional love

Carl Rogers was a psychologist who used to proselytize about the healing power of unconditional love. A lot of other psychologists from different theoretical perspectives disagreed with him and instead promoted the importance of reinforcing or rewarding good behavior while giving negative consequences for bad behavior.

We believe that both camps were right, because kids need to know that their parents love them — always and unconditionally — and parents need to communicate that love no matter what. That love is for your kids as your kids, however, not necessarily for their behavior. Thus, you should give praise and rewards in higher doses when you've caught them doing something right. It's great to dole out special privileges, praise, little gifts, or gratitude when children have done something special that took effort. At the same time, it's important not to reinforce kids for trivial accomplishments or pseudoefforts. Kids don't need praise for breathing. On the other hand, you can give them affection at almost any time.

Humans universally tend to do more of almost anything that gets rewarded or reinforced. The trick is finding out what children find especially rewarding. Sometimes, that's just a smile or pat on the back.

Don't overdo reinforcement. It's a good idea to let kids know when they're doing well, but refrain from doing so each and every time they've done something that pleases you. Psychologists usually recommend rewarding new skills and behaviors fairly frequently and slowly fading the ratio of good behavior to rewards over time. Otherwise, positive reinforcement can quickly become ineffective.

Children often find things rewarding that may not seem rewarding to their parents. A common example is attention, even if that attention comes in the form of mild criticism. If your kids start a pattern of behavior you don't like, be sure to ask yourself whether you are reinforcing them inadvertently by paying attention to that behavior, even if it's negative attention.

Patience and shaping

Raising kids requires lots and lots of patience. Children don't learn new skills or make large improvements in their behavior overnight, so don't expect them to improve by leaps and bounds.

Psychologists have a principle known as *shaping,* which can work wonders. Shaping involves breaking down a big task into small units, and then starting with small goals and building up slowly. So, if a child only does two minutes of homework and needs to do two hours, start with expecting three minutes of homework. Reward and praise improvement and effort. The next day, expect five minutes and gradually increase the homework time to two hours. Reinforce children for each small step they make in the right direction.

A price for bad behavior

We really do believe that the most important elements of parenting are active listening, warmth, acceptance, unconditional love, appropriate reinforcement, patience, and shaping. At the same time, it's quite critical to establish guidelines for unreasonable behavior. Well-functioning families have rules and are clear about what the rules are. The specifics of those rules can vary a fair amount without undue harm to kids. It's just that the rules that exist need to be set, explained, and clear. Children need to hear a firm message from their parents and caregivers: "We have expectations for good behavior, and we expect them to be followed."

Kids being kids, they'll break those rules from time to time. It's almost part of their jobs to break rules, because it's an important way they can learn rules, responsibilities, and consequences. So when your kids break the rules or go over the line, you need to teach them that misbehavior costs something.

Instead of becoming upset when your kids misbehave, try to tell yourself that it's a normal part of growing up and a golden opportunity for them to learn a valuable lesson.

In the next sections, we outline two great methods for teaching kids that bad behavior will cost them.

Time-out

A particularly effective, time-honored strategy for teaching kids that misbehavior costs something is known as a *time-out.* The term comes from the concept that the principle is based on — namely, you're giving the child time out or time away from reinforcement (the things they like or want to do). If you use time-outs consistently when your kids get into mischief, they're very likely to misbehave less often (if you're patient and keep at it).

Here are some basic principles for applying time-outs effectively:

- ✔ Have an area to take your child where he can be observed as well as controlled. Good areas include a chair or a step, or some area of the house that's safe yet devoid of fun things to do (like toys and television sets). The child's bedroom is not an ideal place for a time-out.

- ✔ Time-out can also be delivered outside a restaurant or store, a park bench, or next to a tree — with adult supervision, of course.

- ✔ Time-out should be given for only a few minutes for children ages 2 to 6 and for one to three minutes per year of age for ages 7 to 12. The time-out should start only when the child has quieted down, however. Using a timer that chimes at the end can be useful. It's better to discipline children older than 12 with response cost (see next section).

- ✔ Give a single brief explanation for the time-out (ideally, in ten words or fewer), such as "Don't hit your brother," "You're not allowed to touch the computer," "I asked you to pick up your toys, and you didn't," or "You can't take candy from the shelf without my permission."

- ✔ With kids who are reasonably verbal (usually, older than about 3 or 4), you can delay giving a time-out until you're able to (obviously, you may not be able to give a time out while you're driving in rush-hour traffic). But it's always best to give time-outs as soon as possible.

- ✔ Don't interact with your children during a time-out. If they continue to misbehave, reset the timer, but don't say anything other than "I am adding time to your time-out."

- ✔ Do your best to be emotionally neutral when giving a time-out. Anger doesn't enhance its effectiveness; in fact, it probably makes it less effective and fills kids with anger and resentment.

Time-outs work especially well when you've been spending daily, positive time with your kids. The stronger the bond between parents and their kids, the more effective any discipline strategy is.

Response cost

With this technique, parents take something away from kids that they desire. Things taken away can include privileges, money (fines), later bedtimes, favored toys (for a few hours or days), television time, computer time, and so on. The list is endless.

It's even better if parents make the thing that's taken away fit the "crime" — in other words, if they arrange the consequences to make a certain degree of natural sense. If kids leave their toys out and don't put them away, for example, parents can put the toys in a bag stored in the garage for a few days. Response cost works well with kids clear through the adolescent years.

(Loss of driving privileges can work wonders with teenagers.) However, it's important for parents to make all house rules and expectations for behavior very clear and explicit.

A great book for teaching the principles of reinforcement, shaping, and making bad behavior cost something is *SOS: Help for Parents,* by Lynn Clark, PhD (Parents' Press). Check it out; it's a classic and especially useful for parents of kids ages about 2 to 12.

Removing emotional barriers to effective parenting

We've worked with hundreds of parents and families over the years and consistently found that most of them know much of what they should do to parent their kids. What basic skills they lack, they're able to learn quite readily. Yet they frequently fail to carry out what they know they should do. Sometimes, they lose their temper with their kids far too often; at other times, they fail to set appropriate limits on behavior; at still other times, they set excessive, unreasonable standards.

If you find yourself unable to be the kind of parent or caregiver you'd like to be, we urge you to see a mental-health professional who deals with kids, families, and parents. A good therapist can help you discover what core emotional issues are standing in your way. Needing such help doesn't suggest weakness or mental illness. It merely means that you have the courage to recognize that you want to be the best parent you can be, yet aren't quite there yet.

Following is a partial list of some of the most common emotional issues that often get in parents' way. Consider discussing them with your therapist if you think they may apply to you:

- **Perfectionism:** Perfectionist parents often get caught up in expecting and demanding perfection from their kids. They feel that any misbehavior or failure in school, athletics, or social activities reflects badly not just on their kids, but on themselves as parents as well.

- **Fear of losing their children's love:** Parents who struggle with this concern often have an anxious attachment style that they have carried since their own childhoods. (See Chapter 3 for more information about attachment styles.) Because of this concern, these parents have great difficulty setting limits with their kids, and their kids quickly learn to manipulate their parents by telling them they don't love them!

- **Self-centeredness:** Parents with this problem see themselves as the center of the universe and often disconnect from their kids. They're a bit likely to take on the uninvolved parenting style, discussed earlier in this chapter.

- ✔ **Excessive distrust or worry:** Parents with this issue often worry constantly about potential harm coming to their children. As a result, they overprotect their kids to the extent that the normal drive toward independence becomes distorted. Kids may either act out and rebel or become excessively dependent when their parents overprotect them. A popular term for parents who overprotect and smother their kids is *helicopter parents.*

- ✔ **Excessive guilt or self-blame:** Some parents feel guilty about almost anything they may do wrong as parents. They actually place their kids' needs and desires at the center of the universe. If their kids get upset, they blame themselves for the problem. Their kids quickly learn how to manipulate parents who have this issue.

Considering the Rest of the Family

Families are not entirely comprised of parents and their kids. American families have changed over the last several decades. The traditional family of a mom, a dad, and two kids is no longer the norm. The following sections discuss what families look like today as well as the special, important role played by both siblings and grandparents.

Changing families

If you start digging even a little, you'll quickly compile tons of information about how families have evolved in America. But why wade through all that? Here's the bottom line on a few interesting trends:

- ✔ American families are changing.

- ✔ The once-typical family of husband, wife, and two kids has become a minority.

- ✔ More than 25 percent of children are being raised by a single parent.

- ✔ One of every two children will live in a single-parent family at some time or another.

- ✔ Over the past few decades, there has been a huge increase in the number of children living with aunts, uncles, grandparents, and other relatives.

- ✔ Almost 30 percent of couples living together are childless.

Gay and lesbian parents

There are well over a half-million same-sex couples in the United States. That figure is probably conservative, because some same-sex couples don't publicly identify themselves as gay or lesbian. According to Gary Gate, senior research fellow at the University of California-Los Angeles School of Law, more than a quarter of those couples are in the process of rearing children. Studies have consistently found that children being brought up by same-sex couples do at least as well on measures of social behavior and development as children being brought up by heterosexual couples.

A study recently published in the journal *Pediatrics* (2010) said that children born to lesbian mothers are not only well adjusted but perform better academically, have higher self-confidence, and are less likely to break rules or be aggressive than children reared by heterosexual couples. The study's authors, Annette Gartell of the University of California at San Francisco and Henry Bos of the University of Amsterdam, speculate that lesbian mothers may be more involved in their children's lives and stress open communication, although other interpretations of these findings are certainly possible. More research is needed to clarify these results and broaden the sample to include same-sex male families.

Families are changing in lots of other ways as well. It's no longer unusual to find children being reared by grandparents or other relatives. People are living together in quasi-families, which have no official ties either legally or in terms of formal relationships. Instead, the members come together to help each other out because of financial necessity, convenience, or help with child care. The tasks remain the same, whether or not the family is traditional. Rearing children takes love, time, patience, and money.

Seeing how siblings affect one another

Relationships among siblings can vary from love to hate and swing back and forth from day to day. Sibling rivalry starts almost at the moment of conception. Most parents claim that they treat their children fairly and without favoritism, but research on siblings invariably discovers that some kids identify unfair competition and inequality; thus, they often harbor deep resentment.

When children believe (accurately or not) that one or more of their siblings get better treatment than they do from their parents, the sibling relationship is likely to be very negative. Sometimes, parents can intervene and make sure that they pay extra attention to their jealous children's concerns. However, in some cases other factors such as the need to attend to a new baby or the needs of a child with disabilities make it difficult to satisfy everyone's needs.

Gaming

One of the challenges facing families today is the seduction of computers and video games. Electronic toys are available in the infants' toy section. By the time children start school, many are masters of mice. Most parents are aware that time spent playing *violent* video games increase the incidence of aggressive thoughts in children, teens, and even adults. Many parents worry that exposure to violent games makes it easier for young people to become violent. A direct link between gaming and actual violence isn't yet clear, but the evidence suggests that it is likely true.

Perhaps more surprisingly, there are also reasons to be concerned about the use of nonviolent video games. Several studies have shown that video games compete for study time and interfere with grades and homework performance. In other words, they may do more harm than good.

For example, an interesting study reported in the journal *Psychological Science* (2010), by Robert Weiss and Brittany Cerankosky of Denison University, looked at a group of boys who didn't own video games. The researchers reviewed the boys' academic achievement and behaviors; then they randomly selected half of this group of boys to receive free video games and waited four months. At that time, they took another look at how the two groups were doing. Those with the free video games had lower reading and writing scores and more behavior problems. The more they reported having played with the games, the worse their achievement scores came out.

Findings like these suggest that even educationally based video games probably should receive thorough testing and validation before any claims about their helpfulness are made.

On the other hand, there's no question that video games may improve specific motor skills as well as provide good entertainment for kids and adults alike. Thus, we aren't about to suggest their elimination from the home. The problem comes about when the games are especially violent or when the time spent gaming becomes excessive.

Because the sibling relationship often lasts longer than any other relationship, when troubles exist, it's wise to intervene during childhood. Parents or concerned caregivers should consider getting help from a mental-health professional to come up with a treatment plan for the family that can improve this critical connection. Otherwise, sibling conflicts have been known to continue unabated for a lifetime.

Bringing grandparents into the mix

Children and grandparents lucky enough to have one another benefit mutually. Some grandparents are designated primary caregivers; others are sources of regular babysitting, backup help for emergencies, occasional visits, or holiday fun. The type of role you assume as grandparent obviously affects the nature of the relationship you end up having with your grandchild.

For most grandparents, however, the first rule of grandparenting is that as much as you love your grandchildren, they're not your own. Even though you've learned valuable lessons about parenting throughout the years, you're not the boss. It can be excruciatingly painful to watch your adult children make mistakes with their kids, but your advice will rarely be listened to, no matter how reasonable and rational it is. The general rule of thumb is "Zip your lips."

Okay, we have four grandkids, and believe it or not, we occasionally slip up. In fact, it's really hard to keep our mouths shut. After all, we're not only grandparents, but also parents and psychologists who work with and write about kids all the time. But guess what? For us, giving advice as grandparents still doesn't work. As much as we try to cleverly slip in advice, we still get glassed-over looks from our adult children, reminiscent of the way they looked during our lectures in their teen years. Go figure.

If you can't resist and must give your adult children parenting advice, use your own past parenting mistakes (we all made them) to illustrate your point.

It's much easier to be patient with your grandkids than it was with your own kids. Part of that is because of maturity, and lots of that is because grandkids usually go home after a while. In addition, grandparents rarely feel as much ego involvement in helping with their grandchildren as they did in rearing their own kids. Therefore, let your adult children know that you understand how hard it can be to bring up children. Be there when you can; give them a break but have your own life as well. When conflicts about how to rear children arise, wise grandparents respect the guidelines of their adult children. After all, the kids are theirs to rear. Did we mention zip your lips?

Chapter 9

Optimizing Education

*P*arents have options when deciding where and how to have their kids taken care of and educated. Many parents express confusion when faced with these decisions. They wring their hands over whether to send their kids to day care or whether they need to stay at home to maintain control of how their kids are reared. They wonder where to send their kids to school.

In this chapter, we first look at how to evaluate various educational and child-care options, such as day care, home schooling, charter schools, magnet schools, public schools, parochial schools, and private schools. We give parents questions to help them identify the critical issues so that they can make a good decision. We also help them weigh the pros and cons of a variety of child-care and educational settings.

Next, we step back and take a look at how school-wide programs and policies can enhance the achievement of four goals of childhood: controlling impulses, getting along with others, developing appropriate self-esteem, and achieving potential.

Evaluating Schools and Child Care

Not too long ago, most children attended neighborhood schools and stayed at home with their parents until school age. A minority of kids went to parochial schools, and a smaller number went to private schools. The choices were pretty limited and frankly easy to make. Times have changed. Today, parents are presented with many options for child care as well as education. Child-care options include in-home care provided by parents or others, day care at private providers' homes, and professional day-care centers.

Education options range from home schooling to charter schools (publicly funded independent schools), public schools, *magnet schools* (public schools with specialized curricula), private schools, and parochial schools.

The decision about how and where to educate a child is extremely important, but many research studies show that children can be educated successfully in a variety of settings. Think about President Abe Lincoln. He learned to read in a log cabin!

Visiting facilities and asking basic questions

Before we get into specifics, here are a few general ideas to consider when choosing any school, day-care provider, or day-care center. Arrange a visit to the facility. Be sure to call ahead and make an appointment. Stay a while and observe. Then think about the following issues and questions:

- ✔ Does the home, building, or classroom seem clean, cheerful, and positive?
- ✔ How friendly and approachable are the staff members?
- ✔ Do the staff members or provider seem to genuinely enjoy working with the kids?
- ✔ How does the school or provider handle discipline?
- ✔ Do the providers maintain regular communication with parents?
- ✔ Do the kids seem to generally get along and follow the teachers' or provider's instructions?
- ✔ Look at the children. Do they seem comfortable and busy?
- ✔ How much physical activity do children get during the day?
- ✔ Do the calendar and hours fit with your needs?
- ✔ Is the school or home location convenient for you?
- ✔ Is the school or day-care center accredited and licensed by the state?
- ✔ What do other parents have to say about the school, provider, or day-care center?
- ✔ Does the school, center, or home serve nutritious snacks or meals, and if so, does it make special considerations for food allergies?
- ✔ Ask for a copy of the school's mission statement. For an individual child-care provider, ask what her goals are for the children under her care.
- ✔ How do *you* feel walking around this school, home, or center?

Revealing research on day care

Back in 1991, the National Institute of Child Health and Human Development began a process to answer the important questions about how spending time outside the home affects young children. Scientists and parents alike were extremely curious as to whether the huge shift toward day care was a good thing or a bad thing. The hope was that day-care centers and preschools would provide a boost to children's academic skills. The fear of many was that day care would disrupt the usual bonding or attachment process between parents and children, which might lead to future emotional and behavioral problems.

Several universities participated in the study and followed more than 1,000 children from diverse backgrounds. They recruited the babies at around 1 month of age and continued to assess and observe them regularly until age 15. Findings were published in the journal *Child Development* in 2010. Some of the major conclusions were as follows:

✔ In the first three years, the quality of mothers' care had more influence on the mental and emotional health of children than did whether or not the kids received child care.

✔ Teenagers who received high-quality child care (regardless of whether that care was provided by relatives or nonrelatives) scored slightly higher on academic achievement tests and lower on measures of behavioral problems (such as impulsivity and risk taking). High-quality child care was distinguished by warm, supportive caregivers who also provided good opportunities for learning.

✔ Teenagers who received the largest total number of hours in child care by nonrelatives exhibited slightly higher problems with impulsivity and risk taking. However, the effect was small, and the quality of child care probably matters the most.

Evaluating schools, day-care centers, and day-care providers is a heavy responsibility. It's helpful when possible to take along a friend or relative with you on a school visit. Sometimes, another person will notice things that you don't and have a useful additional perspective. You may want to bring a written list of questions you want answered. Take notes so that you can remember important details, especially if you're observing more than one facility.

In the next two sections, we zero in on issues specific to evaluating and considering different types of day-care and educational options.

Looking at day care

Moms and dads all over the world bond closely with their babies. In most industrialized countries, after all-too-short maternity leaves, babies are cared for by people other than their parents. Handing a precious baby to another for care frequently gives rise to feelings of anxiety, guilt, and fear. Parents of young babies want to be sure that their offspring are taken care of with expediency and, more important, with loving kindness.

Almost 70 percent of mothers with children under the age of 18 work. Back in 1948, this figure stood at less than 20 percent. For most of these mothers today, economic necessity or career interests send them back to the workforce shortly after giving birth. The radical change in the way society cares for children spawned research questions about the effects of day care on young children.

Looking at pluses and minuses of child-care options

When evaluating child-care options (at home, with relatives, in a center, and so on), you need to consider many factors, including your own individual circumstances, income, and needs. No single option will be the right one for everybody. Table 9-1 gives you some of the pros and cons for the various day-care options. Please note that these are merely possibilities. What's a pro or con for one person may actually be the opposite for another. Furthermore, cons can sometimes be overcome with creative problem solving.

Research shows that for parents faced with deciding about day care as opposed to in-home care, the most important issue appears to be the quality of care the child receives, both during time at home as well as at any day-care center (see the nearby sidebar "Revealing research on day care"). It's probably a good idea to keep overall time in day care within reasonable limits to the extent possible, but parents needn't worry that their kids' lives will be ruined by day care. In this section, we help you evaluate child-care options.

Table 9-1	Pros and Cons of Child-Care Choices	
Setting	**Pros**	**Cons**
At home with one or both parents	Child benefits from close contact with parents. Child is comfortable in a familiar setting. Parents get to see every nuance of their child's development day by day.	At-home child care may restrict the economic and career possibilities of one or both parents. Child misses opportunities to interact with other kids and adults.
At home with a caregiver other than the parents	Child is in a comfortable, familiar setting that's convenient for parents, as transportation usually isn't needed.	It's difficult to find reliable, trained people for this duty. Having backups available can present a challenge. Sometimes, caregiving practices are not consistent with what parents want. Often, kids do not receive activities designed to enrich their cognitive and emotional development.

Setting	Pros	Cons
Care by relative, whether in home or at relative's home	Child is likely familiar and comfortable with the caregiver. Caregiver is likely attached to child. This option is often more convenient than some other options.	It's more than a little awkward to fire a relative if things aren't going well, which can cause family conflict.
Day care at another person's home	This option is often less expensive than preschools and professional day-care centers, and can foster attachment and relationships among the kids present.	When the day-care provider is not available, backup plans may be challenging. It can be difficult to evaluate the quality of care provided. Background checks can't easily be conducted on other adults who may come and go in the household. Often, kids do not receive activities designed to enrich their cognitive and emotional development.
Day care at a professional center	These centers often provide activities designed to promote cognitive, social, and emotional development. They are usually licensed and inspected regularly. It's relatively easy to evaluate the quality of care provided by observation. Backup plans are needed less often because such centers are not dependent on a single person to deliver care.	These centers can be relatively expensive. Care may be somewhat less personal. Staff turnover may be high. Child may have to adjust to routines that are different from those at home for eating, napping, and toileting. When a child is sick, an infection may spread quickly through the entire group.

No matter what day-care setting you choose, always have a backup plan. Schools sometimes close; bad weather happens; kids get sick; traffic snarls; cars break down; and stuff happens!

Asking the right questions about day-care providers

In addition to the issues we discuss in "Visiting facilities and asking basic questions," earlier in this chapter, here are some specific questions to guide your selection of day care for babies and preschoolers:

✔ How many adults will be responsible for how many kids? Legally mandated ratios vary significantly from one locale to another. Although there are no definitive ratios, the American Academy of Pediatricians recommends that there should be one adult for every three infants, one adult for every four children ages 13 to 30 months, one adult for every five children ages 31 to 35 months, and one adult for every eight children ages 4 and 5 years old. These guidelines are ideal. You may not be able to achieve this ratio, but try to come as close as you can.

✔ How secure and safe are the facility and playground area? Many preschools have video cameras to record what's going on — a nice touch. In terms of home-care providers, are electric plugs capped, cabinets locked, and potentially dangerous objects and poisons placed out of reach?

✔ If the child needs to be taken off site, are car seats appropriate for the child's age available?

✔ How does the day-care center approach feeding and toileting issues? Nutritious food should be provided but never forced on kids. At the appropriate ages, kids should be given opportunities to learn toilet training in a caring manner.

✔ What is the policy regarding sick kids? Is there a sick-care option that protects the other children? Are children required to be up to date on immunizations?

✔ Are there extra charges for late pickup?

✔ Are you allowed to visit at any time you want? (The answer should be yes!)

✔ What is the education and training of the child-care providers, and have they been required to obtain criminal background checks?

✔ Are the directors reachable and open to an occasional phone call?

✔ Do the staff members know first aid and CPR?

Sorting through school options

Many parents want to know which educational option will maximize their children's achievement: a parochial, public, magnet, in-home, private, or charter school. Overall, the qualities of an individual school are more important than the type of school, but even those qualities can be tough to interpret. The data from standardized test scores often isn't as consistent as you'd like to think, for example. But don't worry — in this section, we discuss various school options, achievement scores, and critical questions to ask when evaluating a school.

Looking at the pluses and minuses of various school types

Many parents, even those with limited resources, have choices about where to send their kids to school. The questions we suggest in "Considering critical issues about individual schools," later in this chapter, should help guide that decision, but there's more to consider. Table 9-2 shows you some of the likely pros and cons for each type of school setting. Please keep in mind that these pros and cons don't always apply to each specific school; they are merely tendencies.

Table 9-2	Pros and Cons of Educational Choices	
School Setting	*Pros*	*Cons*
Public schools: Schools supported by public funds and provide free education.	Public schools are free other than school supplies. These schools are usually located close to the home or free transportation is provided. Kids are exposed to and learn to get along with a diverse group of other children. These schools often have lots of choices for classes and extracurricular activities. By law must provide services to kids with special needs. Public schools have strict criteria for teacher credentials.	Public schools vary widely in academic achievement outcomes. They often have quite large class sizes. Because all kids are welcome, they typically have more discipline and behavioral problems than other school settings. They often have difficulty disciplining or firing teachers with problems.
Charter schools: Public schools operated independently from the local schools and have different curricula or instructional methods. They are free from some regulations and restrictions governing typical public schools.	Charter schools are free other than supplies. They often encourage innovative approaches to instruction and offer interesting alternatives to standard public schools. Charter schools usually encourage parent and community involvement. They can lose their charter after three years if they underperform academically.	Sometimes, charter schools have excessive administrative costs. They have not consistently demonstrated superior academic achievement and don't always serve children with special needs. Sometimes charter schools have a high teacher turnover due to longer work hours and greater responsibilities. Commute times may be longer and transportation not always provided.

(continued)

Table 9-2 *(continued)*

School Setting	Pros	Cons
Magnet schools: Schools that are publicly supported but have specialized curricula such as arts, science, or technology and draw from students communitywide.	Magnet schools are free other than supplies. They give students an option to specialize in specific areas of interest and/or talent.	Commute times to magnet schools is sometimes longer and transportation not always provided. These schools neglect core academic subjects in some cases and emphasize specialized curricula.
Private schools: Run and paid for by tuition and/or support from contributions by individuals or corporations. Free from some regulations and restrictions governing public schools. Have their own admission and discharge criteria.	Sometimes private schools provide an unusually enriched curriculum, standards, equipment, texts, and achievement scores. They usually have fewer discipline and behavioral problems than public schools. Highly committed teachers have smaller class sizes than public school teachers.	Private schools often fail to address students with special needs. They can be quite expensive. Kids attending private schools have less exposure to diverse groups of children. Teachers are sometimes not required to have teaching credentials (which may be mitigated in some circumstances by unusual accomplishments in other areas). Commute times may be longer and transportation not always provided.
Private boarding schools: Children live at the school, which is paid for by tuition and/or support from contributions. Free from some regulations and restrictions governing public schools. Have their own admission and discharge criteria.	Boarding schools can provide unusually enhanced curricula, standards, equipment, and achievement scores. Children can learn independent skills. Students often make lifetime friends. Generally fewer discipline, behavioral, learning, and emotional problems than public schools although some of these schools specialize in educating children with those problems.	Costs are very high in most cases. Children can become quite homesick, and their parents may miss their presence as well. Parents miss out on watching their kids develop week in and week out. Parents are often not as involved in the educational process as with other school settings.

School Setting	Pros	Cons
Home schools: All states allow parents to educate their own children at home. These settings are free from some regulations and restrictions governing public schools.	Home schools can provide individualized instruction as well as flexibility of curriculum. Parental control over content, which may be consistent with moral or religious values of the family, is possible with home schooling. There is flexibility of scheduling. No time is wasted on incidentals such as taking attendance or passing from room to room. Exposure is limited to crime and bad influences.	Home-schooled children have fewer opportunities to benefit from diverse groups and social activities found in larger settings. There is usually less variety in courses and in extracurricular activities. Often parents lack expertise in certain subject areas and have difficulty teaching. Parents can have problems separating the roles of teacher versus nurturer. Home schooling takes huge amounts of parental time and commitment.
Parochial schools: These are run and funded by private religious organizations. Also free from some regulations and restrictions governing public schools.	Parents choose schools that are consistent with their spiritual beliefs. These schools tend to have fewer behavioral and learning problems Class size is often smaller. Can include religious education within the general curriculum.	Parochial schools sometimes lack money or resources to keep up with technology and equipment. Parents may have to pay tuition for their students to attend. Students are exposed to a less diverse population. May not have as many opportunities for extracurricular activities.

Although occasionally confusing, the increase of school options means more choices for kids and parents. With choice comes responsibility. Those who make decisions about education must keep in mind the individual needs of the children and help parents by providing information so that they can make informed decisions.

Achievement scores: Weighing statistics

If you read your local newspaper, you're bound to run into articles describing the state of your city and state schools. These articles routinely report on graduation rates, achievement scores, criminal activity, dropout rates, and more. If you pay attention, you may notice a lot of inconsistencies in the data. So do we.

Leaving no child behind? Knowing your rights

In the United States, educational reform called the No Child Left Behind Act was enacted in 2002. A thorough review of this legislation goes beyond the topic of child psychology and development. However, a few facets of the law have relevance that all parents should know about:

✔ **Choice.** Parents of children attending schools that fail to meet standards for two consecutive years have the option to ask the school district to provide transportation to a school that has met standards.

✔ **Help.** Kids that are below grade level for two consecutive years and are attending

schools that don't meet standards are entitled to tutoring or other assistance.

✔ **Scientifically supported methods.** Teachers or school districts must use methods that are scientifically based for teaching reading and math. They will no longer be able to adopt the latest fad unless evidence backs up the new approach.

For more information, go to the No Child Left Behind Web site at www.nochildleft behind.gov. Parents need to know their rights and advocate on behalf of their children.

Unfortunately, these reports are based on a slew of different types of measurements and sometimes outright manipulations. School districts have been known to use outdated tests and tests with inappropriate statistical norms, and in a few known cases, they have allowed blatant deception and fraud. In many cases, teachers have been encouraged to teach test materials directly.

Until quite recently, the majority of states had not adopted a universal, national standard for assessing achievement. Thus, many states assessed their students with highly idiosyncratic tests based on each state's particular curriculum. This enabled some states to claim extremely high levels of proficiency in reading, math, science, and writing, but when tested on national standards, students appeared to fall quite short.

Some achievement tests have been carefully constructed and *normed,* meaning that the test compares an individual student's scores with those of a large group of other students. These tests allow you to compare your student with others in a reliable, valid manner. Examples of such tests include the Woodcock Johnson Test of Achievement, the California Achievement Test, the Iowa Test of Basic Skills, the Stanford Achievement Test, the Comprehensive Test of Basic Skills, and the National Assessment of Educational Progress exam (also referred to as the Nation's Report Card).

In addition to wondering about the quality of the assessments, many professionals have lamented the failure of our school systems to keep up with the rest of the world in terms of achievement. Simply teaching students to take tests has not resulted in better test scores or increased their ability to adequately participate in an ever-changing world. Schools that focus exclusively on teaching specific academic skills are likely to produce underachieving students who lack critical emotional, behavioral, and motivational tools.

Some studies have suggested that private schools have a slight edge in obtaining higher achievement scores, but there is a huge difference from one private school to another. Furthermore, many private schools (as well as some magnet and charter schools) are able to choose which students they accept while freely discharging underperforming or misbehaving students. Thus, the public schools end up with a larger population of students with special needs, language barriers (English as a second language), and behavioral problems of various sorts. There are many examples of public schools and some private schools (as well as charter, magnet, and home) that have miserable track records while others produce impressive outcomes in student achievement.

Considering critical issues about individual schools

Evaluating each school individually with care may be more useful than deciding on which type of school to send a child to. When evaluating an individual school, don't hesitate to ask school administrators, teachers, or admission counselors about the following issues and concerns:

- ✔ **Safety:** Ask about crime rates and how the school handles disruptive students. Most schools now require background checks for all adults interacting with students, including volunteers and substitute teachers, but you should ask about this. Is a licensed school nurse or other medical care available?

- ✔ **Academic standards:** How many students in the school perform at grade level in math, science, and reading? How do the students perform on *standardized* achievement tests compared with students at other schools in the area?

- ✔ **Teacher education and continuing education:** Inquire about the licensure of the teaching staff and whether or not they update skills through continuing education. Some charter schools have teachers who are not certified, which could be good in some cases (such as when they employ a scientist who has a PhD but no teacher certification per se), but the practice of employing uncertified teachers should be examined carefully.

- ✔ **Homework policies and expectations:** A good school will generally expect students to do homework on a routine basis.

- ✔ **Parent/teacher communication:** Some schools have sophisticated communication strategies through the Internet. Whatever the method, though, good schools will make a concerted effort to communicate regularly about student performance, homework completion, discipline, and so on. There should be some kind of Parent Teacher Association to facilitate parental involvement and communication. Regular individual parent/teacher conferences should be held.

- ✔ **Facilities, technology, learning tools, and equipment:** How current are the textbooks, computers, and audiovisual equipment? Are the teachers adequately trained in the use of that equipment? Does the school have a well-stocked and well-run library?

- ✔ **Curriculum:** What subjects are offered? Are subjects like art, physical education, and music offered? Ideally, you want a well-rounded curriculum as opposed to one focused solely on core subjects.

- ✔ **Individual needs:** Are there opportunities for enrichment for gifted students? If a child has special needs, are these needs supported and accommodated? Are there tutors or extra instructional time to help students who are falling behind? If a child is not keeping up, what provisions are there to assess that child's issues?

- ✔ **Extracurricular activities:** What clubs (drama, debate, language, technology, and so on), sports, or other activities are available to students? Are these opportunities made available to all students?

- ✔ **Class size:** A debate has raged for years as to whether or not class size influences the quality of children's education. Although studies have produced conflicting data, it does appear that class size matters, especially in the early elementary years. For those years, certainly a goal is to have fewer than 20 students per teacher, ideally supplemented by a teacher's aide or assistant.

- ✔ **Graduation, attendance policies, and dropout rates:** Schools with high graduation and low dropout rates tend to show higher achievement scores. Good schools have policies about attendance and promptly notify parents about problems.

Good administrators welcome such inquiries and see them as indicating that you're an interested, involved parent. And if you're an administrator or teacher, be thrilled that the parents of your students care enough to ask.

We also realize that many families have few or no options regarding which school their children attend. Due to economic issues or location, they may have only one school that will work. Even in those cases, it's still a good idea to ask the same questions to show you that are an interested, committed, and involved parent.

Promoting Positive Policies in Schools

The school years provide the foundations of many skills that children carry on into adulthood. School policies and procedures can do much to encourage the development of the four goals of childhood, noted in the introduction to this chapter and elaborated on in Chapter 3. Here, we articulate some policies that are consistent with achieving the childhood goals of self-control, healthy self-views, good relationships, and motivation for academic achievement.

If you're a parent, get involved in the Parent Teacher Association. Find out more about the policies at your child's school. Ask about how these goals of childhood are addressed. Volunteer for programs that help kids improve self-discipline, make friends, and achieve to the greatest potential.

Fortunately, policies aimed at one problematic childhood issue often help with other problems. School strategies aimed at developing balanced, healthy self-esteem may reduce school bullying, for example, because research has shown that bullies tend to have an overly inflated, narcissistic view of themselves.

Working together: Cooperating with others

The ability to work independently as well as in groups involves skills that are usually taught throughout the school years. *Cooperative learning* is an educational term that involves students working together, usually in small groups, to accomplish a goal. This style of learning has been shown to improve academic achievement, increase social skills, decrease disruptive behavior, and increase persistence. This type of group work involves teacher supervision and planning. To be considered cooperative learning, certain elements must be present:

- ✔ **Accountability:** All members of the group must do their share of the assigned work.

- ✔ **Interdependence:** To accomplish the goal, everyone has a part to play.

- ✔ **Interaction:** Whether face to face, on a conference call, or in a Webinar, the group needs to meet to share progress and give feedback.

- ✔ **Interpersonal skills:** In working together, group members develop improved social skills, such as leadership, conflict management, decision making, and communication.

- ✔ **Processing of progress:** Group members meet to discuss how the group is doing in meeting its objectives. They talk about what is going well and what problems have come up. They bring up ideas to improve the functioning of the team.

Cooperative learning is *not* having a teacher assign a group of students a task and walking away. When this happens, one or two students often take over and do the work while others sit back.

Parents and teachers should look for opportunities to provide cooperative learning experiences whenever possible. Cooperative learning promotes interpersonal skills, self control, and the flexibility needed to function well in ever changing, increasingly interdependent job environments.

Cooperative learning abilities translate into job skills. We recently took a tour of the New York City offices of a major international corporation. There were no cubicles. Long lines of tables with computer stations ran parallel, almost resembling a college classroom. Tucked against the walls were multiple sets of four chairs surrounding low tables. Cozy, closed-off breakout rooms, which included high-tech equipment, were scattered throughout the space. This layout allowed the staff to work alone yet easily meet in small groups.

Squelching bullies

Bullying in schools is a serious problem that affects many children. Studies suggest that 15 to 30 percent of schoolchildren report having been bullied at one time or another and that almost 10 percent of students are the victims of bullying at least several times each month. Victims are at high risk of having low academic achievement as well as of becoming depressed, anxious, or lonely. They often suffer from extremely low self-esteem. For some victims, bullying occurs over a period of years.

Kids left on their own rarely confront bullies although they know that bullying is wrong. Some children fear that confronting bullies will result in retaliation. Other times children who witness bullying, fail to respond because they simply don't know what to do. Therefore, school administrators need to implement clear school-wide programs, policies, and procedures aimed at ameliorating bullying. Here are a few suggestions:

- **Administrators should set up an effective method for tracking and collecting data on bullying that goes on in schools.** Parents and teachers alike should have full and open access to this data. Pretending that the problem doesn't exist only encourages it to continue.

- **Antibullying efforts need to be sustained over time.** Simply holding a few meetings during a given school year will not have much impact. Programs can be systematically improved over time, and data suggests that they become more effective when sustained.

- **Schools should implement a program that has been shown by research studies to reduce bullying behavior.** Some programs may actually make bullying worse, so beware. One example of a program that has been found to be effective is the Olweus Bullying Prevention Program, which significantly reduced bullying in schools in Sweden and Norway. This program also has been replicated and found to be effective in schools in the United States. The program is based on four overriding goals:

  - Increased awareness on the part of all concerned about the problem of bullying and aggression.

  - Inclusion of both parents and teachers in a collaborative fashion to address the problem.

- Explicit rules about bullying that are made clear to parents, teachers, and students alike. These rules lay out the need to prohibit bullying behavior and to help and include students who have tended to be left out of activities.

- Provision of both support and protection for students who have fallen prey to bullying.

Be aware that relatively little is understood at this time in terms of which components of most antibullying interventions are most critical and useful. Studies are under way that should clarify these issues, but they will take considerable time and money to complete. Eventually, these programs will no doubt become more focused and effective. In the meantime, it's important to do something about bullying, and implementing a program that research has found to be effective is a good start.

Kids who develop good friendships, healthy self-views, control over their impulses, and a sense of competence are much less likely to be bullies or bullied. See Chapters 3 for considerable additional information about how teachers, parents, and other caregivers can foster positive environments for children and see Chapter 6 for more information about bullying.

Finding fair, firm discipline

If Johnny is throwing spit balls in class, he isn't learning to read, and when the teacher takes time from her instruction to discipline Johnny, she isn't teaching reading to the other students. From minor incidents of disruption to major rule violations, misbehaving students take time and attention away from education.

One approach to managing bad behavior in schools has been to send unruly or disobedient students out of classrooms. Unfortunately, suspension is a short-term solution. Kids who are suspended are more likely to underachieve, drop out of school, engage in illegal behavior in their neighborhoods, and enter the juvenile justice system, so the school benefits for a short time, but the overall cost to society is much larger.

To decrease discipline problems and increase opportunities for learning, educators turned to psychology for help. School-wide approaches to discipline were developed, using research on human behavior and the principles of learning. The result is called *Positive Behavior Support* (PBS). PBS helps teachers and administrators establish rules, reward good behavior, reduce discipline problems, and encourage good social skills.

Here's how PBS works:

▶ **When kids follow the rules, they get positive attention or rewards.**
Rewards can come in the form of enthusiastic praise, stickers, or extra
time on a favored activity. Kids who put in good effort can also be given
special high status responsibilities such as line leader or office messen-
ger. Parents can follow up at home by reinforcing homework efforts with
a slightly later bedtime, an extra story, or some other special treat.

▶ **When they misbehave, they suffer mild but consistent consequences.**
Consequences can include a brief time-out (see Chapter 8 for information about how to provide time-out) or temporary loss of privileges
(such as recess or free time). When kids come home with negative
reports from teachers, parents may want to fine their kids part of their
allowance, restrict privileges, or restrict access to certain toys or games
for a while.

Teachers model and reinforce appropriate social skills. Teachers can do
this by noticing and rewarding kids when they demonstrate kindness, polite
behavior, or cooperation. For example, a teacher may say, "Great job of sharing your markers with Susie!" or "I love it when you say thank you." Teachers
model good social skills by showing kindness, respect, and empathy.

See www.nasponline.org for more information about positive behavioral
interventions and support. Multiple studies have shown that schools using these
methods have decreased problem behaviors and improved school climates.

Not all rewards work for all kids nor do all discipline strategies work for
every kid. Sometimes parents and teachers have to be creative and flexible in
searching for rewards and consequences that hit home for different kids. For
example, Shelly loves stickers and works hard to get them. However, Steve
cares less about stickers but he does just about anything for a little extra computer time.

Recognizing real effort

Some schools attempt to make every single student feel special. They treat
their students as though they're all superstars. Everyone is promoted, and no
one is allowed to experience a sense of failure. Many schools have adopted
special curriculums in order to promote uniformly high self-esteem regardless of what students do.

In fact, type the term "self-esteem curriculum" in your favorite search engine,
and your computer screen will inundate you with information. You could
spend the next five years downloading and printing it all. You'll see a pleth-
ora of creative, interesting ways to teach students of all ages to feel good
about themselves and their talents. These programs often teach students to

proclaim, "I'm special," "I can do anything," and "I'm the best!" They're based on the assumption that positive self-esteem will inevitably lead to better academic performance, as well as good emotional adjustment.

If you dig a little further, you'll also see criticisms of such curricula. Careful reviews of the literature suggest that the relationship of self-esteem and achievement is quite thin at best, and almost no evidence supports the idea that general, unfocused attempts to raise self-esteem do anything to promote greater effort or achievement. Furthermore, an extensive body of research has shown that inflated self-esteem in the form of narcissism has been connected to aggression, violence, and a variety of other problems. Other studies add to these concerns about unfocused attempts to raise self-esteem by demonstrating that the more people focus on themselves (something called self-absorption), the more poorly they perform on tasks that require memory, focus, and speed.

Don't think that we're recommending that schools should ignore their students' emotional well-being. After all, we believe that a balanced, healthy view of one's self is a hallmark of good emotional health. But this goal isn't readily accomplished by most self-esteem curriculums. Instead, we recommend that school policies focus on encouraging student effort, developing skills, and providing help to students who need extra assistance.

Chapter 10

Building the Right Village for Kids

*I*deal communities for kids provide quality education, recreation, transportation, clean air, open spaces, and parks, all within a safe environment. These opportunities should be accessible to every resident —young, able, handicapped, or old. Healthy communities also encourage a sense of togetherness and have access to good food and health care.

In this chapter, we take a look at the community factors that maximally support children's health and welfare. The neighborhood where kids grow up can affect their overall physical and psychological health. Common sense tells you that kids living in areas that have high crime rates; crowded, unsafe housing; or poor schools are at a disadvantage compared with kids growing up in secure neighborhoods with access to good educational opportunities. Other qualities in the neighborhood matter, too.

We discuss what goes into building an ideal community for children and families. Great places to live have multiple things to do, including places to sit, play, and socialize, as well as art, music, and interesting food. We describe how a community can encourage the health and safety of its citizens through cohesive, collaborative action. Throughout the chapter, we tell you what you can do to improve your community.

Investigating Infrastructure

The *infrastructure* of a community consists of the basic facilities and services needed to support the lives and well-being of its residents. Such services and structures include water supplies, roadways, parks, gas and electric power, schools, post offices, public safety, senior centers, communications, sidewalks, libraries, and prisons. Aesthetics of architecture and landscaping also affect the overall quality of a community. These collective elements can enhance or impede healthy child development.

Suburban neighborhoods, for example, sometimes support healthy child development by providing safe culs-de-sac for kids to play in. Yet suburban sprawl also substantially increases parents' commute time to and from work, robbing them of valuable time with their children. Thus, suburbia provides both advantages and disadvantages for children and families.

Getting from place to place

Empty parks, libraries, and public squares do little to promote community cohesiveness. Residents' ability to get to these places depends on safe and convenient transportation. Communities that provide easy access and dependable modes of transportation help improve the mental and physical health of children and families.

Until recently, the symbol of affluence for many American families was a big house on a big lot. However with increasing energy costs, traffic, and time spent commuting, the price of living in suburban splendor can be isolation. Often, suburban kids can't safely walk, ride their bikes, or take public transportation to attend after-school activities. With the rise of single-parent households and working parents, many children miss out on those opportunities because parents aren't available for transportation.

Increasingly, families are looking for a different way of life. City planners and architects are responding with new designs for neighborhoods. Multiple-use communities are being built so that people can live, work, shop, play, and gather within one neighborhood. This approach integrates public spaces with offices, stores, walkways, and homes. These communities encourage walking, bike riding, and visiting among neighbors. They help develop community cohesiveness, which in turn reduces crime and vandalism while helping people connect.

These new and sometimes revamped multiple-use communities are not common or even practical in many areas of the country. In many communities, economic reality makes multiple-use projects unrealistic. That's because, people simply can't afford to build new houses or move to neighborhoods resplendent with shops and grocery stores. In the meantime, improvements can be made so that existing areas are more conducive to healthy pursuits. Citizens can organize to support government policies and politicians that promote healthy communities.

These improvements should focus on

- Improving ways for people to get to and from public spaces
- Adding dedicated spaces for walking or jogging
- Making sure that all public areas are well lit

- ✔ Ensuring the presence of ramps and slopes at intersections so that people using wheelchairs or walkers can cross streets safely
- ✔ Making sure that sidewalks are sufficiently wide for wheelchairs or walkers
- ✔ Creating safe bike lanes
- ✔ Ensuring that traffic lights have separate signals for pedestrians

Promoting parks

Parks give people places to be active, which improves physical and mental well-being for both children and adults. When the adults who take care of children are happy and healthy, they're better able to take good care of kids. Also, parks are great places for children and adults to play and socialize.

When children have access to parks, they tend to exercise more. Crime rates are lower in areas that have parks. Furthermore, fewer children visit the emergency room when they have safe places to play and don't have to play in the street.

Parks are also a good investment for the overall community. Areas that have open spaces, trails, and parks have higher property values than similar areas without parks. In addition, parks provide natural sound barriers and can decrease air pollution.

If you are considering a new neighborhood, check to see whether the community has open spaces and parks. And if you have children, be sure to take time to walk or play in nearby parks.

Creating Community Cohesiveness

A community can be a place that either enhances or diminishes the lives of its citizens. Actively promoting well-being requires organization and work. Community organizers need to canvass neighborhoods and set up meetings to discuss priorities and goals to go after first. (Usually, it's a good idea to tackle one goal at a time.)

Funding for communitywide projects is sometimes available through collaborative efforts with local businesses, which have an investment in the community. Government and not-for-profit agencies also offer various programs that can help. Just search the Internet for "funding for community programs," and you'll discover many resources.

Mentoring minds

One way to enhance the lives of children in your community is to mentor them. A variety of research studies have shown that children who have committed, caring adults as mentors are far more resilient than those who don't. By *resilient,* we mean that these kids are relatively more able to deal with hardships and traumas that may come their way. They're more likely to end up as emotionally secure adults in spite of encountering childhood difficulties.

You can find out more about mentoring by contacting Big Brothers Big Sisters at www.bbbs.org. You can also ask your local school district if it needs tutors or mentors. Encourage your friends and neighbors to do the same.

Cleaning up

Neighborhood cleanup programs can do wonders for a community. Litter, broken glass, and poor sanitation stand out like neon signs welcoming criminal activity. Pristine environments, on the other hand, communicate the message that neighbors are on the lookout for one another.

If your neighborhood has a cleanup program consider volunteering a few hours a month. If not, talk to your neighbors or attend a local political meeting to see whether you can help organize an effort to cleanup.

Such cleanup efforts usually take place on weekends. The most effective programs occur regularly, such as the first Saturday of every month. That way, everyone knows when to expect to pitch in, and organization is simplified. Furthermore, regular efforts work much better than occasional, halfhearted approaches do.

Cleanup may focus on removing trash, painting over graffiti, boarding up broken windows, cleaning weeds out of vacant lots, or trimming out-of-control shrubbery in medians and intersections. More ambitious efforts involve enhancement projects such as designing and building a park.

Collaborating on healthy goals

An interesting array of options for improving a community's overall health and well-being are available. You can find models of effective community programs for almost any goal you can imagine. Here are just a few:

- ✔ **Child and infant safety-seat programs:** Some communities attempt to provide these seats free to families in need, and they often require attendance at short courses that teach proper installation of the seats.

- ✔ **Safe-sleep programs:** In some communities, educational programs teach parents and caregivers how to ensure safe sleep for infants as a way to prevent Sudden Infant Death Syndrome (SIDS).

- ✔ **Community obesity programs:** These programs promote healthy eating habits and exercise for both kids and adults. Obesity has become an epidemic, and these programs support communitywide efforts to combat it.

- ✔ **Maternal- and infant-care programs:** These undertakings are designed to improve prenatal maternal care, ease the birth process, and provide parenting information and resources.

- ✔ **Community drug and alcohol programs:** These programs address major causes of childhood injuries — vehicular accidents and domestic violence — by addressing the contributing factor of substance abuse.

Getting good food and health care

Traveling from home to work, school, or shopping or for health care takes time and money. When neighborhoods don't have options close by, some people can't get what they need because they lack financial resources or have problems with mobility. Many poor neighborhoods don't have sufficient mental or physical health-care choices within walking distance, so some residents delay preventive care and access only expensive emergency care when they're in extreme pain. In the long run, this kind of health care is far more expensive than regularly scheduled doctor visits. Regular exercise and good food helps keep kids and adults healthy.

The best diet for children and adults includes multiple servings of fruits and vegetables, whole grains, low-fat dairy products, and small portions of meat or beans. Try shopping for this diet in most local convenience stores, however. Good luck. Good food is found in abundance in most full-size grocery stores, which usually have lower prices than those of small independent groceries or convenience stores. Unfortunately, many people living in inner-city neighborhoods lack easy access to these prices and products, because multiple studies have found that there are more supermarkets and healthy food choices in affluent neighborhoods.

If you live in a neighborhood without adequate food or health care, consider getting involved in local politics to help support political efforts that improve the health of children and adults. Because this problem is largely economic, government financial support is usually needed to convince large grocery stores to invest in poorer neighborhoods.

Rallying around recreation

Recreation refers to the activities that people do, usually for pleasure, during free time. Activities such as swimming, hiking, camping, playing sports, boating, and even watching television can be considered to be recreation. Playing video games or sitting in front of computer screens can be entertaining too, but they haven't been associated with improved health or well-being. By contrast, time spent in active, physically challenging recreational pursuits can lead to improved mental and physical health. Therefore, in this section we discuss how neighborhoods can encourage healthy activities.

Communities can support recreational opportunities by making a range of sports teams or skill classes for children and adolescents available at little or no cost. Participation in sports benefits children by improving their physical strength, stamina, and coordination. Success improves self-confidence and self-esteem based on developing real skills. Playing by rules under the guidance of adults helps kids control their impulses, get along with others, learn about winning and losing, and even do better in school.

When deciding on a sport for any particular child, parents should consider looking for the following qualities in a community sports program:

- ✔ **Safety:** Coaches and team leaders should always put safety first. They need to make sure that kids are getting plenty of water (kids themselves don't always know when they need to drink water) and are well protected from the sun. They should provide all equipment and enforce the rules that apply to each sport. Kids should never be pushed to the point of exhaustion. Finally, all sports programs should require preparticipation physical exams.

- ✔ **Supervision:** Any good community recreational program needs adequate adult supervision, especially for young children.

- ✔ **Age appropriateness:** Children younger than 8 years old shouldn't be expected to play highly competitive sports, and if they participate in a sport that has winners and losers, coaches and parents shouldn't make a big deal about the outcome. The joy of playing needs greater emphasis than the joy of winning even for children older than 8.

Be aware that excessive repetitions of a movement (as in pitching or certain swimming strokes) may not be ideal for young bodies. Also be aware that weight training has a high potential to strain preadolescent children. If your child is involved in this sort of sport, talk to your child's doctor about any concerns.

- ✔ **A level playing field:** Children need to practice the skills required for a sport without pressure. Those skills should be taught in lessons or on a beginning-level team. Putting kids on teams more advanced than their current skill levels can result in teasing, humiliation, or physical injury.

✔ **A range of options:** Some kids have a hard time playing team sports, so they should consider an individual sport such as martial arts, swimming, tennis, or golf. Ideal communities have a wide range of options including ones that are free or low cost to participants.

✔ **Sportsmanship:** One goal of organized sports is developing good character. Children should be encouraged to have fun, be respectful, and increase their skills. If coaches or adults are concerned only about winning, children will miss out on valuable lessons.

Securing safety

If you don't have basic safety, you don't have much. Kids in unsafe neighborhoods tend to grow up feeling vulnerable and anxious. Sure, anxiety can be treated (see Chapters 14 and 16 for more information about treating these issues), but preventing a problem from emerging in the first place is a better way to go.

Fortunately, the people in neighborhoods can do certain things to improve safety. The next sections show you how.

Watching neighborhoods

By far the most widely known and implemented strategy for improving the safety of neighborhoods is the Neighborhood Watch program, which began in the late 1960s. The program began in the United States, and similar programs have been implemented in countries including the United Kingdom, South Africa, Norway, Canada, Australia, and Russia.

These programs tend to be local rather than national in scope and you can type the name of your town or state along with the term *neighborhood watch* into your Internet search engine of choice for information in your area.

With such broad appeal, you would assume that these programs universally improve neighborhood safety. Unfortunately, reviews of the literature have not always found that to be the case. Although many, if not most, of these programs appear to help, they also seem relatively ineffectual in combating crime. We don't know the exact reasons for this variability, but it's likely due to how effectively each program is carried out and how involved the neighbors become.

Neighborhood Watch is based on the idea of citizens organizing to collaborate with law enforcement in combating crime. Some of these groups focus solely on crime; others have broader goals, such as looking out for terrorism, collaborating with community development groups, and cleaning up the environment (see the pertinent sections earlier in this chapter). At their best, Neighborhood Watch programs improve safety and enhance a sense of community and cohesion.

Starting a Neighborhood Watch program is easier than you may think, although it does take some time and patience. Many police departments provide brochures or starter packets filled with information about how these groups work.

Here's how the process generally works:

1. **Someone in the neighborhood decides to host an organizational meeting.**

2. **The host or other designated person goes door to door, collecting the names, addresses, and phone numbers of those who are interested in participating.**

   It's not a bad idea to include children and adolescents in the program; they have eyes and ears too.

3. **The host schedules the initial meeting.**

   It's a good idea to provide simple refreshments or ask people to bring along potluck items.

   Ideally, the host asks the police and fire departments to send representatives to the meeting. These public officials can talk to the neighbors about what they can do to prevent crime and keep the neighborhood safe. Their suggestions depend on the specific types of crimes and dangers in the neighborhood.

4. **At the initial meeting, attendees choose a neighborhood block captain and define their goals.**

   The block captain serves as a liaison with the police and fire departments. As for goals, some groups merely want people to stay vigilant about what's going on in the neighborhood and to report suspicious activities of any sort; others may want volunteers to patrol the area regularly — not as vigilantes, but as watchful eyes and ears.

5. **Group members post Neighborhood Watch signs around the neighborhood.**

   These signs may serve as crime deterrents in and of themselves. Talk to your police department about where to obtain these signs in your community.

Sometimes, it takes a while to get people involved in a Neighborhood Watch program. If you keep at it, however, people will increase their participation rate. Persistence pays off.

If your neighborhood contains non-English speakers, consider getting materials translated into those residents' languages.

Lobbying for lower speed limits

In some neighborhoods, speed limits are set quite high; traffic buzzes along at 40 to 50 miles per hour (mph) right next to houses and playgrounds. In places like these, the overriding philosophy seems designed around the idea of doing anything it takes to zip people to and from work. Convenience rules.

We happen to live in Corrales, New Mexico, where speed-limit signs range from 15 to 25 mph in most places, 30 mph along the main thoroughfare, and 35 mph along a couple of very short stretches. People ask us how we stand these low speeds, but you get used to them. Yes, it probably takes an extra five minutes or so to get through town, but you also sense that kids and people cycling and walking along the roads (and lots of them do) are much safer when cars crawl along like that.

Lower speed limits aren't especially popular, but they do increase safety and reduce fatalities in collisions. If you want a safer neighborhood, consider lobbying your local city or town council for reduced speeds and perhaps even (gasp!) putting in a few speed bumps.

Part IV
Spotting Troubled Development

The 5th Wave   By Rich Tennant

"Let's see if we can identify some of the stress triggers in your life. You mentioned something about a large wolf that periodically shows up and attempts to blow your house down..."

In this part . . .

We look at how normal child development can get interrupted — in other words, child psychopathology. We begin with a look at what happens when babies are born too early or with genetic disorders. Then we discuss problems that interfere with learning, including learning disabilities, attention deficits, and intellectual challenges.

Next, we describe the growing problem of children born with autistic-spectrum disorders. We follow this discussion with an exploration of the emotional and behavior problems that challenge children and those who care for them. Finally, we look at how trauma and abuse affect children.

We alert parents and teachers to possible signs of trouble and what steps to take when they have concerns about the development of a child they care for. When a child has problems, early identification and intervention improves long-term adjustment.

Chapter 11

Facing Physical Problems

*T*aking care of children is tough. Nevertheless, most children have caring adults who volunteer to feed, clothe, shelter, educate, and nurture them. What a tremendous, awesome, and sometimes quite frightening responsibility that is. Lots of new parents are overwhelmed by the sheer magnitude of the day-in-and-day-out obligations of parenting.

Taking care of kids who are normal, whatever that means, is incredibly hard. Now think about how difficult it is when normal development is complicated by health problems and physical challenges.

In this chapter, we look at some of the difficulties children and those who care about them can face. These problems range from small bumps in the road to disabling or life-threatening conditions. Knowledge is a powerful and necessary first step in addressing these obstacles.

Kids with physical complaints should be thoroughly checked out by a pediatrician. In some cases, they may actually have emotional problems and may be using a physical complaint as a way of expressing their distress. See Chapter 14 for more information about this type of problem.

Previewing Prematurity

Babies born prematurely (before they're fully developed) often need extra care and attention. Between 11 and 13 percent of all babies are born prematurely — in other words, before the 37th week of pregnancy.

In this section, we review the various problems associated with premature birth. First, we note the primary causes of early birth. Then we look at dealing with the physical needs of premature babies. Finally, we discuss some of the challenges these babies often face down the road.

Noting the causes of early birth

Premature birth occurs for many reasons. In some cases, preterm birth occurs because a woman is unable to safely carry her baby to full term. Doctors simply don't know why some women deliver early. Many risk factors have been identified, and sometimes, a cause can be determined. Here are some of the most common threats to full-term births:

- Teenage pregnancy
- Two, three, or more fetuses
- Previous delivery of a preterm baby
- Poor prenatal care
- Premature rupture of the membranes surrounding the fetus
- Poor nutrition
- Stress
- Use of certain drugs or alcohol
- Infections
- Diabetes
- High blood pressure
- Hormone imbalances
- Structural abnormalities in the mother

Taking care of premature babies

Many preterm babies, especially those who are born close to full term, are healthy and go home shortly after birth. Others require a bit of extra watchful care and time in the hospital to grow. Still others require specialized care in a neonatal intensive care unit (NICU). With advanced medical care, babies weighing a bit less than 2 pounds and as early as 24 weeks gestational age have a good chance of surviving.

Babies born too early come into the world not as well prepared to deal with life outside the womb as do those who hang out in the womb for the full term. The health of premature babies varies, depending on the development of their lungs and other organs, their weight, their gestational age, genetics, the health of the mother, infections, and other factors. Taking care of premature babies requires medical expertise, technologically advanced equipment, and tender loving care. Areas that will be assessed by the medical caregivers include

- ✔ **Breathing:** Babies born too early don't have fully developed lungs. *Respiratory distress syndrome* (RDS) is caused because babies' lungs don't fully expand. *Apnea* involves periods when premature babies stop breathing. Both of these conditions are closely monitored and treated with medication and, when necessary, with mechanical assistance for breathing.

- ✔ **Jaundice:** This quite common condition occurs when there is too much bilirubin in the blood. *Bilirubin* is a chemical that's normally processed in the liver and eliminated. Jaundice causes babies to have a yellowish tinge to their skin and the whites of their eyes. Treatment for jaundice involves placing babies under special lights to help the body eliminate excessive bilirubin.

- ✔ **Warmth:** Preterm babies don't have enough body fat to keep them warm. They often need to be kept in incubators or under warmers to keep their body temperatures normal. Some NICUs encourage placing the babies on their parent's chest to help them keep warm. This practice likely promotes critical bonding between infant and parents as well.

- ✔ **Weight:** Weight gain is a major goal in the NICU. Babies may be fed intravenously or through a tube directly into their stomachs. Breast milk, pumped from the mother and fortified with extra calories, vitamins, and minerals, can be fed through a tube that goes through the nose or mouth into the stomachs.

- ✔ **Other conditions:** Premature babies' hearts may not be fully developed, requiring medication or surgery. They can also have bleeding in the brain or problems with blood vessels in their eyes, and they're at greater risk for infections than babies born on time.

After life-threatening issues are addressed, premature babies need what all babies do: love. Hospitals now encourage parents to spend time bonding with their babies even when the babies are getting intensive care. Babies benefit when they have attention from adults who love them.

When the premature baby goes home, the need for special care and attention continues. Health, growth, and development should be closely monitored. A premature baby requires frequent feeding and may be fussier than a full-term baby. It can take a premature baby a couple of years to catch up to full-term children.

Understanding problems preemies have later on

The outcomes of babies born early vary from totally normal to major physical and mental disabilities. Generally, babies born the earliest with severe health issues are at risk for more problems than babies born closer to term, but there are no absolutes. Following are some of the areas of concern:

- ✔ **Chronic lung disease:** Babies whose lungs were not well developed may have continued lung problems (including asthma) that may improve with age.

- ✔ **Problems with vision or hearing:** Abnormal growth of blood vessels in the eye can cause mild or severe damage, requiring the child to wear glasses later in life or even resulting in blindness. Another vision problem that's common among children born prematurely is strabismus (lazy eye). Babies born early are also at risk for hearing problems.

- ✔ **Cerebral palsy:** This condition involves damage to the area of the brain that controls body movements and muscular control. It can be caused by bleeding of the brain or lack of oxygen. Cerebral palsy can be very mild and almost undetectable to very disabling.

- ✔ **Problems with learning:** Children born too early are at greater risk for learning problems and attention-deficit disorders. These problems range from mild to severe. See Chapter 12 for descriptions.

Many babies born early show absolutely no problems later. Those who have problems benefit from careful monitoring and early intervention.

Reviewing Genetic Disorders

Genetics is the study of how living things inherit and express certain traits or tendencies. Babies inherit eye color, height, skin color, and many other traits from their parents (see Chapter 2 for more information). Children can also inherit abnormal traits caused by genetic anomalies. These disorders range from mild, undetectable defects to major disabilities.

Looking at types of genetic disorders

Three broad types of genetic disorders have been identified: single-gene disorders; chromosome abnormalities; and multifactorial disorders, which involve the interaction of genetics and environmental factors such as the health of the mother, exposure to toxins, diet, and exercise.

Single-gene disorders

Single-gene disorders result when a gene is missing or altered. These disorders are passed on to children by various combinations of dominate or recessive genes from the parents. There are thousands of known single-gene disorders, including these relatively common ones:

- ✓ **Cystic fibrosis:** Cystic fibrosis causes mucus buildup in the lungs and digestive organs. Children who receive good medical care can be expected to live until middle adulthood. Cystic fibrosis can be detected prenatally.

- ✓ **Phenylketonuria (PKU):** This disorder involves abnormal protein digestion, resulting in mental retardation if not treated. PKU can be detected prenatally or at birth and treated with diet.

- ✓ **Fragile X syndrome:** Boys are more likely to have symptoms of this disorder than girls. Fragile X is the most common inherited cause of mental retardation, although not all children with the disorder are retarded. Some have problems with learning and attention. Many have problems with getting along with others. Fragile X syndrome is detectable prenatally through amniocentesis.

- ✓ **Sickle-cell anemia:** Abnormal blood cells cause problems with the heart, and kidneys, and frequent episodes of intense pain. Sickle-cell anemia can be detected before and at birth, and is most common in African Americans and Latinos.

- ✓ **Duchenne muscular dystrophy:** A progressive disease involving weakness in the muscles and increased disability, sometimes death. Some forms can be detected prenatally and at birth.

- ✓ **Hemophilia A:** Problems forming blood clots can result in death from bleeding. Hemophilia is common in certain royal families in Europe. It can be detected prenatally or at birth.

Chromosome disorders

Chromosome disorders occur when a chromosome is changed, added to, duplicated, or deleted. Many pregnancies in which the zygote (see Chapter 2) has these abnormalities are spontaneously aborted, often before the mother knows that she's pregnant. Disorders that involve chromosomes include

- ✓ **Down syndrome:** This condition involves an extra chromosome and results in distinct facial characteristics such as a rounded face, thick tongue, and slanted eyes. Children born with this syndrome are often quite affectionate and have extremely easygoing temperaments. (See Chapters 2 and 3 for more information about temperament.) They tend to be slow learners, but with extra attention and stimulation, they can become independent and *occasionally* show average to above-average abilities. They have shorter life spans due to early aging.

✔ **Turner syndrome:** This syndrome, which occurs only in females, involves abnormalities in the reproductive system. When Turner syndrome is caught early, girls with this disorder can be treated with growth and sex hormones, but they are always infertile and often shorter in stature than average. Problems with mathematics and visual spatial skills are also common.

Multifactorial disorders: Combining genes and environment

As science advances, more and more genetic connections to diseases are being discovered. Most disorders appear to be caused by genetic mutations combined with factors related to the environment. One problem with this knowledge is that at this time, no one can predict how much of the disease process is controlled by genetics and how much by the environment.

A boy may be born with a genetic predisposition for high blood pressure (thought to be a multifactorial disorder), so as an adult, he is vigilant about his health, eats right, and exercises regularly, and does not develop high blood pressure. Another child with the same genetic disposition and an equally healthy lifestyle may develop high blood pressure. In many cases, scientists don't yet know who will or who will not end up expressing their genetic predispositions or why.

Here are a few of the common disorders thought to be produced by an interaction of what goes on in the world and inherited tendencies:

✔ **Diabetes:** Insufficient insulin causes abnormal levels of sugar in the blood. Early-onset diabetes seems to be more genetically determined than triggered by environmental influences. Late-onset diabetes also runs in families but seems to have more environmental determinates.

✔ **Cleft lip or palate:** Babies are born with incomplete closure of the roof of the mouth and/or the lip. One of the most common birth defects, cleft lip or palate can be surgically repaired or substantially improved. These disorders tend to run in families, but drug use or illness during pregnancy may make them more likely to occur.

✔ **Heart defects:** These abnormalities can range from mild to severe. Treatment includes medications and sometimes surgery. In most cases, the cause of these defects can't be determined, but familial factors and prenatal exposure to toxins are potential influences.

Getting genetic counseling and testing

Genetic counseling involves a medical professional discussing risks and providing information to an individual or couple preparing for conception.

Prenatal testing is available for some of the known genetic disorders. Genetic counseling is recommended for couples who are considering conceiving a child and have one or more of the following risk factors:

- ✔ Family members with a known genetic disorder
- ✔ Previous miscarriages or stillbirths
- ✔ History of infertility
- ✔ Members of the same biological family
- ✔ Members of an ethnic group with elevated risk
- ✔ Age (woman over 35 or man over 40)

Genetic counseling is available to provide information only. Some parents prefer not to know whether they are carrying a child with a genetic disorder. Some parents know that they are likely to give birth to a child with a problem but strongly believe in carrying out any pregnancy. Others may choose to terminate a pregnancy if they are carrying a child that will likely suffer. Some potential parents choose either to adopt or to use egg and sperm donors rather than conceive if they carry strong genetic risks. Many genetic disorders are expressed in mild forms with few symptoms; some can be seriously disabling. Decisions about genetic counseling and what to do with the information is highly personal and difficult.

Whether genetic testing has been carried out prenatally or not, it also occurs shortly after birth. About a day or so after a baby is born, a few drops of blood are taken from his heel. This blood test is sent on to a laboratory, where screening for genetic disorders is conducted. In the United States and many other countries, this test is required and looks for more than 20 conditions. (U.S. states vary in the number of conditions they mandate screening for.) Many of these conditions can be treated, controlled, or even prevented by early treatment.

Regulating the Body: Growing, Sleeping, and More

The body has numerous rhythms that regulate all its functions. You have rhythms for eating, growing, sleeping, and eliminating waste. Unfortunately, as all parents of newborn babies know, these rhythms don't adjust to the vagaries of the outside world immediately upon the baby's arrival. The next three sections discuss a few common conditions that include a lack of coordinated bodily rhythms.

Not all problems are neatly categorized as being purely physical in nature. The disorders discussed in this section all involve the body, but psychological factors and learning often contribute to their development.

Failing to thrive

Failure to thrive (FTT) is a relatively common condition. The term is used to describe an infant who is significantly underweight or whose rate of weight gain falls well short of expectations. Pediatricians also factor in height and head circumference when making this diagnosis. Signs of failure to thrive have been observed in as many as 10 percent of children in primary health-care settings (which often include family doctors, nurse practitioners, physician assistants, internists, and pediatricians).

There are numerous causes of failure to thrive. Generally, these causes fall under the broad categories of organic medical problems or environmental factors. A partial list of medical causes of FTT includes

- Endocrine problems or deficiencies
- Various blood disorders, such as anemia
- Edema from renal kidney disease or liver disease
- Cancer or HIV
- Cerebral palsy
- Heart disease
- Respiratory problems associated with cystic fibrosis or bronchopulmonary dysplasia
- Vitamin deficiency caused by celiac disease
- Maternal illnesses such as hypertension, preeclampsia, anemia, or advanced diabetes
- Maternal consumption of alcohol, tobacco, or other drugs of abuse

So-called *nonorganic or environmental* causes of FTT are also wide ranging. A partial list of these factors includes

- Emotional deprivation of the baby because of parental depression, hostility, withdrawal, or serious emotional disorders
- Poverty causing poor nutrition or substandard living conditions
- A lack of parenting skill or preparedness for parenting
- Extreme stress on parents

- Blatant neglect or abuse of child
- Extreme stress and dysfunction in the family (divorce, conflict, chaos)
- Being a single parent with few resources or support

Sometimes, FTT occurs for no clear, apparent reason. You cannot assume that poor parenting or parental neglect is at work just because a physical cause can't be found. We simply don't always know the answer.

It is not uncommon to see a mix of internal and external causes of FTT, and sorting them all out requires diligent evaluation.

The main way to avoid problems with FTT is to take your baby in for regular well-baby checkups. If a physical condition is responsible, it may be possible to diagnose and treat it, and growth may resume a normal path. If psychosocial problems are involved (whether primarily or solely), we recommend a consultation with a *pediatric psychologist* (a psychologist who specializes in the assessment and treatment of psychosocial issues associated with various medical conditions).

Not sleeping through the night

Infants about 4 to 6 months old sleep off and on through the day and night, and parents can't do much about that irregularity. Frankly, many parents find these months quite exhausting and frustrating, because their own sleep is affected greatly. After those first four to six months, however, there's a good chance that your baby will sleep close to six or eight hours sometime during the night. By the time they're 1 year old, the majority of kids sleep pretty much through the night. There is considerable variation, however, and it's not uncommon for kids to awaken from time to time up to the age of 4 or so.

When illness and stress cause FTT

Dr. Chuck Elliott (co-author of this book) once treated a 2-year-old who had FTT due to a medical condition. Specifically, the child suffered from glycogen storage disease, a metabolic problem that prevents appropriate processing of starches. His disorder meant that his parents had to get him to eat every two hours or provide his nourishment through a gastronasal tube. The anxiety surrounding eating became intense, and the toddler responded to the tension by refusing to eat. The parents reported having to "hang from chandeliers" to get him to eat; in other words, they did everything and anything they could to induce him to eat. Sometimes, their efforts worked. Too often, they didn't. Chuck and a team of other pediatric psychologists intervened and taught the parents strategies for instilling regular eating habits. The toddler wasn't cured of his disease, but he learned to eat on a much more regular basis.

Be sure to check for sleep difficulty if your child is having trouble at school. When kids aren't sleeping well from whatever cause, they often don't do well in school or act out. Sometimes they are mistaken for having problems with attention or learning when they actually have a sleep problem.

Hindering sleep

The following list describes some of the most common mistakes that parents make when attempting to teach good sleep habits to their infants and young children:

- ✔ **Don't overstimulate the baby just before bedtime.** Try to make the couple of hours before bedtime calm and relaxing.

- ✔ **Don't try to soothe your little one by placing a bottle of juice or formula in her crib.** Having a bottle in the mouth is not good for developing teeth.

- ✔ **Don't place toys in an infant's crib.** For an infant younger than 6 months old, an empty crib is necessary to prevent suffocation. After that time, items such as a blanket or stuffed animal can serve as transition objects and help a little with fears of separation.

- ✔ **Avoid inconsistency.** Bedtime does not have to occur at exactly the same time each night — variations of an hour or two probably won't cause much problem — but avoid wild swings in bedtimes.

- ✔ **Especially for kids younger than 5 or 6 years old, don't use bedtime as a punishment for bad behavior.** You want your child to associate bedtime with feeling good.

- ✔ **Avoid giving the child food or drinks that contain caffeine, such as chocolate or cola before bedtime.** Caffeine is a stimulant that keeps kids awake! Furthermore, caffeine and useless sugar found in many drinks are unnecessary and unhealthy.

- ✔ **Don't expose the child to bright artificial light in the few hours before bed.** Bright lights have a stimulating affect that can keep kids awake.

Don't place your infant on his stomach to go to sleep; rather, place him on his back. This practice has been shown to reduce the incidence of Sudden Infant Death Syndrome (SIDS). For more information, check out www.nichd.nih.gov/sids.

If you find your infant or toddler's sleep problems exhausting to the point that your mood deteriorates or anger flares, be sure to get help. You may start by asking a close friend or relative to give you a night or two off by providing child care. However, if your problems persist or seem overwhelming, consider seeing your doctor or a mental health professional. Stressed-out, upset parents are likely to just make things worse and are at increased risk of abusing their kids even if they have no intention of doing so.

Helping sleep

On the other hand, there are a few good practices that parents can try to help their infants and young children sleep through the night:

- ✔ **Make bedtime pleasant.** Make the time just before bed special, but not too stimulating. Try reading a book to your child at this time. Lullabies and/or rocking are good too.

- ✔ **Keep regular routines throughout the day for naps, meals, play, and so on.** Babies adjust to regular routines much better than unpredictable chaos.

- ✔ **Be sure your baby is exposed to light in the morning and dim lights in the evening before bed.** Darkness helps bring on sleepiness and bright light does the opposite.

- ✔ **See how your baby reacts to baths.** Some babies are calmed by a warm bath before bed, but don't bathe your baby just before bed if yours finds baths stimulating.

- ✔ **Consider massage therapy.** Some very limited data suggests that massaging infants may help them acquire regular sleep patterns sooner than babies who don't get massages. Massage is great for preemies too.

- ✔ **Consider using a white-noise generator or fan.** Background sound often soothes babies.

- ✔ **Fill 'em up before bedtime.** Babies are likely to sleep longer on full stomachs. Make the last feeding shortly before bedtime.

Even with parents' best efforts, problems with establishing a regular sleep pattern sometimes persist. If the child's problems go past the age of 12 months or so, you should consult a pediatrician, who may call in either a child psychologist or a pediatric psychologist for assistance. Effective programs are available based on setting firm limits, special strategies for systematic ignoring, and sometimes rewards (depending on the age of the child and other factors).

Night terrors

Night terrors are episodes that typically occur one to two hours after the child falls asleep — they generally do not appear connected to nightmares. The child will suddenly sit up, screaming and crying. High arousal occurs, as demonstrated by a fast heart rate, sweating, and rapid breathing. The child is usually inconsolable and may be difficult to awaken. Although night terrors are scary for parents, the child usually does not remember them.

Night terrors occur in up to 5 percent of children and are most common between the ages of 3 and 12, although they typically begin at the lower end of that range. Most of the time, night terrors fade away by adolescence, if not before. If your child experiences night terrors, your pediatrician should check her out, although physical causes are rare. If night terrors occur frequently or for many months, a child or pediatric psychologist should be consulted because stress, worries, and anxiety sometimes underlie the problem and can be addressed by a professional.

Sleepwalking

Sleepwalking is a bit more dangerous sleep problem than night terrors, because sleepwalking kids run the risk of falling down stairs or out of windows. Sleepwalking is quite common between the ages of about 4 and 12. The main thing parents must do is make the child's sleeping area safe by securing windows and doors, as well as blocking stairways. Having the child's room on the first floor is a good idea when practical.

Sleepwalking usually fades away after a while and doesn't require any particular treatment. However, in severe, chronic cases, parents may want to try anticipatory awakenings. Essentially, they track sleepwalking episodes and awaken their child 15 minutes before the typical time sleepwalking occurs. They keep the child up for a few minutes and then let him go back to sleep. This procedure often takes care of the problem within a couple of weeks.

Sleep apnea

Sleep apnea is a sleep problem experienced by perhaps 1 to 3 percent of children. Generally, it involves repeated episodes of airway obstruction during sleep. Symptoms include unusual sleepiness during the daytime, loud snoring, heavy irregular breathing, long pauses in breathing, unusual sleep positions, and changes in color. Sleep apnea is a serious condition and should always be assessed by a child's pediatrician and often a sleep specialist. Sometimes, it can be taken care of by removal of adenoids or tonsils; at other times, a machine is used to blow air into the nose to keep the airways open.

Taking on toileting problems

Most kids achieve fairly reliable bladder and bowel control by the age of 4 or 5. Among kids who succeed at learning this control at an earlier age, many experience at least occasional accidents until the age of 6 or 7. By that time, continued accidents or the sudden appearance of relapses in appropriate toileting is usually considered to be problematic. Some professionals recommend active intervention for these problems if they are still occurring after the age of 4 or so. Problems with urinating fall in the category known as *enuresis,* and problems with uncontrolled defecation are labeled as *encopresis.*

Enuresis

Lack of control over urinating during the daytime is called *diurnal enuresis,* and nighttime accidents are called *nocturnal enuresis.* Boys tend to have this problem more often than girls do. Professionals have noted a variety of physiological causes of enuresis, but these probably account for at most 10 percent of all cases. These causes can include muscle spasms in the bladder, trauma to the spinal cord, urinary-tract infections, sleep apnea (see the preceding section), and diabetes. Thus, children exhibiting enuresis should be carefully evaluated by a pediatrician.

The vast majority of cases that don't have physical causes can be successfully treated. Daytime enuresis can be dealt with by frequent, monitored bathroom visits along with structured rewards. Nighttime enuresis is most often treated with a device known as the pad and bell. A pad is placed under the child; this pad is connected to a bell or alarm that sounds when moisture triggers the circuit. In most cases, the alarm awakens the child. Typically, the child will gradually learn to awaken earlier during urination and eventually before urinating. After six to eight weeks, kids are generally dry without accidents.

Pediatric psychologists work with enuresis frequently. They can add additional strategies to the pad and bell, as well as daytime routines that make treatment more effective for a larger number of kids. Seeking consultation with a pediatric psychologist does not necessarily mean your child is suffering from any type of emotional disorder per se.

Encopresis

Encopresis refers to accidental passage of feces into a child's underwear after toilet training would be expected to have occurred. Perhaps 1 to 2 percent of children experience encopresis, and boys who have this problem greatly outnumber girls who do. Many parents incorrectly assume that encopresis is a voluntary act on the part of the child and resort to harsh punishment, which only makes things worse.

In actuality, encopresis usually occurs because a child has been holding on to or retaining his feces. Often, this retaining begins because of a painful bowel movement. Retaining the stools results in constipation. Eventually, the colon becomes clogged or impacted and distends, which makes passing stools more difficult. As the colon stretches, the child loses the usual sensations of needing to eliminate. Stools start to seep or leak around the blocked area, which causes staining that the child may not even feel.

Symptoms of encopresis include lack of appetite; leakage of stool; unusually large, hard stools; abdominal pain; resistance to bowel movements; and constipation. If your child shows evidence of encopresis, you should have him seen by his pediatrician for a workup. Pediatricians may be able to fix this problem just by using stool softeners, mineral oil, suppositories, increased liquids, and sometimes enemas. High-fiber diets and lots of liquids can help maintain the colon in better condition. If the problem persists, pediatric psychologists work with this problem with techniques based on helping parents remain calm and using a structured program that rewards kids for learning better bowel habits and diet.

Looking at Chronic Illness in Kids

All kids get sick from time to time. In fact, getting sick helps children build immunities. Try going to a preschool in the winter months. Half the kids will likely have drippy noses. Most children get through the early years with a few bumps, bruises, high fevers, flu viruses, and colds.

About one of five children in the United States, however, suffer from chronic health problems. Chronic health conditions interfere with a child's day-to-day life; last longer than a few weeks; and require lots of home health, medical, and sometimes hospital care. In this section, we discuss conditions including asthma, diabetes, and cancer. (In the following section, we cover hospitalization and pain management.)

Kids with serious health problems are especially vulnerable to developing anxiety or depressive disorders (see Chapter 14 for more information). Be on the lookout for symptoms of these problems, and get help if you see them.

Analyzing asthma

Asthma is an especially common chronic health problem, afflicting about six million kids in the United States alone. Asthma is a disease of the lungs involving inflammation and narrowing of air passages. Symptoms of asthma include coughing, wheezing (a whistling sound made while breathing), shortness of breath, and tightness in the chest. Minor wheezing, especially during colds, does not always indicate asthma, particularly in younger children, who have narrow airways. Thus, a physician must make the actual diagnosis of asthma based on a careful assessment of any given child's lung functioning. Most kids who have asthma show signs of it before the age of 5. If you see symptoms in a child, be sure to have the child checked out.

Like many other disorders, the causes of asthma are a little complicated. It does appear to have a strong genetic component. It also may be caused by respiratory or viral infections that happen during infancy or young childhood. There's also a rather counterintuitive speculation known as the *hygiene hypothesis* that asthma may be caused in some cases by an overly clean environment in young childhood, which interferes with proper development of the immune system. Scientists have observed that kids who grow up on farms with exposure to dirt and animals as well as kids who have attended day care (and thus are exposed to more germs and such) acquire asthma at much lower rates than children without such exposures.

After a child is diagnosed with asthma, caregivers must take precautions to track what appear to be triggers for acute episodes of asthma and try to reduce exposures to those triggers. Triggers can be rather wide ranging and include dust mites (which happen to be almost impossible to eliminate), perfumes, cleaning agents, chalk dust, exercise, dander from cats or dogs, pollen, cold air, smoke, and so on.

From a psychological standpoint, asthma poses lots of challenges for kids. They must participate in identifying triggers. They are called upon to monitor their symptoms and carefully adhere to medical regimens that can include various long-term control medications (designed to prevent or reduce acute flare-ups) and medications designed for quick relief of acute flare-ups. Kids often report feeling embarrassed about their condition and its treatments. Especially when not well controlled, asthma can lead to problems with anxiety and/or depression as well as other emotional and behavioral problems. (See Chapters 14 and 15 for more information about these types of problems.) Some kids even discover that certain strong emotional states (such as intense laughter, crying, or acute stress) can cause flare-ups.

Asthma is not thought to be caused by strong emotions, but these can serve as triggers to flare-ups.

Some parents worry about letting a child with asthma participate in sports. Most kids with asthma lead reasonably normal lives and can participate in many types of sports. Their activities may require a little adjustment and careful monitoring, but well controlled asthma needn't keep them on the sidelines.

Dealing with diabetes

Diabetes is a disease in which the level of blood sugar (glucose) rises or falls to dangerous levels. Glucose provides energy for the body and is regulated by a hormone called insulin. People with diabetes do not produce enough insulin to keep the levels of glucose in the bloodstream normal. There are two types of diabetes:

- ✔ **Type I:** This type, usually diagnosed in childhood or early adulthood, is also known as juvenile diabetes. Children with type I diabetes produce little or no insulin. Their immune system, which normally fights off germs, attacks and destroys insulin-producing cells. Children with this disorder must have their blood sugar monitored frequently and almost always require daily injections of insulin to control their blood-sugar levels.

- ✔ **Type II:** This kind of diabetes was formerly uncommon in children. However, parallel to increased rates of obesity, the rate of diabetes in children and adolescents is rising quickly and steadily. In type II diabetes, insulin is still produced by the body, but the amount may be insufficient, or the body seems to be unable to use the insulin to regulate blood sugar. This type of diabetes is thought to be largely preventable with healthy diet and regular exercise.

The symptoms of diabetes in children are the same as in adults, but children may not be as aware of them because they don't experience them as being painful or uncomfortable. A doctor should be consulted if a child has unexpected weight loss, unusual thirst, frequent urination, blurred vision, slow-healing sores, frequent infections, or excessive fatigue.

Diabetes can be managed, but management requires hard work, including dietary changes, frequent monitoring of blood-sugar levels, and perhaps painful injections. Children and their families are often understandably quite upset when they get a diagnosis. The diagnosis usually means big changes in lifestyle. There is often a sense of loss or sadness and sometimes anger.

There are many ways that families and caregivers can provide information and support to children and adolescents with diabetes. Consider checking out www.jdrf.org or www.diabetes.org for information about diabetes and children and how you can help kids cope.

Because the control of both asthma and diabetes require adherence to various routines and medicines as well as lifestyle adjustments, many kids will either rebel or develop emotional problems in dealing with their condition. Caregivers should be on the lookout for resistance to the doctors' recommendations or emotional struggles by the child. A referral to a good child or pediatric psychologist is often a good idea.

Confronting cancer

Cancer occurs when cells in the body go wild, dividing rapidly, pushing out normal cells, growing into lumps or tumors, and becoming misshapen. They can spread to other areas in the body and rob the body of nutrition, sapping strength, destroying organs or bones, and causing weakness.

Cancer in childhood is relatively rare. The most common childhood cancer is leukemia, followed by lymphoma, brain cancer, and bone cancer. Cancer treatment for children is similar to that for adults and can include chemotherapy, radiation, surgery, and bone-marrow transplants.

When a child has cancer, the whole family mourns. Family members worry that the child will suffer and are terrified by the possibility of death. That's why mental-health professionals are often part of the cancer treatment team. They can provide support for family members, answer questions, and help prepare the child for treatment.

Cancer treatment involves destroying healthy cells along with cancer cells. These life-saving treatments sometimes cause impairments in functioning. Most of these problems get better with time, but especially when treatment requires destruction of brain cells, long-term effects are possible. Children

recovering from cancer should be monitored for learning or attention problems. Families should talk to their treatment teams about any concerns.

Helping Kids Deal with Pain and Hospital Care

In addition to the various physical anomalies, challenges, diseases, and conditions we discuss in earlier sections, children also often deal with pain and/
or hospitalization. Hospitalization and pain are never easy for kids, but you
can help children manage them a bit easier. The next two sections give you
some ideas about how.

Managing pain in children

Various illnesses, injuries, and treatments for medical conditions unfortunately cause children to suffer pain. A wide variety of chronic diseases
can cause problems with pain for kids, such as muscle and joint disorders
(including juvenile arthritis and multiple sclerosis), certain cancers, irritable
bowel syndrome, hemophilia, and sickle-cell anemia (see "Single-gene disorders," earlier in this chapter).

For decades, children have received less pain medication than adults who
have similar chronic diseases and problems with pain. Some health-care
providers have assumed that children don't feel pain as sharply as adults
do, and others have expressed concerns that kids could become addicted to
pain medications more easily than adults do. Both of these ideas are untrue.
Therefore, if you're a care provider for a child who has pain associated with a
chronic medical condition, ask about pain medications.

In addition to pain medications, a variety of psychological and mind–body
approaches have shown some effectiveness in the treatment and management of chronic, disease-related pain:

- ✔ **Yoga:** Exercises that improve flexibility, circulation, and often aid in pro-
  ducing mental calmness as well.

- ✔ **Hypnotherapy:** Uses imagery to help kids calm themselves and reduce
  the experience and perception of pain.

- ✔ **Massage therapy:** Designed to relax kids' muscles and tensions that may
  be making their pain worse.

- ✔ **Cognitive behavioral therapies:** Various methods designed to help kids
  relax, feel calmer, and reduce their experience and perceptions of pain.

Unfortunately, kids sometimes must cope with acute injuries (such as burns, broken bones, and head injuries) as well as painful or distressing medical treatments (such as bone-marrow aspirations, lumbar punctures, and chemotherapy). Sometimes, they can be sedated or given powerful short-term pain medications. When medications cannot be administered or prove to be inadequate, both hypnosis and cognitive behavioral therapies have shown significant promise in helping children cope and get through these difficult experiences.

Some kids who experience serious injuries or even extremely painful, repeated medical procedures may develop Post Traumatic Stress Disorder (PTSD; see Chapter 14). Symptoms to watch out for include hyper arousal, irritability, poor sleep, anger, and attempts to avoid reminders of the distressful events.

Hospitalizing kids

Kids with chronic health conditions sometimes need hospital care. Kids are often frightened by the unfamiliar setting, the possibility of discomfort or pain, and the unknown faces of hospital staff members. Depending on the situation and the age of the child, parents can help children cope with hospitalization. Whenever feasible, it's great if at least one parent or close relative can spend the night with hospitalized children, especially when they are young or seriously ill.

Hospitals that care for children often have Child Life programs that employ specialists who help parents and children cope and prepare for hospitalizations. Be sure to ask. Sometimes, hospitals also have pediatric psychology departments that can be quite useful, especially for severe or chronic conditions and issues.

We have a few general rules of thumb for helping hospitalized kids, depending on the age at which they are admitted:

- ✔ **Birth to age 1:** Babies don't really understand what's going on. It's important for parents and family members to spend as much time as possible with the infant. Take pacifiers, bottles, and favorite toys or stuffed animals.

- ✔ **Preschoolers (2 to 4 years old):** Preschoolers have a rudimentary understanding of what's going on but mostly know that they're in a strange, scary environment. Read stories to the child about doctors and hospitals (the hospital's Child Life program may have books available). Take favorite toys, blankets, or stuffed animals.

Books for kids with problems

The following books are designed for use by kids. They address a variety of problems, such as depression, anxiety, anger, and attention problems. For minor problems, these resources sometimes suffice as the sole means of helping a child. For more serious issues, they're a great place to start, but you'll probably want to consider getting additional help for your child.

Books on anxiety:

Cat's Got Your Tongue?: A Story for Children Afraid to Speak, by Charles E. Schaefer (Magination Press)

My Anxious Mind: A Teen's Guide to Managing Anxiety and Panic, by Michael A. Tompkins and Katherine A. Martinez (Magination Press)

Books on intervening with anger:

How to Take the Grrrr out of Anger, by Elizabeth Verdick and Marjorie Lisovskis (Free Spirit Publishing)

A Volcano in My Tummy: Helping Children to Handle Anger, by Eliane Whitehouse and Warwick Pudney (New Society Publishers)

Books to help with ADD and ADHD:

The ADHD Workbook for Kids: Helping Children Gain Self-Confidence, Social Skills, and Self-Control, by Lawrence E. Shapiro (Instant Help Books)

Sometimes I Drive My Mom Crazy, but I Know She's Crazy About Me: A Self-Esteem Book for Overactive and Impulsive Children, by Lawrence E. Shapiro (Childswork/Childsplay)

Books that answer questions about autism:

All Cats Have Asperger Syndrome, by Kathy Hoopmann (Jessica Kingsley Publishers)

Different Like Me: My Book of Autism Heroes, by Jennifer Elder (Jessica Kingsley Publishers)

Books on defeating depression:

Beyond the Blues: A Workbook to Help Teens Overcome Depression, by Lisa M. Schab (Instant Help Publications)

When Nothing Matters Anymore: A Survival Guide for Depressed Teens, by Bev Cobain (Free Spirit Publishing)

✔ **Middle childhood years (5 to 12 years old):** You can prepare kids of this age up to a week ahead of time. These kids will want to know about their illness and are probably curious about why they have it. Explanations should be given that are concrete and straightforward. Kids need to be able to express their fears and concerns openly. Some children at the upper end of this age range can benefit from brief counseling before their hospitalization because they may find it easier to open up with a counselor than with their parents. It's still a good idea to bring favorite toys, books, and games from home. For older kids in this age range, some of the ideas (such as texting) in the next bullet on teenagers may help as well.

✔ **Teenage years (13 to 18 years old):** Teens may act braver than they feel. Make sure that they have plenty of information about their condition and what hospitalization is all about. Parents can help teens write down questions they may have for the doctors and nurses before their admission. Teens may have concerns about how they will look to their friends, whether they will have privacy in their hospital room, what will happen at school and with other activities that they miss out on, and whether they will be in serious pain. They will want to know what to expect when they return home as well.

Family members should visit, even if the teen seems to be withdrawn and sullen. Friends should also be encouraged to visit or keep in touch via texting or other means. Teens should be allowed to bring their music and gaming devices when possible. This age group may find counseling ahead of time especially useful.

Chapter 12

Understanding Problems That Interfere with Learning

Children must master basic reading, writing, and arithmetic skills to become independent adults. When children struggle with learning in school, parents, teachers, and other professionals try to figure out what's going on. Often, they discover that children have learning disabilities or attention deficit disorders that are responsible for underperformance in school.

In this chapter, we describe the early signs of learning disabilities and attention disorders. Then we discuss what the various types of learning disabilities and attention deficits look like and how they're diagnosed. We also explain the difference between a learning disability and slow learning, and show how emotions can get in the way of achievement in school.

Seeing Risk Factors for Learning Problems

Unfortunately, lots of problems that interfere with learning aren't really noticed until the child is in school and not doing well. That's because you can't really tell whether a child will have trouble learning to read, write, or perform math until it's time for her to learn those skills. But you can tell whether a child is showing problems with developing normally.

Many times, parents will ask their child's doctor when something doesn't seem right or they notice that their child appears to be a bit behind other kids. When doctors share parents' concerns, they can refer a young child to a specialist. Those professionals can look more closely and evaluate whether the child's development is proceeding normally. Such specialists include pediatricians, speech and language pathologists, occupational therapists, physical therapists, and psychologists.

Diagnosing an infant, toddler, or preschooler with a specific type of disorder can be pretty unreliable, however, because kids change, grow, and get better. So instead of getting a definitive diagnosis, most kids who show some problem with development often receive a broad diagnostic label that can easily be changed or dropped later on.

Developmental delay is the term used to describe a wide variety of minor or major problems in early development. Some of these delays simply get better with time; others require intervention; still others last throughout childhood.

In this section, we cover various forms of developmental delays. These delays can occur in all areas of development, including talking, listening, understanding language, paying attention, performing large movements (such as walking or running) or small movements (such as grasping or coloring), and mastering social skills. Kids with developmental delays have a higher risk of having trouble learning in school.

A child who might have a developmental delay is eligible for specialized evaluation (at no cost to parents) to determine how to best support and help the child. The National Dissemination Center for Children with Disabilities Web site (www.nichcy.org) has information about the process of assessment and available interventions.

Lots of perfectly normal children have one or more of the symptoms or concerns reviewed in the following sections that could indicate a developmental delay. These overviews are not provided for the purpose of home diagnosis. If you have a concern, please consult or refer the child to a professional who is trained in the diagnosis and treatment of children. That person will tell you whether you have reason to worry.

Noting trouble talking and understanding

Most children start talking around their first birthday, but lots of normal kids vary. We know kids who didn't say a word until they were almost 2 years old but then started talking in sentences. Other kids start blabbing at 8 or 9 months and never seem to stop.

Developmental delays that deal with language can involve communicating and/or understanding:

- **Communicating:** *Expressive language* refers to the way someone communicates with words. When children do not talk before the second birthday, they should be checked out. By 2 years of age, most toddlers can put a couple of words together to make a sentence such as "More juice" or "No nap." By age 3, sentences should be up to 3 or more words long.

  Kids with developmental delays that later develop into learning disabilities may have trouble pronouncing words or can't seem to remember the right word. They may be slow to learn colors, shapes, numbers, letters, or names.

- **Understanding:** *Receptive language* refers to how someone understands words. Young children should be able to understand what others are saying. By a few months of age, most babies will turn and look at people when they talk. By the time they're 1 year old, they should be able to follow simple directions like "Bring me your blanket" or "Don't touch; it's hot."

Many problems could cause delays in expressive or receptive language, such as hearing problems, infections, problems with attention, or learning disabilities. That's why it's critical to get a comprehensive evaluation, usually starting with the child's pediatrician.

Looking for delayed movements

Kids with developmental delays often have problems with movement. Compared with kids who don't have these delays, these kids are at greater risk for later being diagnosed with a learning disability. They may sit up or walk somewhat later than expected, or they may have trouble holding crayons to draw, or they may seem sort of clumsy.

Signs of potential learning problems also show up in other, more subtle ways, such as these:

- They don't seem to have a good idea of where their bodies are in the world. They take corners too closely, bump into walls, or hit their heads on furniture.

- They may have low muscle tone; seem to lack stamina; have early problems with chewing; tend to drool; often have their mouths open; and fall easily, especially when tired.

- They frequently spill things or knock them over.

- They have trouble thinking about how to do something physically and then carrying out a plan.

✔ They may have trouble using small objects that require precision handling, such as puzzles, building toys, and crayons. They dislike coloring or painting.

✔ They may have difficulty understanding sizes, shapes, or the dimensions of objects. They don't master concepts like bigger, smaller, under, and over as soon as other kids do.

✔ They easily get lost in familiar places or seem to have poor memory about places. As they get a little older, they may have trouble knowing left from right.

Although kids with one or more of these symptoms have a greater risk of developing learning disabilities, sometimes they improve or grow out of the problem. Also, a few of these kids continue to demonstrate a few motor problems but don't end up with a learning disability.

Improving motor skills

When children get extra help, many developmental delays can be resolved or at least improved. The following example illustrates what early identification and early intervention can do.

William is born after a long labor and difficult delivery. In his first few weeks, he's a quiet baby who sleeps a lot. When his mom, Alexis, takes him to his first checkup, the doctor is a bit concerned about his lack of weight gain. He tells Alexis that she should try to keep William awake during his feedings and that she should bring him in for another weight check in a couple of weeks. When Alexis returns with William, she describes a very different baby. Now, she reports, William is fussy and seems to take hours to breast-feed.

The doctor tells Alexis not to worry so much, because William has gained some weight, but he suggests supplementing her breast-feeding with formula. Alexis vows to relax but remains concerned, especially because she has only two more weeks of maternity leave.

The next few months seem like a blur. Alexis is exhausted from work and the responsibilities of being a new mother. At 6 months of age, William has yet to sleep more than a few hours in a row.

At William's six-month checkup, the doctor is concerned about some of William's motor development. William has not yet attempted to roll over, and his head and neck control are more like those of a 3-month-old than those of a 6-month-old. The doctor reminds Alexis that all babies develop differently, however. He encourages her to put William on a blanket on the floor with some toys so that he'll have more opportunities to develop his motor skills.

At 10 months of age, William is not sitting up independently. He rolls over but doesn't seem to be ready to learn how to crawl. The doctor refers him for an evaluation by a team of professionals, including a speech pathologist and a physical therapist. The team concludes that William shows a delay in motor skills. He is given the label "developmentally delayed" and is provided two hours of therapy a week.

Therapy involves teaching his mom and his daycare provider specific exercises to help William develop motor skills. By 18 months of age, William's motor skills catch up with those of other kids his age and therapy is discontinued.

Sensing problems getting along with others

Many children with developmental delays seem to have no problem getting along with others. In fact, lots of kids with delays are very popular and have great interpersonal skills. But problems in social skills can also be red flags warning of future challenges. When children show the following symptoms, the problem may be worth checking out:

- ✔ They avoid playing with other children when given the opportunity to do so.
- ✔ They get frustrated by other children easily and quickly.
- ✔ They become unusually overwhelmed and excited by other children.
- ✔ They seem to be unusually gullible and dominated by other kids.
- ✔ They act inappropriately with other kids.
- ✔ They are usually rejected by other kids.

Noting when kids can't sit still or listen

Little kids are normally pretty active, but you can expect kids to be able to quiet down after periods of active play. We have four grandchildren under the age of 6. When they all get together, they run around the house, screaming and laughing. Our two dogs usually get into the action. So the commotion seems pretty out of control to us. But they can settle down to something more tame after a while. We can sit them at a table with some paper and markers, and the concentrated quiet is an amazing contrast to the preceding chaos.

Some kids don't seem to be able to make that kind of transition. They go from one activity to another and have trouble sticking with something quiet. They have trouble focusing or sitting still. They may have difficulty following directions and appear to be inattentive. These kids (and their caregivers) may need extra help in helping them adjust (see Chapter 17).

Often kids who appear overly active and distractible improve with time. However, some of them ultimately receive a diagnosis of attention deficit hyperactivity disorder (for more information on this disorder, see later in this chapter).

Children develop differently and on different timetables. Young children tend to be exuberant, enthusiastic, and distractible. This does not mean that they have a disability; it's just too early to tell!

Struggling with Reading, Writing, and Arithmetic

Learning disabilities (LD) occur when children do not perform as well as expected in listening, speaking, reading, writing, reasoning, or mathematics. The struggle that they have with any given type of LD can vary from quite mild to profound. These problems occur in children who appear to be perfectly normal in most other ways. In other words, they do not appear to have trouble seeing or hearing, or to have obvious brain damage.

No one knows the exact cause of LD, but genes contribute, and it's thought that subtle brain differences sometimes account for the problem. Almost 9 percent of school-age children have a diagnosis of LD, which is the most common reason for children to receive special education. These kids may have other challenges, such as emotional problems or economic deprivation, but the learning disorder isn't caused by emotional disturbance or poverty.

Kids with LD are sometimes accused of being lazy or not motivated. This is rarely the case; they have problems learning specific skills and want to succeed in school just like other kids.

Kids with LD can usually be taught to compensate and sometimes overcome their difficulties, especially if they're provided accommodations and specialized instruction. Kids with LD usually grow up to be productive and sometimes brilliant members of society. Many very talented, creative people had disabilities as children, including Albert Einstein, Thomas Edison, Cher, and Tom Cruise.

We like to describe LD as being a pothole in a road: Kids learn to jump over it, go around it, or sometimes just plow through. The road keeps on going, and they keep traveling forward.

The next section describes the signs and symptoms of possible learning disabilities seen in school age children.

Understanding signs of learning disabilities

During elementary school, basic reading, writing, and arithmetic skills need to be mastered. Learning disabilities can interfere with achieving these foundational skills. Following are some signs that children might have a learning disability. These symptoms become apparent when children begin school. (We discuss preschool signs of possible problems earlier in this chapter.)

✔ They have trouble associating sounds with letters. A common task is matching pictures to beginning sounds. A picture of a cat, a dog, and a bat are presented, for example, and the child needs to draw lines across the paper to the first letters of the names of those objects: *c, d,* and *b.*

✔ They have difficulty rhyming words and don't seem to understand what rhyming means.

✔ They may have problems breaking words into syllables and don't seem to hear the sounds as being separate (despite having normal hearing).

✔ They may be able to sing the alphabet song but can't say the letters in order when they're asked to start in the middle or to stop and start.

✔ They don't easily memorize common words in books, such as *the, it, does,* and *do.*

✔ They can't seem to sound out three-letter words even after learning the sounds.

✔ They have trouble copying words off the blackboard or from books.

✔ They reverse letters both in spelling and reading. It's normal to reverse *b* and *d* in the early grades, for example, but kids with disabilities continue to reverse letters.

✔ They may rely on visual memory (sight words) and not master phonics, even with adequate instruction.

✔ They have trouble learning basic math facts and often confuse arithmetic signs. They may add instead of subtract, for example, because they "see" a plus sign instead of a minus sign despite having normal vision.

✔ They have a great deal of trouble solving word problems.

✔ They can't tell time on an analog clock.

✔ They struggle with reading and read slowly. They can get through a passage but can't answer questions about the content. If the same passage is read to the student out loud, the child is more likely to be able to answer such comprehension questions.

✔ They can memorize spelling words with lots of effort but forget them by the following week. They reverse letters and misspell common words.

✔ They have trouble memorizing dates in history, days of the week, and months of the year.

✔ They have difficulty memorizing geography lessons (states, capitals, and countries).

A good place to start when a kid shows signs of trouble learning is the child's primary-care provider. Make sure that the child takes hearing and vision tests. Also discuss and deal with any health issues that may be affecting the child.

Investigating learning disabilities further

If a child shows signs of a learning disorder (see previous section), has adequate or corrected vision and hearing, is otherwise healthy, and struggles in school, further investigation should be started. In the past, many school systems subscribed to a wait-and-see approach. Officials suggested that the child be held back, or assumed that a child just lacked maturity and would eventually catch up. This wait usually meant a wait for failure. That approach did not work, and children who were not helped almost always fell farther behind. (See Chapter 17 for information about effective treatments.)

When a child has been identified as possibly needing more help, most schools have teams consisting of parents, teachers, and educational specialists who meet to see whether any accommodations can help the child in a regular classroom program. These accommodations include

✔ Additional individual tutoring

✔ Increased parent–teacher communication

✔ Seating in the front of the class

✔ Frequent monitoring of progress by the teacher

✔ Changing teaching methods or building up basic skills

Sometimes, adjusting a few things in the classroom and providing some extra attention are all that a child needs to succeed. At other times, these interventions do not address the child's needs, and a more comprehensive evaluation of the problem is required. A comprehensive education evaluation involves interviewing the parents about developmental history, reviewing educational progress and records, making classroom observations, and performing individual specialized testing.

Testing a child who might have a learning disability is usually done by a team of professionals. The team is often headed by a school or educational psychologist. Depending on the child's needs and the concerns of parents and teachers, the team may also include the child's teacher, a speech and language pathologist, a neuropsychologist, an audiologist (hearing specialist), a clinical psychologist, or an occupational therapist. (See Chapter 18 for more information about testing and test scores.)

Labeling learning disabilities

Depending on whether you're talking to a physician, a psychologist, or an educator, you may hear different words used to describe a learning disability. Although the situation is slowly changing, many school systems give kids extra help for a reading disability but not for dyslexia, yet a reading disability is a disorder that involves trouble with reading, and dyslexia is also a disorder that involves trouble with reading. You see, kids who are labeled as having a learning disability in the area of reading are almost always dyslexic too.

Other terms for specific learning disabilities include dyscalculia (difficulty with math),

dysgraphia (problems with writing), auditory processing disorder (problems listening and discriminating sounds or language), communication disorder (problems speaking or understanding language), and visual processing disorder (problems understanding visual information, such as letters, maps, and symbols).

The specific definitions of these terms change from one textbook to another and from one profession to another. Don't get too worked up about the terms; just know that learning disabilities can come in many forms.

Attending to Attention Problems

If you're reading this book, in all likelihood, you probably went to school for some years. Think back. Do you ever recall drifting off during a class? Maybe you were thinking about something that happened last week or what you were going to do on the weekend, or perhaps you were just looking out the window. Suddenly, you realized that you'd completely lost track of what the teacher was talking about. You may have been concerned that the teacher would call on you, and you had no idea what was going on. Perhaps you can remember that uneasy feeling when you worried about getting caught daydreaming.

Or maybe you didn't daydream but instead felt restless and hated sitting at your desk. You remember getting in trouble for fidgeting or leaving your desk to sharpen your pencil. You couldn't wait for recess or gym class. When the teacher asked the class a question, sometimes you waved your hand in the air or blurted out answers before being called on, only to be criticized for interrupting. Possibly you rushed through your school work, talked too much or too loudly, and had trouble standing in line.

Most children and adults have some trouble paying attention or staying still from time to time. But when lots of these problems crop up every day at home, at school, or at work, they may be signs of a disorder. Attention deficit/hyperactivity disorder (also known as ADHD or ADD) is a common condition often diagnosed during childhood. A little more than 8 percent of school-age children have been given a diagnosis of ADHD or ADD by a professional, according to survey results published by the Centers for Disease Control and Prevention (CDC).

Seeing what attention disorders look like

With ADHD, symptoms are often apparent when a child starts to experience problems in school. An example of a fairly typical child with ADHD follows.

> **Owen** can't stop grinning as he walks into his new classroom. Floor-to-ceiling windows stretch along one wall, offering a view of the courtyard and playground beyond. Colorful charts and maps adorn the walls. Shelves hold plants, books, baskets of art materials, and even a cage with a real live snake. Banners strung above the teacher's desk proclaim, "Welcome to Third Grade!"
>
> His teacher stands inside the door, greeting all the children with a smile. She lets the children pick their own desks, which are arranged in clusters of four. Owen dashes over to a desk near the back of the room — right next to the snake and with a good view of the playground. He doesn't know it yet, but he's starting one of the worst school years of his life.
>
> Owen's teacher believes in letting children learn by exploring their environments and doing group projects. She allows lots of freedom and encourages movement. Owen has trouble sitting still and is easily distracted. He spends a lot of recess time in the classroom because he hasn't completed his assignments. His teacher patiently explains to him that he needs to develop better self-control. She wonders how to reach him. He spends most of his time daydreaming or wandering around the room. By midyear, Owen is spending time in the office for not listening to the teacher. Everyone is frustrated.

Owen shows signs of an attention disorder. He may need more structure than the teacher is providing in her engaging classroom. Many kids with these difficulties are labeled disobedient, like Owen. That's why it is so important to notice signs of trouble, have a child evaluated if indicated, and get help early.

Just because children have trouble paying attention or seem to be overly active does not mean that they have ADHD or ADD (see the sidebar "Watching out for the wrong diagnosis"). Many other problems — such as side effects of certain medications, childhood depression, anxiety, or learning disabilities — can cause kids to have similar symptoms. Diagnosis of these complex disorders requires assessment by a trained medical or mental-health professional.

Watching out for the wrong diagnosis

The number of children getting a diagnosis of ADHD has grown significantly over the past three decades. Actually, ADHD was rarely diagnosed 50 years ago. So what's happened, and why do rates of ADHD vary so much from place to place? The CDC reports that fewer than 6 percent of children in some states are diagnosed with ADHD, and in other states, more than 9 percent of children get this diagnosis. Are kids born in some states more likely to become hyperactive? Probably not. Many people wonder whether professionals are diagnosing some children incorrectly.

An interesting study suggests that problems with diagnosis are quite real. Data was collected from national surveys and from health records. Researchers found that a certain age group was 50 percent more likely to be diagnosed with ADHD. Were these kids brain-damaged, exposed to toxins, or born prematurely? No. This group of kids had the bad luck of being born just before the kindergarten cutoff; they were the youngest kids in their classes. The kids were simply less mature than their classmates. This rather astounding research is no surprise to many of us who have practiced in the field. For those who want more information about the study, see the *Journal of Health Economics* "Measuring Inappropriate Medical Diagnosis and Treatment in Survey Data: The Case of ADHD" by William Evans, Melinda Morrill, and Stephen Parente, September, 2010.

Counting the costs of attention problems

ADHD is also one of the most common reasons parents seek help from their family doctor or a mental-health professional. Kids with this disorder have some mixture of hyperactivity, impulsivity, and inattentiveness. Almost half of kids with ADHD also have a learning disability (see "Struggling with Reading, Writing, and Arithmetic," earlier in this chapter). The combination of LD and ADHD can make school quite difficult and require lots of extra help from educational and mental-health professionals.

Kids with ADHD also have a significantly higher rate than their peers of experiencing the following problems:

- Underachievement in school
- Injuries (both mild and serious)
- Emergency-room visits
- Hospitalizations
- Anxiety and depression
- Behavior problems

- Problems that interfere with friendships
- Traffic tickets (after they get their driver's license hopefully!)
- Drug or alcohol abuse
- Cigarette smoking
- Motor vehicle crashes (again, after licensed to drive)

Associating pesticides with ADD or ADHD

As with many disorders, the exact causes of ADHD are not really known. The disorder runs in families, so genetics are likely culprits. Kids who are born too early or have difficult births are also more likely to have ADHD, so those issues probably increase the risk. Furthermore, children with brain damage caused by genetics, birth, or injuries run a greater chance of having ADHD than kids without brain damage. Environmental factors such as exposure to lead or other toxins are also probable causes or contributors to problems in the area of attention.

Pesticides are environmental toxins that are considered to be possible causes of ADHD. Organophosphate pesticides are designed to kill insects by attacking their nervous systems and are also commonly used in solvents, plastics, and lubricants. Concerns have been expressed about the possibility that exposure to pesticides could cause problems in children's nervous systems. In fact, a recent study reported in the journal *Environmental Health Perspectives* looked closely at the relationship of pesticide levels in pregnant mothers and highlighted these concerns.

The study involved testing for levels of pesticide in pregnant women twice during pregnancy and in their babies after birth. Then the researchers tested the children for ADHD when the children were 3½ and 5 years old, using comprehensive psychological measurements. They found that exposure to pesticides substantially increased the incidence of ADHD, and the more exposure prenatally, the higher the risk of ADHD.

For those readers who want more information about the study or want some fascinating bedtime reading, the title of the article is: *PON1 and Neurodevelopment in children from the CHAMACOS Study Exposed to Organophosphate Pesticide in Utero* by Brenda Eskenazi, Karen Huen, Amy Marks, Kim Harley, Asa Bradman, Dana Barr, and Nina Holland, Center for Children's Environmental Health Research, School of Public Health, University of California, Berkeley and Emory University, Rollins School of Public Health 2010. For more information, see: `http://ehp03.niehs.nih.gov/article/info%3Adoi%2F10.1289%2Fehp.1002234#abstract0`.

Granted, many of the participants in the study on ADHD and pesticides were farm workers who would be expected to have higher than average exposure to pesticides. However, most experts today believe that any exposure to pesticides should be as limited as possible. Unfortunately, residual pesticides cannot be *completely* washed or peeled off common fruits and vegetables. The obvious choice is to wash your foods carefully and eat organic foods when you can. But those foods are not always available and are often much more expensive. Experts advise that people who are concerned should cut down on the worst offenders (as determined by the U.S. Department of Agriculture), such as celery, peaches, strawberries, apples, and blueberries. Fresh foods that are lower in pesticides include onions, avocados, corn, pineapples, peas, and mangos. Still eat your fruits and vegetables; just take care when you can.

Looking at the symptoms of ADD/ADHD

Kids with ADD/ADHD have a variety of symptoms. These symptoms involve hyperactivity, impulsivity, and problems focusing and paying attention. First, we discuss hyperactivity and impulsivity that almost always occur together. Then, we review problems with attention.

Exhibiting hyperactivity and impulsivity

Hyperactivity and impulsivity are two symptoms that all kids have, but kids with ADHD have a lot more. All children like to run around and play. They sometimes seem to have boundless energy and bounce from activity to activity. These tendencies are perfectly normal. Going from the playroom and the playground to sitting in rows quietly working can be a difficult transition for any kid. It's no surprise that symptoms of hyperactivity often go unnoticed until children start school.

Young kids tend to act without thinking. This impulsivity is also perfectly normal. Ask any 5-year-old boy why he jumped out of a tree or hit his sister. He'll probably say, "I don't know," and he'll probably be telling the truth.

In fact, a little impulsivity stays with most kids off and on throughout adolescence and even into early adulthood. Ask your 18-year-old daughter what she was thinking of when she got a huge tattoo of a rattlesnake wrapped around her arm, and she might say, "Snakes are wicked" (or something equally puzzling).

Although a degree of hyperactivity or impulsivity is expected in kids, it can also become a major obstacle. When it rises to the level that interferes with school, causes problems in relationships, or gets kids into trouble, it could be a symptom of ADHD. Most children display a few of these traits and do not have ADHD, however. To constitute a disorder, these symptoms must occur frequently over time and get in the way of everyday functioning.

Here are some common signs of hyperactivity and impulsivity in children:

- ✔ They're always moving and can't sit still. They tap their hands and feet, shift their bodies, and fidget.

- ✔ They have trouble staying in their seats. They are restless and wander around. They have trouble sitting still at school, a long restaurant meal, or dinner. Young children with this symptom may run in halls, climb on furniture, or pace. Older kids might be able to stay seated but dislike it and feel confined.

- ✔ They get overly excited and rambunctious. They can be noisy and loud. They talk too much, interrupt others, and are often intrusive.

- ✔ They answers questions without thinking, blurt out responses before being called on. They have trouble thinking things through and complete assignments without carefully reading directions.

✔ They act without thinking and make decisions without considering consequences. They have difficulty taking other people's perspective. Although they are often very loving and kind, they sometimes hurt others due to impulsivity.

✔ Impatient, they want to get done fast, go fast, and hate waiting in lines. They rush through school work and feel restless when tasks require thoughtful consideration.

✔ They often like excitement and relish danger. They may take risks and be willing to do things for attention.

Although it's not part of the official diagnostic criteria, one additional item that concerns many parents is what we like to call the Mall on Saturday Phenomenon. Kids with MSP disappear among the shelves, touch things they're not supposed to, and want everything *now*. We like to ask how a child behaves in a crowded store. Almost inevitably, parents whose kids have ADHD sigh very loudly just before they answer the question.

Spacing out

Inattention is another symptom of ADHD. Many kids have a mixture of hyper-activity, impulsivity, and inattention, but some kids just have trouble staying focused. Some professionals use the ADD diagnosis for kids who are not partic-ularly hyperactive or impulsive but have trouble paying attention, but for now, the official name remains ADHD — predominately inattentive. (If you want more information about the reasons, see the sidebar "Labeling ADD and ADHD.")

TECHNICAL STUFF

Labeling ADD and ADHD

Psychologists, psychiatrists, and other mental-health providers use a book called the *Diagnostic and Statistical Manual of Mental Disorders:* Fourth Edition (DSM-IV), which describes symptoms and provides the official names of emotional and behavioral disorders. When the current manual was developed, the authors used the name *attention deficit/hyper-activity disorder* to describe both the disorder that primarily involves inattentiveness and the disorder that involves hyperactivity and impul-sivity. Their rationale was that ADHD and ADD symptoms often occur together. This can be confusing because many people see ADHD and ADD as being two separate disorders.

For clarity, we talk about both ADHD and ADD. But realize that until the next edition of the *DSM* is published, the official diagnoses are

✔ Attention Deficit/Hyperactivity Disorder, Predominately Inattentive Type

✔ Attention Deficit Disorder, Predominantly Hyperactive-Impulsive Type

✔ Attention Deficit Disorder, Combined Type

Oh, we almost forgot Attention Deficit/ Hyperactivity Disorder Not Otherwise Specified, a name reserved for people who have problems but don't quite fit the other categories. Sorry; we didn't design the system.

Inattentive symptoms can make life pretty darn difficult, especially in school. To result in a disorder diagnosis, the symptoms have to be negatively affecting a child's life. Every child has difficulty staying focused from time to time, but those with ADD really zone out. Here are some of the common problems of inattention:

- ✔ They make lots of careless mistakes. They may not follow simple directions not because of lack of skill but because of poor attention. Their mistakes include adding instead of subtracting, filling in the wrong bubbles on answer sheets, and missing the point of a question.

- ✔ When tasks require long periods of attention, these kids lose track. For example, they can't focus on long passages in a book, lecture, or conversation.

- ✔ Sometimes they seem to not hear others although their hearing is normal. Parents often complain that these children do not listen, even when spoken to directly.

- ✔ They have trouble finishing tasks such as school assignments or chores. They may starts things but quickly lose interest.

- ✔ They're disorganized. They may have trouble taking on big projects. Sometimes they fail to grasp where to start something like a science project or a paper. They have amazingly messy backpacks, rooms, and desks.

- ✔ They don't like things that require staying focused and may rebel when given long assignments or repetitive practice.

- ✔ They are notorious for losing homework, jackets, mittens, keys, or books. They might do their homework but forget to put it in the backpacks. They require lots of reminders and often fail to keep appointments.

- ✔ They get distracted easily. Kids with ADHD can be sitting in a classroom listening to a teacher and then get involved in watching something out the window or another child doodling on a piece of paper.

Learning Slowly

Some children develop slower than others. Some of those slower-to-develop kids catch up with time or extra help, but others don't catch up. The latter children may have an intellectual disability. *Intellectual disabilities* involve limited intellectual capacities across a broader range of areas than learning disabilities involve (see "Struggling with Reading, Writing, and Arithmetic," earlier in this chapter). Intellectual disabilities include both impaired intelligence and problems with everyday functioning.

Intellectual disabilities are diagnosed only after comprehensive evaluations by trained professionals.

Sometimes, children with intellectual disabilities have a known genetic disorder, such as Down syndrome or Fragile X (see Chapter 11). Other kids may have not had enough oxygen during birth or shortly thereafter and suffered brain damage as a result. Others were born to mothers who abused alcohol during pregnancy, so the children developed fetal alcohol syndrome. Some children may have had strokes or severe head injuries. But for many children with intellectual disabilities, the causes are unknown.

The term *intellectual disability* is becoming widely adopted and replacing the older term *mental retardation*, but *mental retardation* is still used by many to describe people with an intellectual disability. Some advocacy groups have suggested finding terms other than disability to describe this problem.

Impaired intelligence

Intelligence is the ability to learn from the environment and to use that learning to adapt to the environment. Intelligence cannot be fully measured by a single test, but an intelligence test can be one important piece of information that is used in the diagnosis of an intellectual disability. Generally, those with an intellectual disability score in the bottom 3 percent of children in their age group who take the test.

Many factors come into play in diagnosing impaired intelligence. Cultural background must be considered, because some IQ tests may not be as appropriate for kids from diverse backgrounds. Furthermore, not all kids perform up to their potential on intelligence tests due to problems with motivation, attention, and emotional issues. Some children are uncomfortable taking a test and, due to anxiety, don't do well. Other children lack interest in the test and don't try very hard. Still others are distracted or restless, which can interfere with their performance. That's why a single test should never be the only source of information considered in making a diagnosis.

Problems with everyday functioning

Leading an independent life involves much more than learning how to read, write, and perform arithmetic. *Adaptive behavior* refers to the everyday skills necessary to get through the day. Broadly, these abilities have to do with thinking, communicating, getting along with others, and practical skills such as taking adequate care of the body. The list of adaptive behavior is very long, but here are some examples:

✔ Eating independently

✔ Using communication to get needs met

✔ Fixing food

✔ Bathing

✔ Toileting

✔ Combing hair

✔ Taking medications independently

✔ Dressing

✔ Cleaning one's room

✔ Understanding money

✔ Telling time

✔ Enjoying leisure activities

✔ Being a friend

To be diagnosed as intellectually disabled, a child must test in the lowest 3 percent in his or her age group in intelligence *and* two areas of adaptive functioning. Considering adaptive behavior as well as intelligence prevents children who do poorly in school or on intelligence tests but function well outside school from being classified as intellectually disabled.

Seeing how emotions challenge learning

Any disorder that disrupts emotional functioning (see Chapter 14) can also interfere with learning.

Think of the brain as having a certain amount of electrical energy. When the brain is fully engaged in learning, 100 percent of the resources from the brain are going to that task. The light is bright. But in a child with an emotional disorder, a certain amount of the available electricity goes to fighting depression, feeling anxious, being angry, or worrying about what might happen next. Hypothetically, if an emotional disorder takes 25 percent of the energy, the learning light dims.

That is one reason why it is so important to look at all the reasons a child may not be learning. It's not always a disability. It's important to treat children's emotional problems to keep the light of learning bright.

Chapter 13

Addressing Autism Spectrum Disorders

*I*n the Southwest, after a storm blows over, the skies usually clear, and a rainbow frames the valley with the mountains as a backdrop. Sometimes, the glow seems magical, lighting up the sky. At other times, the colors fade quickly, or a smaller rainbow appears below the first. Rainbows appear as a spectrum of colors that vary in shade, depth, and intensity.

Autism, like rainbows, comes in a spectrum. It varies from mild to severe; the symptoms can be bright, bold, or faded, or can even disappear.

We devote this chapter to autism, a highly complex disorder that has increased by *600 percent* in the past 20 years according to the Centers for Disease Control and Prevention (CDC), a government agency that tracks health across the United States. We review the most common symptoms of autism and how they affect children, as well as dispel some of the myths and misconceptions about this disorder. Then we discuss the intriguing gifts that sometimes accompany autism disorders.

We really like working with kids with autism. They can be fun, challenging, and interesting. Don't ask us why, but some adults feel quite annoyed when they encounter autistic kids, who often have quirky habits and behaviors. If you care for or work with children with autism, make sure that you enjoy yourself, and if you have a kid with autism, be aware that some people aren't ready for the challenge. Protect your kid from those who don't appreciate their unique gifts. All kids deserve to be loved and appreciated.

Defining and Describing Autism

Autism is a complicated *neurodevelopmental disorder* (an abnormality in the way the brain is wired) that's usually first diagnosed in childhood and that has various effects on social development, communication, and perception. Kids diagnosed with the identical label of autism can look, act, and think very differently from one another, and the exact nature of their symptoms and the severity of those symptoms can change over time.

Only professionals who are experienced and well trained are able to make a diagnosis of autism (as well as other types of developmental disorders). Lots of normal kids or kids with other disorders sometimes have a few similar symptoms and eventually grow out of them, whereas symptoms of autism are chronic and negatively affect development. If you're concerned about a child, the first step is to consult the child's pediatrician, who will be aware of appropriate referrals for evaluation if needed.

Recognizing early signs of trouble

This section is a difficult one to write because many babies with the signs we describe don't ultimately develop autism, and we don't want parents or caregivers to worry needlessly. Yet parents and caretakers need to consider these symptoms, because certain strategies can help a baby who has autism symptoms.

If a baby shows worrisome signs, don't ignore them. Professionally and personally, nothing we've seen has made more of an impression on us than the miraculous effects of early intervention. We've seen youngsters who showed all the signs of developing autism being given therapy early on and turning out just fine. We've experienced the anguish of parents who were told that their babies were likely to be severely disabled, and we watched those children grow into productive adults with minor disabilities. We've also been frustrated when parents or professionals decided to hide their heads in the sand, pretending that nothing was wrong or that the babies would just grow out of whatever differences or delays they had. A child doesn't need to have a formal diagnosis to get help.

Early warning signs don't necessarily mean that a child will develop full-blown autism if left alone. Nevertheless, early intervention can't hurt anyone and very well may help a great deal.

Table 13-1 provides a list of early signs or symptoms of autism. These signs don't mean that a baby has autism or will become autistic. The purpose of this information is to increase awareness. If a baby shows worrisome signs, parents and caregivers need to consult the baby's pediatrician, who can refer for further evaluation and possible intervention (see Chapter 17 for information about interventions).

Table 13-1	Early Reasons for Concern
Symptoms	*Discussion*
Differences in the way babies look at things and people	Babies who eventually become autistic don't look around as intently at their environment in the first few months as other babies do. They have less frequent eye contact with others throughout infancy.
Abnormal muscle tone	They have a higher incidence of too-rigid or too-low muscle tone.
Differences in the way babies relate to others	They do look at caregivers — but not as intensely or with as much joy as other babies in the first 6 months do. They may appear to be withdrawn and not smile as much as other babies.
Differences in the way infants interact with caregivers	The ability to have conversations with others starts in infancy. Babies who later develop autism aren't as playful as others. They don't engage in as much give-and-take, such as smiling, babbling, and moving in response to caregivers (about 3 months through 12 months).
Delays and differences in language and communication skills	They don't use sounds or gestures to communicate with others as expected by around 1 year of age. They don't point and make noises to get a bottle, for example, or wave bye-bye or play patty-cake. They don't use words by 18 months; they may repeat sounds or words but not for the purpose of communicating with others.
Losing skills babies have already mastered	If a baby previously communicated, interacted, or had motor skills and then seems to regress, this may be a sign of a problem. Many parents of autistic children report that their child was developing normally and then lost skills.

Certain tests have shown differences in how babies who ultimately develop autism respond visually. At 4 months of age, they appear to prefer higher amounts of visual stimulation. In addition, their pupils don't respond as quickly when stimulated. Although highly promising, tests for these responses are not yet widely available.

Painting a picture of autism

Children may not be diagnosed with autism until they're close to school age or sometimes later, after they have lots of problems in school. By school age, the signs become more noticeable.

With such widely varying symptoms, how can you tell whether a school-age child warrants an evaluation for the possibility of autism? Kids with autism have trouble relating and communicating to the people around them. They also often show uneven development. An autistic child may have skills that seem advanced compared with those of other kids and other skills that are delayed. A boy with autism may be able to recognize and name dozens of brands of cars but be unable to zip up his jacket, for example, or a girl may draw intricate designs but not speak to other people. Autistic kids communicate and relate to the world in so many ways that no one set of symptoms will match any one child with autism.

The following sections, however, give you a deeper sense of how autism can affect behavior, communication, social skills, and perceptions.

Relating to others

Every child with autism is a unique individual (just like every child without autism). So not every child who has autism shows every sign that we discuss. Nevertheless, the following differences in relating tend to be seen more often in children who have been diagnosed with autism:

- **Difficulty with social norms:** Kids with autism can be charming to be around but unaware of social norms such as taking turns and being polite. As they grow older and develop speech, they may be brutally honest — telling the teacher that she has food on her chin, for example, or looking at a stranger and commenting that he has a large pimple on his nose. They don't catch on to social nuances and have difficulty taking another person's perspective.

- **Lack of eye contact:** Kids may not look directly into the eyes of others as much as expected; they seem to look through, not at, other people.

- **Lack of social interaction:** They may not seek out other people to interact with and sometimes don't understand how to share feelings. They're often able to amuse themselves alone for unusually long periods and may even choose to avoid interacting with other kids.

- **Low need for attention and affection:** They may not seek out attention, such as proudly showing a drawing to a parent. Some kids may resist being cuddled and seem less affectionate than most other kids.

- **Delayed or unusual verbal communication:** Their language skills may be delayed, or they may have a good vocabulary but don't seem to know how to hold a conversation. Sometimes, kids with autism memorize favorite videos or speak in strange robotic ways. Their voices may have odd inflections and have a different pace from those of other kids.

- **Delayed nonverbal communication:** An adult may point to something nearby, for example, and the autistic child doesn't follow the point.

✔ **Unusual preoccupations:** Many kids with autism greatly prefer sticking with certain fixed routines and become frustrated and throw tantrums when their routines are changed. Others are preoccupied by certain subjects, such as dinosaurs, car types, or cartoon characters. Older kids with autism may lecture other adults or children about their favorite topic, oblivious to the fact that their listeners aren't really interested.

✔ **Unusual emotional reactions:** The emotions of children with autism frequently seem to be a little off. They may be amused by and laugh at things that other children don't laugh at, or they don't understand or respond to humor. Likewise, they may not respond as expected to discipline, either ignoring it or not understanding what to do.

Relating to the world

Children who have autism relate to the world around them in many different ways. Some kids with autism look pretty much like kids without autism. Some may have ways of interacting with objects that seem pretty strange to others. Again, no two kids are alike, but the following are some of the common ways that kids who have autism may engage with their worlds:

✔ **Unusual styles of play:** Kids with autism may not engage in pretend play or may play in certain restricted, odd ways. They may line up toys in specific order rather than play with them in a meaningful way. They can be drawn to shiny objects or objects that spin around. They may enjoy taking things apart or playing with parts of one toy rather than the whole toy.

✔ **Repetitive movements:** Kids with autism commonly display repetitive motor mannerisms, such as hand flapping or finger twisting or flapping.

✔ **Low tolerance for sensations:** These children can get overwhelmed when the environment is too loud or busy. Sometimes, certain types of noises bother them more than the actual volume of the noises do. Not infrequently, kids with autism become upset by the feel of certain types of fabric or tags on their clothes.

✔ **Likelihood of being overwhelmed:** Various types of sensations, lights, and unexpected events may overwhelm these kids, and when they're overwhelmed, they may withdraw into their own worlds or exhibit what can only be described as a total meltdown.

✔ **High or low tolerance for risk:** These kids sometimes appear to be fearless and engage in dangerous behavior, such as running away from their caregivers at a store or from a line in the classroom. At other times, they act clingy and afraid.

✔ **High or low tolerance for pain:** Kids with autism often have either an abnormally low or abnormally high threshold of pain sensitivity.

Looking at variations in autism

Take a look at a couple of kids, both of whom carry the diagnosis of autism. These two examples illustrate how strikingly different children with autism can be. The first child, Jackson, shows severe signs of autism. The second child, Natalie, has a milder form of the disorder.

> **Jackson** attends a preschool program for kids with disabilities. He's 4 years old and has a vocabulary of a few words despite having had speech therapy since he was 18 months old. He can say "more," "Mama," "bus," and "baba" (a word he uses to indicate that he wants his favorite blanket).
>
> Jackson can't dress himself. He can eat finger foods independently but remains unable to use utensils without spilling. He rarely looks at people and doesn't seek out other children. He lets his mother hug him briefly when he's upset but doesn't want to be held for long periods. Jackson has episodes during which he screams and can't be consoled, especially when his routine is changed or he's in an unfamiliar place.
>
> He rides a small bus to his preschool three days a week. Every day, he looks out the front window of his house, watching for the bus. When he sees it, he repeats the word *bus* over and over while flapping his hands. During the bus ride, he often rocks back and forth. He doesn't interact with other children at school, but he can sit in a circle with the other children without having a tantrum — a skill that took 6 months of work to develop. If Jackson were allowed to do so, he'd sit away from the other children, holding a toy bus and spinning its wheels.

Jackson has been diagnosed with autism. His symptoms are quite disabling. By contrast, Natalie's symptoms are much milder and less obvious. Nevertheless, she too has a form of autism.

> **Natalie** could recite the alphabet by the time she was 18 months old; she was given a child's dictionary when she started kindergarten and promptly memorized all the words. By the time she finished kindergarten, she was reading books at a third-grade level. People who interacted with her invariably concluded that she was a genius.
>
> Surprisingly, Natalie has lots of trouble adjusting to school. She doesn't get along well with her classmates and often fails to complete her assignments. She seems to be disinterested in others and spends all her time reading encyclopedias or dictionaries when she's allowed to do so. Her parents are frustrated after attending numerous conferences at school and having endless discussions with Natalie. She seems to be unresponsive to pleading, lectures, rewards, and even punishments. Her teachers suggest that Natalie needs a complete evaluation.

As you can see, Natalie doesn't seem much like Jackson at all. At first, her parents and teachers were thrilled by her accomplishments and wondered whether she might be gifted (see "When Autism Comes with Unusual Gifts," later in this chapter). In fact, she does have some unusual talents. She also has autism, however, as evident in her odd responses to other kids, her imperviousness to discipline strategies employed by her parents and teachers, and her preoccupation with dictionaries.

These examples are only illustrative. Parents and teachers should not try to diagnose autism. If you have concerns about a child who has symptoms, seek help. Only well-trained professionals who perform a comprehensive assessment can make a diagnosis of autism.

Laying out the autism spectrum

People are often confused by the different diagnostic labels given to children with symptoms of autism. The problem occurs because professionals in different fields develop their own codes or vocabularies. In this section, we attempt to clarify the common names used to describe kids who have similar symptoms.

Labeling a person as having autism, a learning disability, or even depression doesn't give a full picture of that person. Each child is unique, with different strengths and weaknesses. At the same time, labels can guide treatment, protect people with disabilities, and help professionals communicate to maintain good care, so we define the labels that are often applied to children with autistic symptoms because they're commonly used and often confused.

Diagnostic and Statistical Manual of Mental Disorders: Fourth Edition

Diagnostic and Statistical Manual of Mental Disorders: Fourth Edition (DSM-IV), published by the American Psychiatric Association, is the source of most medical and psychological diagnostic terms and definitions. It lists three types of autistic disorders under the broad heading "Pervasive Developmental Disorders":

- **Autistic disorder:** Child must show problems before age 3 in language, social interaction, and play. These symptoms include a variety of the following:

  - Delay in language

  - Problems having a conversation

  - Repetitive or strange language

  - Lack of make believe play

  - Poor nonverbal communication

  - Problems developing relationships with peers

  - Doesn't seem to care about sharing enjoyment with others

  - Doesn't know how to give and take in relationships

- Intense or restricted focus on one activity or interest

- Inflexibility

- Hand flapping, rocking, twisting

- Interested in parts of objects

✔ **Asperger's disorder:** Kids with Asperger's have similar symptoms as those with autism. The main difference between Asperger's Disorder and Autistic Disorder is that children with Asperger's *do not have delays* in language. Children with this disorder are usually not as severely affected as those with autistic disorder.

✔ **Pervasive Developmental Disorder Not Otherwise Specified (PDDNOS):** This category is reserved for children who are impaired in many of the same ways as those with Autistic Disorder or Asperger's Disorder but may not meet all of the specific criteria. PDD NOS is also sometimes known as *atypical autism.*

Diagnostic and Statistical Manual of Mental Disorders: Fifth Edition

Diagnostic and Statistical Manual of Mental Disorders: Fifth Edition (DSM-V) is in the works and should be published in the next few years. Although the DSM-V is still a work in progress, much has been already written about the likely changes in the criteria for autism. The biggest change currently con-templated is instead of having separate categories, there will be one name: *Autistic Spectrum Disorder (Autistic Disorder)* that will be used in place of all three previous categories: Autistic Disorder, Asperger's Disorder, and Pervasive Developmental Disorder. The definition will likely require the same set of problems covered in DSM-IV in the areas of social/communication and restricted/repetitive interests or behaviors.

All of these different labels can be quite confusing and frustrating to parents and people who work with or care about children diagnosed with either Asperger's, autism, or PDD NOS. The new regulations in the DSM-V have some people upset because of the loss of the Asperger's diagnostic category. That's because *Aspies* (a term often used to describe people with Asperger's, even among those who have it), often have special abilities and skills that distin-guish them from those with autism. Other times, they don't have special skills but are somewhat less impaired overall. Thus, parents of kids with the Aspie label often like to have people see their kids as distinguished from those with the more serious category of Autism.

Individuals with Disabilities Education Act

Many children with autism require special-education services. The Individuals with Disabilities Education Act (IDEA) has its own categories for labeling children who require such services, allowing them certain protec-tions under the law, such as individualized educational plans and free appro-priate education such as special tutoring or other accommodations. The federal law refers only to autism, not to Asperger's or PDD NOS.

Under IDEA, autism or autism spectrum disorder is characterized by difficulty in verbal and nonverbal communication, as well as social interactions that adversely affect educational performance. At the same time, most states allow children with the diagnosis of Asperger's Disorder or Pervasive Developmental Disorder Not Otherwise Specified to receive special education services under the category of autism.

Debunking myths about autism

Explosions of myths about autism have accompanied the explosion of diagnosed cases of autism. Here are some of the most frequent of these myths:

- **Myth 1: Kids with autism don't love or form attachments.** Children with autism do love their parents or other close caregivers. Just like kids without autism, they seek comfort and company from mothers, fathers, or other family members. Sometimes, kids with autism feel uncomfortable with physical closeness, which means that they may not enjoy cuddling as much as other kids do, but that doesn't mean they don't love their parents.

- **Myth 2: Kids with autism don't care about other people.** Although they may not show concern in the same way, kids with autism do want others to think well of them. Often the targets of bullies, they want to have friends but may lack social skills. Kids with autism often feel terribly hurt by rejection by other kids. Autistic children and adults do make friends and have meaningful relationships, however.

- **Myth 3: Autism is caused by the measles, mumps, and rubella (MMR) vaccine.** Unfortunately, a physician first reported the link between vaccines and autism in the late '80s. Many parents read about this connection in a respected medical journal and chose not to vaccinate their kids. Choosing not to vaccinate kids led to increased rates of measles but not to a reduction in rates of autism. Since then, studies have not supported a link between the vaccine and autism. Furthermore, the doctor who led the research was paid by attorneys who represented parents involved in suing companies that produced the vaccine. The doctor's research was reviewed by a medical board, which concluded that his article was misleading and dishonest.

- **Myth 4: Mercury causes autism.** Mercury, a neurotoxin, is a component of the preservative thimerosal that was used in vaccines since the 1930s until the late 1990's (and can still be found in some flu vaccines). The rise in autism was thought to be caused by mercury toxicity in the vaccines that children received as infants and toddlers. In recent years, the preservative has been removed from almost all childhood vaccines in the United States and many other countries. Unfortunately, the rate of autism has only continued to rise. Nonetheless, many parents remain passionately convinced that vaccines somehow have a connection to autism.

✔ **Myth 5: Autism is caused by emotionally distant parents.** This has nothing to do with why a child becomes autistic. The myth is left over from the days people blamed their mothers for everything!

✔ **Myth 6: Autistic children are mentally retarded.** Some autistic children are highly intelligent, others have average intelligence, and many are intellectually disabled. Many autistic children have uneven skills — some very advanced and others below average.

✔ **Myth 7: Autism can be cured.** This statement is partly true in that some kids with autism can be given sufficient treatment that their symptoms decrease substantially over time. Therefore, they no longer meet the diagnostic criteria for autism. Most children, however, either don't achieve this "cure" or continue to have some symptoms despite early and intensive treatment.

✔ **Myth 8: Autistic children can never become productive, independent adults.** Many autistic people learn to adapt to their challenges and are able to work and lead meaningful lives. For example, some brilliant college professors, engineers, and scientists likely have undiagnosed, albeit mild, autism. That's because experts suggest that mild autistic symptoms may occur more often in people who are drawn to detail-oriented, technical and scientific occupations. Many others with autism remain profoundly affected and require substantial support as adults.

✔ **Myth 9: All kids with autism have special talents, as portrayed in the movie _Rain Man_.** Although the following section notes that special talents and skills are quite common for those with an autism diagnosis, they're far from universal. Unfortunately, some of these exceptional skills have relatively little practical value.

Looking at increases in autism rates

The rates of autism are increasing. According to the Centers for Disease Control and Prevention (CDC), about 1 in every 110 kids in the United States is diagnosed with autism, and for boys, the rate is 1 in 70. Before the 1980s, autism was quite rarely diagnosed. The CDC compared data from 2000 with data from 2006 and found that the rate of autism had climbed by 57 percent in those 6 years.

There are many arguments about the reasons for the increase, but no one really knows why it occurred. The same culprits are accused for autism as for many other childhood disorders: genetics, environmental toxins, and combinations of genetic vulnerabilities with environmental stressors or toxins (illness, pesticides, malnutrition, or poor care).

Many scientists believe that increased awareness of the disorder and improved diagnosis have increased the numbers, but those two factors don't fully explain the significant increase in the incidence of autism.

When Autism Comes with Unusual Gifts

A surprising number of those who have the label of an autism spectrum disorder have unusual talents or skills. Yet this intriguing issue has generally failed to receive systematic, comprehensive attention by researchers. Only recently have studies begun to address how common these exceptional skills are, as well as their nature and cause. The following two sections describe what these skills look like and how practical they may (or may not) be.

Examining exceptionalities

At one time, experts believed that about 10 percent of those with an autism spectrum disorder also showed signs of unusual talents or skills. Such skills have also been given the label *savant syndrome,* which refers to special areas of expertise or talents that exceed both the level of the person's other overall skills and the average level of skill of people in the general population. Some of these skills can be truly incredible.

Recent research has estimated that perhaps one quarter to one third of those with autism demonstrate unusual talents or skills. More studies will be required before we know the exact percentage, but this estimate fits our personal experience. Males apparently possess these unusual talents more often than females.

Exceptional, unexpected skills are displayed sometimes by people who have intellectual disabilities, brain damage, or brain injuries that may or may not be accompanied by autism. But lest you think that brain damage must be present for these exceptionalities to appear, think again. There are cases of people with no detectable brain injury or other abnormality who have specialized areas of shockingly advanced expertise or talent. No one is sure exactly what causes or enables these talents to emerge, although a few experts have speculated that some type of inhibition or damage to the brain's left hemisphere may trigger the process of developing these skills.

Some of the most common savantlike skills exhibited by those with autism include the following:

✔ **Rote memory:** *Rote memory* refers to the ability to learn substantial quantities of material without necessarily understanding the significance or reasoning that may underlie that information. Thus, a child may be able to memorize huge numbers of words and their correct spellings but not be able to converse fluidly (see the nearby sidebar). Unusual memory often accompanies some of the other skills exhibited by this group of people.

- ✔ **Mathematics:** Those with unusual math skills are often able to perform complex calculations in their heads. Some are able to instantly calculate the day of the week that every holiday falls on for the next hundred years.

- ✔ **Music:** Those with honed musical talent are often able to play various instruments, such as the piano, by ear and may have perfect pitch. Some are able to compose music spontaneously and quite creatively.

- ✔ **Artistic talent:** Painting, sculpting, or drawing are among the talents exhibited in this area. Other spatial skills may include advanced abilities to memorize intricate maps and routes.

- ✔ **Miscellaneous skills:** Various other advanced skills have been reported, including advanced ability to learn languages, extraordinary reading ability, unusual ability to detect and discriminate among smells or touches, and heightened awareness of the exact amount of time that has passed.

A common myth about savant skills is that they occur totally spontaneously without any need to practice or learn them. In actuality, most of those with such talent must practice and nurture their skills for them to blossom fully.

Unfortunately, many kids with autism have savantlike gifts yet are not able to do much with them. There may not be lots of obvious applications for the ability to memorize the phone book, for example. Some kids have little interest in or desire for finding practical applications for their talents, and the skills may not be accompanied by enough general understanding of the world for them to use the skills meaningfully.

Reviewing what to do with these gifts

One challenge that parents and caregivers face when working with children who have autism is finding a way to motivate them to learn. That's because the rewards that work with most kids, such as praise or positive attention, don't always connect with children who have autism. We've seen children who have incredible funds of information about dinosaurs, insects, mammals, types of rocks, names of historical figures, characters in cartoons, and brand names of automobiles, or who can recite scripts from movies and television shows, or who recite mathematical equations for fun yet don't apply their talents in classrooms or connect to other people.

Using children's enthusiasm about a particular subject or skill to reinforce or reward efforts on subjects that don't come so naturally to them can help them progress with challenging subjects. A child who focuses on dinosaurs, for example, could be given a reading task for which he could earn ten minutes playing with dinosaurs for making progress on reading. Or a child with difficulty understanding the need to raise his hand before asking questions could be rewarded for raising his hand by giving him stickers of automobiles for his extensive collection.

Memory and autism: "Feel the burn!"

Way back in the '80s, co-author Laura was a special-education teacher. She and her team teacher taught about 20 children who had a variety of problems, including learning disabilities, emotional problems, conduct problems, and autism. It was a challenging classroom, and the kids could be wild and disruptive, especially after lunch. To settle them down, the teachers started to take them to the gym every day after lunch, setting up a record player and playing a Jane Fonda recording of an aerobic workout. The kids loved it (so did the teachers), and afterward, they were able to come back to the classroom and pay attention to academics more calmly.

One spring afternoon as the teachers were setting everything up in the gym, a storm came through, and the electricity went out. The kids were disappointed. Then one of the autistic students volunteered to lead the group through the

exercise routine. Laura and the other teacher thought, "Oh, right — but what the heck." The boy sat on the chair that usually held the record player. He looked at the ceiling and began the warmup in his best Jane Fonda voice. He flawlessly went through each movement, including Fonda's comments. He had memorized the whole record, including grunts, groans, and other nuances. His best line was "Feel the burn!", which he said with great enthusiasm.

This young man had the ability to memorize long passages of words. He could also repeat game-show scripts and television shows from memory. Like many children with autism, he was quite gifted in some areas. By using these gifts, Laura and her team teacher were able to teach him to read and enjoy literature, but he remained disconnected and unable to form relationships with children or adults.

Caregivers sometimes ignore or discourage the full development of special interests in autistic kids because they see them as deviations that are not to be fostered. This practice could be a serious mistake and inhibit the development of a child's full potential.

In fact, some professionals have suggested that parents, teachers, and caregivers should more actively search for hidden talents in autistic kids, especially given the frequency with which they seem to pop up without active searching. They suggest that it's entirely possible for many autistic kids to have at least one strength that could be developed, even if the particular skill falls short of extraordinary. Many autistic kids appear to have some predisposition toward musical talent that doesn't rise to the full-blown savant-like skills described in the preceding section but that could nevertheless be enhanced and encouraged.

A few experts have speculated that special skills lie latent in most people but require considerable attention and nurturing, perhaps in early development. Research (reported in an international scientific journal called *Philosophical Transactions of the Royal Society: Biological Sciences*) has even indicated that using magnetic pulses to inhibit or suppress the dominant hemisphere sometimes seems to enhance various skills such as drawing, or even proofreading. The fascinating area of autism may ultimately result in exciting new findings about human nature.

Job posting

Wanted: Information Technology and Telecommunication professionals. Must have excellent attention to details, ability to work diligently, and high rates of accuracy and precision. Work involves software testing and development, data entry, quality control, and information processing.

This hypothetical ad could help fill positions in a company originally founded in Denmark but now expanding throughout the world. Thorkil Sonne founded the company Specialisterne (The Specialist; www.specialistpeople.com) in 2004, after his son was diagnosed with autism. Sonne became involved with the Danish Autism Association and then became aware of the high rates of unemployment among adults with autism. He realized that people with autism often have special skills, such as the ability to concentrate on tasks for unusually long periods of time, excellent memory, and the ability to pay attention to minute details.

Sonne's goal is to provide employment for 1 million people with autism around the world. His business model includes assessment and training of people with autism to work on projects that take advantage of their abilities. His focus on harnessing the special skills of autism instead of the disabling features of autism has won him and his business international acclaim.

Chapter 14

Emotional Disorders

*W*e live in a tumultuous, challenging world today. Adults must deal with terrorism, natural disasters, financial calamities, pandemics, and crime. Given such concerns, it's probably not surprising that about 20 to 25 percent of adults in the United States appeared to have a significant emotional disorder of one type or another during the past year alone. Over a lifetime, the percentage of people who have experienced such disorders is far greater, with many experts estimating that at least half of all adults have experienced an emotional disorder.

There are two reasons that the high prevalence of adult emotional disorders are relevant to children. First, the foundation for many adult emotional problems is laid during childhood. Second, when adults have emotional problems, these problems inevitably have a negative effect on kids.

Independently of adults, kids have many issues to deal with too, such as mastering academic skills, learning how to get along with one another, handling bullies, coping with rejection, and so on. It's a wonder that anyone gets through childhood intact. So early intervention has the potential for stopping the cycle of emotional disorders from being passed from generation to generation.

In this chapter, we review the most common types of emotional disorders that affect children. We do not attempt to equip you to make diagnoses of children — that's a job for professionals — but we do give you an idea of what children's emotional problems look like and provide a checklist of early-warning signs. This information should enable teachers, parents, and care providers to refer kids for an evaluation if they're starting down a path toward trouble. Early detection enables early intervention.

Early intervention almost always works better than treatment that's delayed. Therefore, it's crucial to seek further evaluation of children when you have concerns about their emotional well being.

The childhood disorders discussed in this chapter are loosely based on the *Diagnostic and Statistical Manual of Mental Disorders:* Fourth Edition (DSM-IV). In a few cases, we've made note of some changes that are likely to occur in the new edition that's slated to appear in a few years. Many of the changes in the new edition will be somewhat technical and not likely to be of major importance to the typical teacher, parent, or caregiver.

Eyeing Early Signs of Emotional Distress

Table 14-1 lays out some of the early signs of emotional distress that children may exhibit. These signs may not even indicate that a child currently has a diagnosable disorder, but if you see them, a little more investigation may be indicated. Kids commonly demonstrate many, if not most, of these signs, especially at younger ages. For example, it's quite normal for a two-year-old to exhibit a little anxiety about strangers, but not so typical of a twelve-year-old.

In other words, kids outgrow many fears and worries that show up when they're young. You can tell whether the signs you see in a given child are problematic by comparing the child in question with other kids of a *similar* age. Ask other parents and teachers for their input. Again, if you have worries or concerns, consult a professional.

We suggest that you check off each item that applies to a child under your care. Consider consulting the child's pediatrician or a mental-health professional if you have concerns. There's no magic number of items; any you check that persist could indicate a problem. We recommend taking the list in Table 14-1 with you to your child's next appointment.

Table 14-1 is intended to be an overview of possible problems that kids may have. Diagnoses need to be made by medical or mental-health professionals. See Table 14-2, in the next section, for information about when some of the symptoms related to anxiety and fear are normal and when they raise red flags.

Table 14-1   Warning Signs of Childhood Emotional Problems

Check	Symptom	Description
	Changes in appetite	Most kids will vary in the amount they eat from day to day, but if a child starts a consistent pattern of undereating or overeating for more than a week or two, this could indicate a problem.
	Weight loss/gain	Even if eating seems normal, if a child starts losing weight for no reason, his should be checked out. Kids shouldn't be gaining or losing weight in significant amounts quickly unless they're having a growth spurt or they've made a healthy, conscious change in exercise or diet.
	Changes in sleeping or unusual fatigue	Infants will be all over the map, but after children are 2 years old or so, sleep should fall into a reasonably consistent pattern. Be concerned if a child starts oversleeping, wakes up frequently through the night, or stops sleeping adequately. Kids with fatigue may seem listless and lethargic.
	Withdrawal	Lots of kids are shy, but if a child fails to bond with family or close friends, this sign could indicate a problem. Also, when kids who were once attached to their family or friends start pulling back, this trait suggests something of concern.
	Fear and avoidance	Children may refuse to go to school; become frightened of activities; or show extreme fear of various things, such as the dark, dogs, or cars.
	Frequent bouts of crying	All infants cry, sometimes a lot, but if an infant seems to cry for hours at a time, discuss this with her pediatrician. Older kids usually don't cry unless they're frustrated, frightened, hurt, angry, upset, or experience losses. And they may occasionally have tears of joy. However, if a school-age child starts crying almost daily, something could be wrong.
	Tantrums	Again, temper tantrums are normal from time to time in preschool children (usually beginning around age 2 or so), but if they worsen over time instead of improving, you should check further.
	Irritability, meltdowns, and aggression	If a child is easily frustrated and lashes out, an evaluation is called for. Some kids seem to melt down at the slightest frustration and/or when they are in a highly stimulating setting. See Chapter 13 for more information about autism and Chapter 15 for more information about behavioral problems.

(continued)

Table 14-1 *(continued)*

Check	Symptom	Description
	Shoplifting	Sometimes, kids briefly experiment with this behavior for no apparent reason, and they stop quickly. If a child or teen starts taking things of real value or shoplifts often, however, you need to consult a professional.
	Impulsivity	All preschoolers are a bit impulsive, acting without thinking. However, this behavior should start improving gradually by the time they're school age.
	Moodiness or unusual sadness	Kids whose moods shift due to trivial frustrations after age 2 or 3 may have a problem. Moodiness often increases during adolescence, but shifting moods should not interfere with making friendships or with the adult/child relationship overall. A child who frequently looks sad should be evaluated, too.
	Restless nervousness	Kids who appear to be on edge, anxious, tense, or worried much of the time may need help. That's especially the case if the nervousness keeps them from doing things they want or need to do.
	Preoccupations or rituals	Excessive focus on issues such as cleanliness, appearance, food, safety, superstitions, illness, or germs could indicate an emerging problem. Strict patterns of behavior — such as needing to arrange things precisely; engaging in prolonged, precise patterns of dressing or grooming; or feeling compelled to chant certain phrases frequently — also suggest a problem. Most adolescents spend a bit too much time grooming, but we're talking here about behavior that goes on for hours at a time.
	Hurts animals or sets fires	This behavior is not a normal part of childhood. Kids who do these things are at high risk of developing other, serious problems. See Chapter 15 for more information on behavior disorders.
	Excessive aches and pains	Kids often experience what's known as growing pains. When aches and pains start interfering with a child's going to school or engaging in sports or other activities, you should consult a medical professional.

In addition, if your child shows sudden changes in behavior or mood of any kind, consider exploring the issue further with a mental health or medical professional.

Exploring the Anxiety Disorders

Almost all kids feel anxious and fearful at times, in part because a certain amount of anxiety fosters healthy development. If kids felt no anxiety at all, it would be difficult to teach them to be concerned about their safety, the value of studying for tests, or the importance of behaving correctly. At the same time, evidence suggests that today's children suffer from serious symptoms of anxiety at far greater rates than children did 40 or 50 years ago.

So as someone concerned about kids, how can you tell the difference between "normal" anxiety and anxiety that warrants legitimate concern and possible referral for an evaluation? Table 14-2 shows you what's normal, expected childhood anxiety as opposed to what raises a red flag.

Table 14-2 is intended to inform you about common, typical fears that many, if not most, children have at one time or another. These fears are usually nothing to worry about if they occur at the ages indicated. If a child you care about has anxiety or fear that seems to be unusually intense, or that causes her problems with schoolwork or daily living, you should seek a professional opinion.

Table 14-2	Normal Childhood Fears and When to Worry	
Fear	**Normal Ages of Occurrence**	**When to Worry**
Separation anxiety shown when the primary caregiver leaves the child's presence	Quite typical between about 6 months and 2 years	After the age of 3 or 4 years, this type of anxiety should be quite mild. Otherwise, it's worth checking out.
Anxiety and fear demonstrated when strangers show up	Quite common between 6 and 10 months	This fear is not problematic unless it occurs after the age of 2 or 3. Even then, kids may be somewhat shy, which is a problem only if it seems to be severe.

(continued)

Table 14-2 *(continued)*

Fear	Normal Ages of Occurrence	When to Worry
Fear of new, unfamiliar kids the same age	Quite common from ages 2 to 3	You should be concerned if this fear has not started to abate shortly after age 3.
Fears of darkness, monsters, and animals	Frequent between the ages of 2 and 6	This type of fear should begin improving by the age of 6 or so.
Fear of school	Typical of kids age 3 to 6 or so, although they usually calm down fairly quickly when they're left at the setting; sometimes shows up again briefly when a child transitions to middle school	Kids should not be showing this problem more than mildly after the age of 6 or briefly when they start middle school. If it continues, it's a concern. Sometimes, the fear is due to bullying at school. Consider checking with a child's teachers or school counselor to see whether that's going on.
Fear of being judged or evaluated negatively by others	Very common in teenagers	Generally, this fear will gradually reduce through adolescence, but it's not rare or particularly troubling if it continues through the late teens. If it is severe enough to cause a child to avoid desired activities (sports, parties, debate clubs, and so on), it should definitely be checked out.

Sometimes, childhood anxieties go away on their own, but treatment typically is in order when they continue past their normal age of occurrence. That's because some of these kids eventually develop other problems. Chronic, untreated anxiety, for example, is often a risk factor for the development of depression. The following sections cover most of the full-blown anxiety disorders that occur during childhood. (Post-traumatic stress disorder is another anxiety disorder that occurs during childhood, but we cover that one in Chapter 16.)

Separation anxiety: Fear of being left

As we show in Table 14-2, earlier in this chapter, fears about separation from parents or caregivers frequently beset young children as early as 6 months of age and can continue to the age of 2, sometimes even a year or two longer.

After that time, kids who show lots of distress when they're separated from their parents may have what's called *separation anxiety.* Many times, these kids worry about something bad happening to their caregivers or parents. They sometimes worry about going to bed by themselves. Some of these kids complain about physical problems — like stomachaches, headaches, or similar ailments — when they must be away from their parents. Frequently, they have nightmares with themes about separation.

Although separation anxiety is quite common in kids, it probably should be treated if it continues much past the age of 4 and seems to be causing a child significant distress. School counselors see this problem often and can be a useful resource.

Social: Fear of other people

Social phobia refers to fear of being judged or evaluated by other kids and/or adults. Children with this problem try to avoid meeting new people, performing, or interacting with others. They greatly fear embarrassment and humiliation.

But as Table 14-2 notes (refer to "Exploring the Anxiety Disorders," earlier in this chapter), some fear of negative evaluation is quite typical of adolescence. The difference between a disorder and typical teenage concerns can be a fine line, but you should have your child evaluated if he can't get himself to join activities with other kids, refuses to go to parties, or avoids activities that most kids his age are engaging in.

A little shyness is pretty normal and not a big worry, but when shyness starts interfering with a child's enjoying life, that's another issue. Many times, parents and teachers don't see this problem until a child is age 10 or so, but you can actually pick up on it when the child is 3 or 4 if you're observant. Be on the lookout for problems with speaking up or making friends and avoidance of other kids on the playground, which could be signs of social phobia.

General: Worried all the time

Generalized anxiety disorder (GAD) is a type of anxiety involving a variety of symptoms such as restlessness, fatigue, tension, trouble concentrating, and especially excessive worrying. GAD occurs fairly often in today's kids, but it's far more common in adolescents than in younger children. Kids with GAD have excessive worries about a wide range of problems, such as friendships, family, safety, and school. They frequently complain about aches, pains, or gastrointestinal symptoms. They have trouble concentrating and sometimes appear to be irritable. They often can't go to sleep easily and seem to be restless. They are true worrywarts.

GAD almost always interferes with kids' quality of life and sense of well being. Therefore, such symptoms should be evaluated and treated by a mental health professional if they persist for more than a few weeks. The only exception would be worrying that occurs in response to truly understandable concerns such as a parent's loss of a job or home. Even then, treatment should be considered if a child fails to adjust within a couple of months.

OCD: Rituals and urges

Obsessive-compulsive disorder (OCD) is a disorder that includes either obsessions, compulsions, or both. The vast majority of OCD cases include both obsessions and compulsions, although you can technically have the diagnosis with either one. *Obsessions* refer to unwanted, highly disturbing thoughts, urges, or images that jump into the child's mind such as an urge to harm or kill someone even though he doesn't want to do so. They occur over and over again, and the child very much wants to stop them but can't. These thoughts can be about almost anything you can imagine, but some of the most common ones include fear of germs, illness, intruders, harm to parents or caregivers; urges to hurt someone; and visions of doing something embarrassing or abhorrent.

Compulsions involve a wide-ranging list of behaviors, actions, or rituals that children with OCD feel driven to repeat again and again. Especially common compulsions include the need to wash hands excessively (sometimes for hours every day); the need to arrange things in a precise order; repeated counting of things like steps, ceiling tiles, or stairs; and hoarding things of little or no value. Usually, compulsions are carried out as a way of helping the child temporarily reduce feelings of distress associated with obsessive thoughts (such as washing hands to reduce fear of germs).

Although obsessions, like urges to harm people, could sound like a behavior disordered child (see Chapter 15), there's a huge difference. The child with OCD feels *horrible* about having such thoughts whereas the behavior disordered child literally *wants* to carry them out.

OCD occurs in approximately 2 percent of teenagers and has a typical age of onset of between about 10 and 21. Sometimes, it appears as early as age 4, with boys getting it at a younger age than girls. OCD rarely goes away on its own, so treatment is almost always a good idea. Fortunately, treatment for OCD tends to be highly effective. See Chapter 17 for more information.

Lots of kids carry out a few rituals, like not stepping on sidewalk cracks or avoiding superstitious things like black cats and walking under ladders. You have to worry about OCD only when the behavior starts taking up a lot of time or seems to be causing a child significant distress. For extensive, additional information about this disturbing yet fascinating and highly treatable disorder, consider reading our earlier book *Obsessive-Compulsive Disorder For Dummies* (Wiley Publishing).

Although somewhat controversial, some doctors believe that, OCD in kids may be triggered or caused by a strep throat infection. In these cases, the OCD usually comes on quite suddenly following the infection. OCD caused by such infections is called Pediatric Autoimmune Neuropsychiatric Disorders Associated with Streptococcal Infections (PANDAS). Interestingly, the treatment for PANDAS is exactly the same for as it is for OCD caused by other means (see Chapter 17). There may be some differences between anxiety and OCD problems brought on by PANDAS, but further research is needed to determine whether that's the case and just how firm the connection between PANDAS and OCD is.

Body obsessions

Body dysmorphic disorder involves a strong preoccupation about some perceived bodily defect. By *perceived,* we mean that the defect is not really there at all or that if it is, the child's concern is way out of proportion to the actual blemish.

People with body dysmorphic disorder sometimes seek unnecessary plastic surgery and/or spend excessive amounts of time obsessing over the imagined defect as they gaze into the mirror. This obsession most commonly pops up in adolescence. Again, it's one of those concerns that most adolescents have to a limited degree, but it becomes diagnosable when it causes a lot of distress or takes up inordinate amounts of time.

Body dysmorphic disorder is not officially considered to be one of the anxiety disorders, but the next edition of the DSM-IV is quite likely to lump it into a category along with the anxiety and OCD spectrum of disorders covered in this section.

Phobias: Fear of bugs, snakes, and more

Specific phobias involve extreme fears of specific situations or objects that a child works very hard to avoid. Particularly common phobias include being alone at night, thunder and lightning, dogs, spiders, flying, heights, and snakes.

Please note, however, that most adults and kids have one or more fears of something or other. Fears don't rise to the level of a phobia unless they involve something that causes distress and interference with everyday life. Thus, if a child fears snakes but rarely runs into them because she lives in the city, you probably don't have to consider the fear problematic. However, if her fear is so intense that she can't get herself to engage in outside activities, you're dealing with a phobia that should be addressed.

REMEMBER

As indicated in Table 14-2 (refer to "Exploring the Anxiety Disorders," earlier in this chapter), it's pretty normal for kids to fear monsters, the dark, and animals or bugs between the ages of 2 and 6 or so. A fear of such things at that age would have to be unusually intense or distressing to be considered a true phobia.

Minding Mood Disorders

Just like adults, kids sometimes have emotional problems with their moods. Sometimes, they become sad and depressed. At other times, they show a very different mood problem, as they seem to bounce off the walls in a burst of rapid activity, with decreased need for sleep and rapid talking. The next two sections discuss the primary types of mood problems you might see in children.

Depression: Sad all the time

Fortunately, young children don't suffer from major bouts with depression very often, but depression can occur at almost any age. Depression can have various levels of severity and can fall into a few subtypes, but all forms of clinical depression involve sadness, low moods, and loss of interest or pleasure in usual activities or life itself that persists for several weeks or longer. Kids aren't particularly good at understanding when depression hits them; thus, you can't rely on them to tell you whether they're depressed. Caregivers simply have to look out for the signs of emerging depression:

- **Preschoolers:** These kids may withdraw and fail to show appropriate signs of attachment to their caregivers. (See Chapters 3, 4, and 5 for more about attachment problems in young kids.) They may fail to establish normal sleep and feeding routines and/or fail to gain weight as they should. (See Chapters 5 and 11 for information about sleep, feeding, and body rhythms.) They won't be very likely to complain about low self-esteem or feelings of intense guilt.

- **School-age children:** These children demonstrate a wider array of depressive symptoms than younger kids do. In addition to having problems with sleep, weight changes, and withdrawal, they tend to have trouble concentrating, give up easily on tasks, often look fatigued, express a low sense of self-worth, and express feelings of self-contempt and/or guilt.

- **Adolescence:** As in all forms of clinical depression, teenagers have loss of interests, pleasure, sleep problems, and weight changes. They also have low self-esteem and trouble concentrating. Suicidal thoughts and/or attempts at suicide increase in frequency for these kids compared with younger children.

Roughly 5 to 8 percent of adolescents make a suicidal attempt at one point or another. Depression is a very significant risk factor for such attempts. Be on the lookout for signs of depression in teens, and seek a professional consultation if you have concerns. Suicide is the third leading cause of death in teens through young adulthood.

Several decades ago, it was thought that depression in children shows up in quite different ways than it does for adults — as aggression, oppositionality, or misbehavior, for example. Most professionals today do not agree with that thinking, and you should be leery of any diagnosis of depression given to a child who seems to exhibit completely different symptoms.

Bipolar: When emotions go to extremes

Bipolar disorder is a serious emotional problem that typically occurs for the first time in older adolescents and young adults. Although there are subtypes of bipolar disorder, this diagnosis generally involves seriously unstable moods. All of the subtypes mean that the person has experienced at least one or more periods of *mania* — an episode involving euphoric feelings that typically last most of the day for several days. These manic episodes can quickly lead to trouble and include symptoms such as the following:

- **Grandiosity:** Adolescents with this symptom feel that they're above the rules and see themselves as being smarter and better than others. They may even believe that they possess extraordinary powers, such as the ability to fly. Okay, we know that lots of adolescents think that they know more than their parents, but this symptom is more extreme than that.

- **Rapid speech and ideas:** This symptom involves talking with unusual speed and flipping from one topic to another with little need to connect concepts.

- **Euphoric mood:** This symptom involves unusual ebullience for no apparent reason, as though a child is going to his own birthday party, but without the party. The child may laugh outrageously and appear to be giddy. *Note:* Younger kids sometimes show this kind of mood for minutes or even an hour or so, but it's meaningless if it comes in short bursts.

- **Decreased need for sleep:** Teenagers may suddenly seem to need only a few hours of sleep each day. Many teens stay up late at night, of course, but given their choice, most of them would sleep until noon. So if you see a teen that feels rested and energized day after day yet only slept for five hours or less, you're probably looking at a decreased need for sleep.

- **Hypersexuality:** This behavior shows up as excessive flirtatiousness and attempts to engage in risky sexual episodes.

- **Risky behaviors:** Teenagers are often a bit out of control, but this symptom refers to excessive spending sprees, speeding, and other behaviors that could lead to self-harm or harm to others.

Bad temper, bad moods, bipolar, or what?

Diagnosing children with emotional disorders is a bit more challenging than assigning diagnoses to adults, because expectations for children's behavior change rapidly over the years, and children demonstrate more variability in their moods and behaviors than adults do. Thus, diagnoses for children — especially preadolescents — presents professionals particularly problematic conundrums.

A new diagnosis is being seriously considered that would apply to kids who show certain problems after their sixth birthday but before they reach the age of 10. It's called *temper dysregulation disorder with dysphoria,* which is categorized as a type of mood disorder. This diagnosis would apply to children who show excessive, grossly disproportionate temper outbursts three or more times each week. Moods between outbursts are generally quite negative (irritable, sad, resentful, and/or angry), and such kids must show clear periods of more than a day in which they show signs of euphoric or elevated mood (such as mania). This diagnosis emerged in part due to the belief of some professionals that irritability reflects a mood disturbance similar to euphoria in adults. Again, this diagnosis is not without its critics, and it will be interesting to see how the whole controversy ultimately plays out.

Bipolar disorder also can include episodes of *hypomania,* which are similar to the previous symptoms of mania, but not quite as intense and disabling. It requires a professional to make that distinction.

Professionals have increasingly debated how common bipolar disorder is in younger kids. Many professionals believe it to be quite rare in kids and alarmingly overdiagnosed, especially in preadolescent children; others take the opposite perspective. This controversy is currently unresolved. For now, it seems to be prudent to focus on symptoms of bipolar disorder involving adolescents and wait to see how the debate plays out with regard to younger children.

Most typically, bipolar disorder in children begins with an episode of depression, followed at some point by a period of mania. Whether it begins with depression or not, most of those with bipolar disorder also experience depressive episodes that range from mild to severe. Adolescents tend to cycle from one phase to another more rapidly than most adults with this problem do.

See the nearby sidebar "Bad temper, bad moods, bipolar, or what?" for information about a new diagnosis for kids with elements of bipolar disorder that's currently being considered.

Looking at Miscellaneous Problems

We're not finished yet! Unfortunately, kids sometimes suffer a host of additional emotional problems. Although anxiety and mood disorders are the most common ailments confronting kids, children can also develop a wide variety of problems, such as failure to talk, loss of touch with reality, tics, pulling out hair, fascination with fire, physical aches and pains, and unhealthy habits and eating. The following sections provide an overview of these issues.

Selective mutism: Choosing silence

Kids with *selective mutism* consistently fail to speak in situations in which they are expected to speak (such as school). Yet they know how to talk perfectly well and generally do so in at least some situations with apparent comfort (such as at home or with their parents). Sometimes, kids stop talking for a little while, but this diagnosis is not considered until they've avoided talking for at least a month in certain specific situations or settings.

As you can imagine, this problem shakes parents up. Fortunately, it's relatively rare, occurring in fewer than 1 percent of children. Unfortunately, no one really knows for sure why selective mutism occurs. However, there are a lot of myths about selective mutism, such as these:

- ✔ **The child must simply be stubborn.** No one knows the cause(s) of selective mutism for certain, but stubbornness is probably not the culprit. Anxiety and a predisposition toward being highly inhibited may set the stage, but we don't know for sure. It's possible that various subtle events in the child's family or learning environment also play a role after that. In either case, firmly insisting that the child talk doesn't seem to work and may even make things worse.

- ✔ **The child will inevitably outgrow this problem.** Well, the frequency with which children outgrow this problem is a bit controversial. It appears that most kids do grow out of it, but left untreated, selective mutism can last for years.

- ✔ **The child must have suffered abuse.** No evidence suggests that abuse is especially more prevalent among children with selective mutism than among those who don't have it.

- ✔ **The selectively mute child must have a learning disability.** As much as any other child, a selectively mute child may have a learning disability, but learning disabilities do not appear to be the cause of selective mutism.

If selective mutism continues for more than a few months, treatment should be sought, because if a child fails to speak in various settings, the problem will ultimately disrupt normal educational, occupational, and/or social development. There's a wide range in the severity of this problem, but all cases deserve attention.

Schizophrenia: Losing touch with reality

Fortunately, psychotic disorders in which people lose contact with reality are quite rare in young children. *Schizophrenia*, the best-known of these disorders, typically includes a range of symptoms, such as these:

- **Delusions:** *Delusions* are unshakeable false beliefs that are clearly untrue in spite of what other people think and evidence that contradicts these beliefs.

- **Hallucinations:** *Hallucinations* are perceptions of voices, sounds, sensations, or smells that simply aren't there.

- **Peculiar speech:** The person may exhibit grossly disorganized, incoherent, and disconnected speech.

- **Restricted range of feelings:** The child appears as though someone pushed his "emotional mute" button. He shows reduced pleasure and joy as well as sadness or anger.

- **Catatonic behavior:** *Catatonic behavior* refers to various types of unresponsiveness, such as virtual paralysis or extreme agitation, that don't change in response to input from others.

Schizophrenia is quite rare before late adolescence, although it is not unheard-of. Other forms of psychosis (such as delusions and hallucinations) are also quite rare in kids, but they are more difficult to diagnose because kids often have some pretty strange beliefs. If you suspect that a child is exhibiting evidence of psychosis, an evaluation is called for. See the sidebar "Detecting psychosis before it happens" for more information on this topic.

In our practices, we've seen some kids diagnosed as psychotic and treated with powerful antipsychotic medications. Sometimes, the child turned out to have severe OCD (refer to "OCD: Rituals and urges," earlier in this chapter); at other times, they actually appeared to have suffered significant trauma or abuse and used make-believe stories as a way of coping. Occasionally those with autism are incorrectly diagnosed with psychosis. In a few rare instances, we've actually seen kids who told their doctors about monsters living under the bed and were given a diagnosis of psychosis. Be sure to get a second opinion on any child who is given this diagnosis, because the medications for its treatment are quite potent and have significant side effects.

Detecting psychosis before it happens

The next edition of the DSM may include a new diagnosis — attenuated psychotic symptoms syndrome — that essentially is designed to detect and treat adolescents before they actually develop a full-blown case of schizophrenia. This diagnosis is based on the assumption that it's possible to detect a prepsychotic condition in the hope that early treatment may stave off schizophrenia, which can be more difficult to treat after it becomes entrenched. So-called prepsychosis is demonstrated when teenagers have a reasonably intact sense of reality but have some evidence of delusions, hallucinations, or disorganized speech that is not due to substance abuse and has been occurring with some frequency for a while.

The goal is clearly a noble one, but critics of this strategy have been coming out of the woodwork. They note that at best, one out of three or so of the kids given this diagnosis will ultimately develop schizophrenia in its complete form. They fear that the diagnosis will lead to immediate administration of antipsychotic drugs to thousands of kids who would never become schizophrenic. The problem with such drugs is that they can have serious side effects, the most frequent of which include substantial risks of weight gain, diabetes, and cardiovascular problems.

We have to wonder whether a more prudent approach would be to study and follow these kids carefully and use extreme caution before recommending antipsychotic drugs. During this time, they could also be provided cognitive therapy (see Chapter 17), which has been shown to improve some of the symptoms of schizophrenia, although it's usually combined with medication for the treatment of the full-blown disorder. Also consider reading Chapter 17 for information about the limitations of medications, especially for kids.

Understanding irrepressible tic disorders

Tics are repetitive, rapid movements or sounds that a person feels an irresistible urge to engage in. People can suppress these urges, but usually only for a while. They get worse under stress but sometimes go away for a while when a person is totally focused on some engaging activity, such as playing video games or a musical instrument. Tics typically fade during sleep.

There are two types of tics: motor and vocal. Particularly common *motor tics* include jumping, grimacing, sniffing, blinking, shoulder shrugging, and grooming. Common *vocal tics* include throat clearing, tongue clicking, repeating specific words, snorting, and grunting. As you can imagine, tics can be highly embarrassing for children, especially during adolescence.

Kids sometimes acquire tics as early as 2 years of age. Sometimes, the behaviors are quite subtle and barely noticeable unless you're looking for them. At other times, the symptoms can be quite dramatic. Tics frequently get worse from age 9 to 15 or so. Any child may shift in the particular tics he has over time, and the symptoms frequently go through cycles of greater or lesser intensity.

Tourette's syndrome sounds a lot scarier than a tic disorder, but it really just involves two or more motor tics accompanied by at least one vocal tic. The good news is that both Tourette's syndrome and tic disorders often show some degree of improvement over a period of years. If they don't improve enough for a child to no longer feel embarrassment or experience ostracism, there are some treatments that can help.

Trying trichotillomania

You could easily stumble over this diagnosis the first time you try to say it, but it's a lot simpler than it looks. *Trichotillomania* refers to when a child persists in pulling out her hair, which results in hair loss and/or bald patches. As you might imagine, the hair pulling causes a child to feel quite distressed and can result in considerable embarrassment, if not outright teasing from peers. Often, kids with this problem report a sensation of pleasure or relief when they pull out hair.

You might think that hair pulling would be easy to stop, but it isn't. Some kids engage in the behavior for a limited period and stop entirely after a while on their own; for others, the problem waxes and wanes over time; still others demonstrate the symptoms for decades. Trichotillomania quite commonly begins around age 5 to 8, with peak onset around age 13.

Professionals have struggled with how to categorize trichotillomania. The current DSM calls it a type of impulse-control problem. The next edition is likely to categorize it as part of the anxiety and OCD spectrum.

Playing with fire: Pyromania

It's not unusual for kids to experiment briefly with setting fires. They are often fascinated by lighters and matches. An unknown but fairly small number of kids evolve into deliberately setting fires frequently out of an intense fascination with or curiosity about fires. They typically experience some tension before setting the fire and feel relief or pleasure as they watch it burn. They don't set the fires to get back at anyone, cover up a criminal act, or obtain financial gain. They're simply fascinated by fire.

As you can imagine, pyromania can land a kid in a heap of trouble. The fires that they set can easily go out of control and cause great harm. If you know a child with what looks like excessive fascination with fire, evaluation by a mental-health professional is called for.

Complaining about aches and pains

Almost all children complain about stomachaches, headaches, or leg pain from time to time. These complaints are part of any normal childhood and can have a wide variety of physical causes. Such minor pains usually go away after a few hours or fade overnight. Obviously, if they appear to be severe or unusually persistent, you should consult the child's pediatrician to see what's going on.

Sometimes, children report such pains with increasing frequency. A child may complain about stomach pain consistently on Monday before school starts or before various other activities, such as sports. At times, medical investigation into the child's complaints reveals no physical basis for them, or the child's reaction appears to be much greater than would be expected from his physical problem. Some type of *somatoform disorder* may be going on when a pediatrician determines that pains and physical complaints seem to be excessive or exaggerated. These complaints prevent many kids with this diagnosis from participating in a wide range of important life events, activities, and functions.

Somatoform disorders often function as a way to enable a child to escape or avoid activities that may be causing her to feel tense, anxious, or nervous. For some kids, it's a lot easier to complain about a stomachache than to admit anxiety about having to present a paper in front of the class. In other cases, the physical problems don't appear to have quite such an obvious function.

Any child who complains about physical problems should be listened to seriously. Don't ever assume that a somatoform disorder is at play unless a pediatrician thoroughly investigates the complaints. If, after careful review, the pediatrician believes that psychological factors are involved, a child or pediatric psychologist can often provide significant help.

Hassling with habits

Mental-health professionals have at times debated how to categorize various childhood habits, but for now, they put them in a category technically known as stereotypic movement disorders. Although that term may feel like quite a mouthful, *stereotypic movement disorders* refer to a wide range of quite common behaviors that a child feels driven to perform. These behaviors are repetitive and reach the level that they interfere with the child's life or at times even result in bodily harm.

Engaging in self-injury

A diagnosis that's likely to appear in the next edition of the DSM is called *non-suicidal self injury*. This label would apply to children or adolescents who intentionally inflict damage to their bodies in such a way that they experience pain, bleeding, or bruising. We're not talking about body piercing or tattoos, but things like cutting, jabbing, burning, stabbing, or hitting oneself. These kids are not attempting to kill themselves, based on what they have to say and the nature of their injuries (which don't have the potential for causing death). But the behavior and the injuries are not inconsequential, in that nail biting or a simple pick at a scab would not be included in this category.

This behavior shows up most often in adolescents. It is not diagnosed unless it has occurred on at least five or more separate days. The injury also seems to involve difficult negative feelings such as distress, self loathing, depression, and anxiety. The urge is strong, occurs often, and is difficult to resist. Most teenagers who engage in this behavior report feeling significant relief from their distressed feelings after they engage in their self-injury.

Non-suicidal self injury is a difficult pattern to stop, but there are treatments for it. It's important to seek treatment if you see this problem in a child or adolescent. Teens can rarely stop it on their own or in response to their parents telling them to stop. The problem also frequently occurs in a very-difficult-to-treat problem most often seen in young adults known as border-line personality disorder. See our earlier book *Borderline Personality Disorder For Dummies* (Wiley) for more information about this challenging emotional disorder.

Nail biting and skin picking are the most common of the stereotypic movement disorders. In fact, most folks have had at least brief episodes of either skin picking or nail biting at one time or another. Skin picking, for example, is especially common when one feels a rough patch of skin or a scab. These habits can worsen over time, however, and cause scaring, sores, infection, and significant destruction of tissue. These habits usually cause considerable stress and embarrassment, too. There are treatments for skin picking and nail biting, and they should be considered if the behavior becomes severe. Some studies have shown that up to 5 percent of college students continue to pick their skin for more than an hour each day. That's a lot of people and a lot of time consumed by this activity.

Other stereotypic movement disorders include head banging, body rocking, and hitting oneself. Head banging is a behavior that greatly worries parents but usually fades away over time and doesn't typically cause bodily harm. On the other hand, unusually serious cases call for prompt treatment because they could cause brain damage. Because it's hard for parents to determine what's serious and what's not, it's not a bad idea to check with the child's pediatrician for an assessment to see what, if anything, needs to be done for a child who spends significant time engaging in any of the stereotypic movements.

Dealing with eating disorders

All eating disorders affect physical condition because they involve disturbances in nutrition, amount of food intake, and overall health. Thus, any of
these problems should be referred to a pediatrician.

Sometimes, subtle physical causes may be operating in the background of
some of these disorders. Other times, no clear physical cause can be found
and emotional issues appear to be the most likely culprits. In still other
cases, both physical and emotional issues are likely involved. The following
disturbances in eating usually include a significant emotional/behavioral
component and most often require input from mental health specialists.

Note that all of the eating disorders covered in this section could have been
covered in Chapter 11. In fact, we do briefly discuss the diagnosis of failure to
thrive in Chapter 11. And failure to thrive looks a lot like the diagnosis of feeding
disorder in infancy or early childhood. However, if a child has a clear cut medical
cause for not gaining sufficient weight, the term failure to thrive would be more
descriptive than the diagnosis of feeding disorder in infancy or early childhood.

Pica

Professionals diagnose kids with *pica* when they continually appear to be
driven to consume nonnutritive substances such as dirt, plaster, hair, peb-
bles, coal, coins, soap, feces, sand, chalk, or clay and continue to do so for
more than a month. Sometimes, children with this problem habitually chew
on something hard, such as wood.

Believe it or not, it's common for kids to eat a little dirt from time to time.
A little bit of clean dirt isn't going to hurt them. By *clean dirt,* we mean dirt
that's not contaminated with motor oil, leaded gasoline, pesticides, and such.
Exposure to and ingestion of small amounts of dirt may even help prevent
kids from developing allergies. Furthermore, ingestion of small amounts of
nonnutritive substances in kids younger than age 2 or so is quite common.

Researchers have speculated about a wide variety of possible causes of pica.
Some have suggested that certain vitamin or mineral deficiencies may be
involved, but these deficiencies are not often detectable. A few cases may
be a result of celiac disease. Others have surmised that stress, trauma, and
other emotional disorders such as OCD (refer to "OCD: Rituals and urges,"
earlier in this chapter) may play a role in pica. Fortunately, pica appears to
be relatively rare and often fades over time, but serious cases can obviously
affect a child's health and well being. Treatment for pica should be sought
following a consultation with a pediatrician.

Rumination

Rumination disorder occurs when an infant or young child repeatedly brings
food up again, rechews the food, and swallows it again. (Occasionally, the

child spits out the rechewed food instead of swallowing it.) This behavior does not qualify for a diagnosis if it happens only occasionally or for less than a month.

Rumination disorder often causes significant weight loss, as well as stomachaches and digestive upset. The baby also may have bad breath and/or tooth decay. Frequently, infants display an unusual posture, such as arching their backs and throwing their heads back when they bring up their food. No one knows the exact cause of rumination disorder, although significant stress, physical illnesses, or abnormalities in the child–caregiver relationship may trigger or cause the problem. Physical causes of the vomiting are not usually responsible but do need to be carefully ruled out.

Rumination disorder occurs somewhat more often in kids who have other types of developmental disabilities or intellectual disabilities (see Chapter 12 for more information) than it does with kids with no such difficulties. The disorder can occur in the absence of other obvious problems, however.

Rumination disorder is a serious problem. It can lead to weight loss, malnutrition, aspiration pneumonia (from vomit that gets sucked into the lungs), dehydration, and even death. Prompt treatment of this problem is always called for.

Feeding disorder in infancy or early childhood

When a child demonstrates failure to thrive (see Chapter 11) because he falls seriously short on height and weight charts, and no physical cause can be found, a diagnosis of feeding disorder in infancy or early childhood is usually given. Kids with feeding disorders consistently demonstrate problems with eating adequate amounts of food, and they fail to gain weight as expected.

Mind you, lots of kids demonstrate a few minor problems with feeding, yet their weight remains within reasonable limits. For example, picky eating of only certain preferred foods rarely rises to the level of a serious concern and rarely leads to substantial malnutrition. These kids would not receive this diagnosis. Eating problems are not likely to be serious as long as the child's weight doesn't start dropping precipitously.

Kids with serious feeding disorders end up with malnutrition and stunted mental or physical growth if the problem isn't corrected soon enough. These kids often have additional symptoms, such as excessive irritability, lethargy, crying, and constipation. Fortunately, feeding problems can be treated successfully. Sometimes, hospitalization is required for a while in order to bring weight up and establish better feeding habits. Various professionals may be brought in, such as dieticians, psychologists, social workers, and behavior specialists in order to accomplish these goals.

Anorexia

Anorexia nervosa is a diagnosis given to those who severely limit their food intake to the degree that they experience a worrisomely low body weight.

This eating disorder usually does not appear until adolescence (typically, age 14 to 18 or so). It often begins with a highly stressful life event, such as heading off to college for the first time. They seem to be trying to achieve perfection in their bodies and total control over their lives. Unfortunately, they don't know where to stop.

Those with anorexia have great fear of becoming overweight, even though they are seriously underweight. In fact, they often perceive their bodies as being overweight or fat although evidence suggests otherwise. They simply fail to recognize the possibility that they are underweight and that the problem could cause serious effects on their health.

Anorexia nervosa comes in two types:

- **Restricting:** These folks haven't recently engaged in frequent episodes of binge eating or purging (such as by self-induced vomiting or excessive use of laxatives). Rather, they simply seriously restrict their intake of food, sometimes eating virtually starvation diets.

- **Binge eating/purging:** Teenagers with this type of anorexia nervosa frequently engage in binge eating (consuming a gallon of ice cream in one sitting would not be especially unusual) followed by purging (again, through laxative abuse, self-induced vomiting, enemas, and so on).

Because those with anorexia nervosa often try to hide their problem, you should be on the lookout for these potentially telling signs:

- Frequent skipping of meals
- Obsession with eating foods only low in calories and fat
- Making excuses for not eating
- Refusing to eat in public and around other people
- Weighing frequently
- Engaging in unusual eating rituals such as cutting food into very small bites, pushing it around their plates, and eating very slowly or spitting food out after chewing
- Complaining about being fat
- Seeking frequent reassurance about not being fat
- Being interested in cooking for others but not eating much themselves

Anorexia can easily lead to serious physical problems, such as abnormal blood counts, low blood pressure, dental and esophageal erosions, and irregular heart rhythms. In other words, anorexia nervosa can be a life-threatening condition.

Anorexia nervosa has increased in frequency over the past few decades. It is thought to affect about 1 percent of females in their high school years, but the actual percentage is a bit unclear due to the fact that many of its sufferers hide the problem and avoid treatment. It appears that this affliction is considerably less common in males.

Alarmingly, Web sites that actually promote and encourage anorexic behavior have been popping up in recent years. No one knows why this is happening for sure, but the Internet obviously provides an easy conduit for social networking and sources of information — both good and bad. Teens are driven to find out what they want to and they have refined skills for doing so. Although we don't like the idea of spying on teens, if your teen spends excessive time on the computer and/or shows signs of anorexia, a brief review of the site's she's been visiting might be in order.

It can be counterproductive to reassure a teenager that she's not overweight. If you have a concern about an adolescent who is exhibiting signs of anorexia nervosa, a referral for an evaluation and/or treatment is in order. You can't solve this problem through simple reassurance, and you could even make things worse.

Bulimia nervosa

Bulimia nervosa is a diagnosis in which there are repeated episodes of uncontrolled, excessive eating known as binges. Binges occur during a period of up to two hours, in which the person consumes an unusually large quantity of food, such as a full bag of potato chips or cookies. Following the binge, the sufferer attempts to compensate for the gluttonous overeating by self-induced vomiting, excessive exercise (such as two hours or more on a treadmill), enemas, fasting, or diuretics. These binges occur at least once or twice a week for months at a time.

Although quite similar to anorexia nervosa with binge eating and purging, those with bulimia nervosa maintain body weight at normal or even above normal levels even though they're very concerned about becoming overweight.

Like anorexia nervosa, bulimia nervosa often appears during adolescence. It appears to afflict 1 to 3 percent of females during their adolescent to young adulthood years; men have the problem much less frequently. Sometimes, the disorder appears to be triggered by an episode of dieting. Like those who have anorexia nervosa, those with bulimia nervosa often have excessive worries about weight.

Bulimia nervosa can be as life-threatening as anorexia nervosa, even though it does not involve a serious degree of weight loss. The ongoing purges may result in dehydration, irregular heartbeat, erosion of teeth or esophagus, bowel problems, heart failure, or even death.

Bulimics often try to hide their disorder due to intense shame and embarrassment. You should suspect that your teenager is headed toward bulimic behavior, however, if she always seems to need to make a bathroom visit after eating. She also may seek privacy after most meals, sometimes to exercise or purge. Frequent sores in the mouth and gums or even on the fingers (from using them to induce vomiting) are also a possible tipoff. Signs of excessive consumption in a teenager's room (lots of crumbs or tossed food packages) can also indicate binges occurring out of sight. If you have concerns, a referral for evaluation and possible treatment is in order.

Although it's not officially a diagnosis in the DSM-IV, it's likely that binge-eating disorder will be included in the next edition. This problem, like bulimia nervosa, involves eating excessive quantities of food in a period of two hours or less. There is also similar lack of control over the eating. Frequently, the sufferers will feel disgusted with themselves after binges but engage in them at least weekly for several months. The primary difference between binge-eating disorder and bulimia nervosa is that binge eaters don't compensate for their binges by purging or engaging in excessive exercise.

Many teenagers eat a lot from time to time. However, binge eaters will consume a half gallon of ice cream in one sitting or a whole bag of cookies or chips. The quantity can be quite surprising. Be suspicious if you notice the disappearance of such goodies shortly after purchasing them. If you have concerns, consult a pediatrician. Weight gain would be common with this problem as well.

Overeating and obesity

Especially well-informed readers will know that overeating and the obesity that results from overeating is not considered to be an emotional disorder in the DSM-IV and is not contemplated for inclusion in the next edition. Why not? That's an excellent question! Obesity typically leads to numerous health problems. Genes no doubt play a role in the development of obesity, as they do with most emotional disorders, and obesity is caused by learned behavioral patterns of consuming too many calories and burning too few of them.

Emotional issues frequently drive people to overeat just as they lead to eating disorders such as anorexia nervosa and bulimia. For example, some kids who are depressed or anxious overeat to handle those difficult emotions. Still others may overeat because of problems with impulse control.

Thus, emotional influences appear to have as much to do with overeating and obesity as they do with other eating disorders.

But whether or not one considers obesity that results to be an emotional disorder, or not, it has become an epidemic around the world for both adults and children. American children have been no exception. According to the U.S. Department of Health and Human Services, the prevalence of overweight or obese kids from ages 12 to 19 has almost tripled since 1980, and rates have more than doubled for kids ages 6 to 11 during that time. From a psychological standpoint, obesity often leads to shame, embarrassment, ostracism, and sometimes anxiety and depression.

Emotional problems and education

When a child has an emotional problem, learning can be negatively affected. Many emotional problems are invisible to teachers, classmates, and administrators. Kids with disturbances may have problems participating in class or getting work completed. When misunderstood, emotional disorders can lead to very negative outcomes.

Suppose that a boy has OCD. He may have frequent thoughts about getting sick from touching what he believes are contaminated surfaces. His pencil falls on the floor, which to him means that his pencil is contaminated. He stares at the pencil, unable to make himself pick it up. His teacher tells him to get to work, and he sits there, paralyzed with fear. His teacher could misinterpret his behavior as defiant, but instead, he's worried about the germs on the pencil making him sick.

Look at a girl with depression. She might have low self-esteem and believe that she's inferior. When the teacher calls on her, she says that she doesn't know the answer. Again, a teacher might interpret her behavior as unmotivated or even as reflecting a learning disability (see Chapter 12), not knowing the girl believes that she isn't good enough to speak up.

When a child's learning is disrupted or negatively affected by emotions, parents and teachers need to communicate. The child may qualify for extra help through special education. If the child doesn't meet the federal eligibility guidelines for having an emotional disturbance, other options are available in the regular classroom. When caregivers work together with schools, the child benefits.

The effects of obesity on health are indisputable. Furthermore, being overweight or obese as an adolescent more often than not leads to the same problem as an adult. Merely being significantly overweight during childhood substantially increases the risk of developing the following conditions:

- High blood pressure
- Type 2 diabetes
- High cholesterol
- Respiratory difficulties
- Orthopedic problems

The causes of kids and adolescents developing problems with weight are multiple. Evidence suggests that diets are changing (greater consumption of sugars and simple as opposed to complex carbohydrates, for example), portion sizes are increasing substantially, and activity levels are dropping. Interestingly, it appears that kids who spend the most time watching television also have the highest rates of obesity.

Although we have no direct data to back up this idea, we suspect that kids who do well on the four goals of childhood outlined in Chapter 3 (control of impulses and emotions, good relationships, balanced self-views, and achievement) will likely have fewer problems with overconsumption and too little activity and, therefore, obesity. They'll likely have fewer emotional problems overall as well.

Chapter 15

Exploring Behavior Disorders

. . . .

. . . .

Kids misbehave. They don't do what they're told to do. They lie, steal, cheat, and throw temper tantrums. They destroy objects, throw food, and argue with their parents. Fact is, this description fits most kids in roughly the 2- to 5-year-old range. A couple of these behaviors even applied to our Golden Doodle puppy, Sadie. She didn't do what she was told, stole things whenever she could, and ripped up our house more effectively than any teenage vandal ever could. We couldn't leave her out of our sight for more than a few minutes without worrying about what trouble she'd get into next. The good news is that most toddlers (as well as most puppies) develop into pretty well-socialized beings.

On the other hand, far too many kids evolve in a more disruptive, deviant direction. Aggression and violence in youth occurs at disturbing rates across the world, although the United States has more than its share. Those individuals who commit violent and aggressive acts in childhood through adolescents frequently continue their antisocial behaviors after they reach adulthood.

Note that many kids with conduct problems also have Attention Deficit/ Hyperactivity Disorder (ADHD), but it's not inevitably the case. Although ADHD is technically categorized by mental health professionals as a behavior disorder, we chose to present it in Chapter 12 because ADHD almost inevitably creates difficulty for children in school.

In this chapter, we discuss the prevalence of aggression and violence in youth. You can also take a look at the major risk factors that contribute to the problem as well as two diagnostic categories used to describe children and adolescents with such behavior. We also cover the issue of substance abuse, which though technically not a type of behavior disorder, frequently accompanies these problems and increases the risks of behavior disorders occurring.

Looking at the Facts: Behavior Problems

Although the rates of the most serious types of youth violence and aggression appear to have declined somewhat since the mid 1990s, aggression and conduct disorders rates remain at seriously high levels and substantially above where they were 25 to 30 years ago.

According to the Centers for Disease Control and Prevention (CDC), in 2009, almost a third of all students in grades 9 through 12 reported having been in a physical altercation (with males exceeding the rate of females by over 50 percent). Over 17 percent of all youth surveyed in these grades had carried a weapon in the month prior to the survey, with males exceeding females by almost four to one.

The CDC also reports that homicide was the second leading cause of death among those in the 10 to 24 age range. A total of 5,764 youth ages 10 to 24 fell victim to murder in 2007 (more than 15 per day). The numbers rise dramatically for nonfatal injuries with 656,000 youth ages 10 to 24 having actually had to go to the emergency room in 2008 for treatment of injuries that resulted from a violent encounter.

The nation's schools have substantially beefed up policies and security measures to combat aggression over the years, but they have failed to quell aggression and violence entirely on school property. A 2009 survey by the CDC of students in grades 9 through 12 determined that 31% of students acknowledged that they had been involved in a physical fight at school. And almost 17% of high school students admitted to having carried a weapon to school in the 30 days prior to the survey. What's even scarier is that such surveys tend to underreport problems because some students don't feel safe in answering honestly. You can find this and additional information about youth behavior and violence at www.cdc.gov/healthyyouth/yrbs/index.htm.

Violence and aggression are complex and have multiple factors that likely contribute to their development. However, it's likely that treatment and intervention efforts to reduce these problems can be effective (see Chapter 17 for information about types of therapy that work). The section "Crossing the Line from Normal to Not" later in this chapter has more information about how psychologists usually diagnose problems with conduct and behavior.

So whether you are a parent, pediatrician, counselor, nurse, teacher, or anyone else interested in kids; violence and aggression in kids should grab your attention. Kids with behavior disorders are at increased risk of committing violent and aggressive acts. The overall cost to society from youth violence and aggression is virtually incalculable.

Considering the Risks for Behavior Disorders

Because defiance, aggression, and violence are so costly to both youth and society, a wide range of factors have been studied to determine their possible contribution to behavior disorders. Sometimes, you don't know for sure whether these factors directly cause violence and aggression, increase the risk of these behaviors, or occur as a result of violence. Nevertheless, knowledge of these issues may eventually help both prevention and treatment of these behaviors.

Previewing poverty

A combination of poverty and crime in a neighborhood provides a rich breeding ground for a child to fall into criminal and antisocial behavior. Such neighborhoods often have drug dealing, gangs, prostitution, and a poor social fabric that fails to support kids. And kids are highly vulnerable to such unscrupulous influences so it's important to fight against them by any means possible.

Two methods for counteracting these bad influences seem effective. First, excellent schools set up in such neighborhoods can provide mentorship, a secure base, and positive, pro-social activities. Second, close, nurturing family relationships seem able to counteract the effects of poverty. See Chapter 10 for other ideas that communities can consider for enhancing kids' lives.

Exploring problems with peers

When children enter school, they have a whole new set of people influencing the way they think and their behavior. If school-age children are rejected by their peers, they are at much greater risk of developing aggressive and/or violent behaviors. Although some children with conduct problems do seem able to make friends, all too often they make friends with similar-minded peers who also display aggressive tendencies.

The role peers and friends with behavioral problems play can't be underestimated. Thus, parents are right to be concerned when their kids start hanging out with the wrong crowd. Parents need to monitor carefully where their kids go, what they do, and who they hang out with.

Viewing verbal struggles in school

Verbal skills refer to the ability to understand and express ideas and emotions through language. Although usually in the normal range, the verbal skills of kids with behavior problems often lags behind those of kids without behavior disorders. Some experts speculate that verbal deficiencies may make acquiring appropriate control of emotions and impulses more difficult (see Chapter 3 for a discussion of the importance of impulse control). Poor impulse control is a hallmark of those individuals with conduct disorders. Another explanation for the lower verbal skills of these kids could lie in the fact that they are less motivated to spend time reading and learning vocabulary than other kids.

Frequently, children who develop behavior problems also underachieve in school, likely in part due to deficient verbal skills. Although becoming frustrated and underachieving at school doesn't appear to directly lead to violence, it probably does make a contribution. Kids who do poorly in school are at risk for bonding with delinquent peers.

Finding family conflict

Significant family and marital conflict and discord have been strongly associated with the development of behavioral problems. When parents are hostile, violent, or aggressive themselves, they provide poor role models for kids. In addition, poor parenting practices such as excessive harshness, failure to set and follow through with appropriate limits, and neglect all set the stage for behavior problems. Depression, especially on the part of the mother, is also a risk factor. Frequent moves and general family instability disrupt normal development and may additionally increase aggression. See Chapter 19 for information about what parents can do to have better outcomes for their children.

Setting the record straight: Self-esteem

For many decades, parents, teachers, and caregivers speculated that low self-esteem led to violence and aggression. However, this idea has failed to hold up to close scrutiny. A large body of research (much of which Dr. Roy Baumeister and colleagues conducted) now suggests that an overly inflated self-esteem actually may contribute to aggression.

Apparently, kids who see themselves as better than other kids and who *overestimate* their talents and skills, also have trouble holding onto their puffed-up views of themselves. When other kids threaten or challenge them, they often resort to aggression to defend their self-esteem (see Chapter 3 for more information about the development of healthy self views as an important goal of childhood). On the other hand, this fact doesn't mean that low self-esteem is good for kids; low self-views have been associated with depression and anxiety (and less often, aggression), which aren't good either.

Searching for genetics

As is the case for most mental and emotional disorders, genes appear to account for roughly 50 percent of the risk for developing various antisocial behaviors. Experts believe that genes likely exert much of their effects on aggression due to their causing a difficult temperament (see Chapters 2 and 4 for information about the role of temperament in development) and by increasing the risk for greater impulsivity. However, the effects of genes can be amplified or mitigated by interactions with the child's environment (check out Chapter 2 for more information about how genes and the environment interact).

Attaining attachment

Studies suggest that insecure attachment during childhood (see Chapter 3 for information about attachment) likely contributes to the development of antisocial behavior down the road. If the bonds between parent and child are poor, it makes sense that a child may be more drawn to bond with peers. Unfortunately, some of these peers may not adhere to usual societal values. Bonding with peers who have behavioral disorders of their own can have a very negative effect on a child's personal behavior.

For example, a young boy whose parents are serious substance abusers may feel neglected and fail to bond adequately with them. When that boy starts school, he feels extremely needy of finding friends. That neediness may make him highly vulnerable to other kids who want him to join them in reckless, delinquent behaviors.

Seeking sensations

An element of personality that apparently predisposes kids and adolescents toward both behavior disorders and substance abuse is known as *sensation seeking*. People who are prone to sensation seeking crave excitement and stimulation. They feel bored easily and go to great lengths to escape such feelings. People high on sensation seeking tend to drive dangerously, love high-risk sports, engage in unprotected sex, engage in antisocial behaviors, and look for thrills wherever they can find them. Controlling impulses is difficult for them. Therefore, when they feel upset or angry, they are likely to act on those feelings rather than control them as other kids would. It appears that genes play a significant role in how much a person becomes a sensation seeker, but learning and experience also play an important role.

Covering culture

Cultures across the world vary in how they raise kids and in their expectations about both behavior and relationships with others. Thus, you may not find it surprising that rates of conduct problems across the world vary greatly from one country or cultural subgroup to another. In general, areas that place high value on interdependence and the collective good tend to have much lower rates of violence and aggression even in the presence of poverty or crowded conditions. Cultures that place high value on autonomy and independence, such as in the United States, tend to have much higher homicide rates than others. Good parenting can go a long way in overcoming the problem of cultures that tend to have a great deal of aggression and violence. See Chapter 8 for more information about good parenting and family practices.

Minding media

The role media — television, movies, video games, computers, and so on — plays in the development of violence and aggression has been hotly debated for decades. However, studies have begun to compile sufficient evidence to suggest cause for concern. Kids witness literally thousands of murders and violent acts on television before they reach the age of 10. Experts generally agree that the amount of exposure a child has to television violence, especially realistically portrayed violence, does predict the degree of aggression years later. This risk factor is not usually thought to be a major cause of violence and aggression, but it's likely that it makes a contribution. Monitoring a child's media input may not be a bad idea.

Obtaining and using substances

Kids who are aggressive and violent are more likely to circumvent laws and find ways to obtain illegal substances. They are also more drawn to the lure of drugs and alcohol in the first place. Even more importantly, the effects of illegal substance use frequently are such that they cause disinhibition and reduce the capacity to control impulses, which raises the risk of engaging in violent behavior.

Note that kids who abuse alcohol and drugs are at higher risk for exhibiting aggression and violence. The causal direction between substance abuse and behavior problems is a bit unclear (a kind of chicken-versus-egg scenario), but it's likely that substance abuse cuts both ways. See the section in this chapter "Sleuthing Substance Abuse" for more information about the effects and consequences of substance abuse on kids and teens.

Crossing the Line from Normal to Not

Professionals use two official diagnoses to describe disruptive behaviors after they cross the line from normal to abnormal. The first of these terms is called *oppositional-defiant disorder* (ODD); the second is called *conduct disorder* (CD). We discuss both of these behavioral disorders in detail, including examples, in the following sections.

Oppositional-defiant disorder (ODD)

ODD refers to chronic patterns of obstinate, defiant, challenging, confronting, and hostile behavior. Kids with ODD often have a rigid sense of "fairness." They are exquisitely sensitive to whenever they believe they are not being treated fairly. Yet they treat other people outrageously and often quite unfairly.

Noting the symptoms of ODD

The *Diagnostic and Statistical Manual of Mental Disorders* (DSM-IV) that mental health professionals use suggests that the label applies when kids demonstrate at least half of the following types of symptoms for at least six months:

- ✔ Frequent temper outbursts

- ✔ Unusually argumentative with adults

- ✔ Often defiant and refuse to do what they're asked

- ✔ Frequently vindictive

- ✔ Annoyed easily by other people

- ✔ Often demonstrates anger

- ✔ Blame other people for problems

- ✔ Goes out of the way to annoy other people

However, a child is only considered to have ODD if he demonstrates these behaviors in a manner that exceeds the frequency and intensity of his peers to a significant degree. After all, we introduced this chapter by noting that most kids below the age of 5 present challenges with disruptive, aggressive, defiant, and frankly, obnoxious behavior. It's possible that a 2 or 3 year old could receive the diagnosis of ODD, but it's unusual and would require truly outrageous behavior, given that kids at that age are naturally rather defiant and have frequent temper tantrums anyway.

The symptoms of ODD overlap somewhat with the more serious condition of CD (see the section "Conduct disorder [CD]" in this chapter). However, most kids with ODD do not actually develop full-blown CD. About half of them simply continue to demonstrate ODD behaviors and do not progress.

Perhaps a fourth of the kids with ODD improve to the point that the diagnosis no longer applies. Treatment (see Chapter 17) may improve the overall outcomes for kids with ODD.

ODD does not apply to kids who have a problem with only one parent. Thus, a child who gets along with teachers, relatives, and his mother, but argues all the time with his father, does not have ODD. He has a problem in his relationship with his dad.

One problem with all mental health "diagnoses," but which especially applies to ODD, is that diagnoses are based on the same model as diseases. In other words, something you either "have" or you "don't have." However, the symptoms of ODD vary quite a lot over time. It's really more like a dynamic continuum, and kids can at certain times be seen as clearly "having" ODD whereas at other times, the picture isn't so clear. This diagnosis haze is why it's important to work closely with a trained mental health professional.

Seeing ODD in action

Use the following example of Tony to get a feel for what someone with ODD may sound like when talking to his mother about homework.

"Mom, I'm going outside to ride my bike," Tony announces.

Mom replies, "No you're not. You didn't do your homework."

"I don't have any homework," Tony lies.

"Tony, I have your backpack right in front of me. You know that your teacher sends notes to me every day. Right here it says that you are supposed to finish the math assignment that you didn't finish in school for homework," responds Mom.

"That's not fair. She didn't give us enough time in class. It's her fault that I didn't finish," Tony's voice is beginning to get louder.

"Tony, I don't care if it's fair or not," his mother says firmly, "you still have to do homework."

"I hate school, and I don't care what that witch teacher said," blurts on Tony as he starts to put on his jacket.

Tony's mother is beginning to get mad, "Tony, I said you have to do your homework before you go outside."

"You can't make me. I'm out of here," with that, he leaves.

Tony and his mother have many of these conversations. Tony also gets in frequent trouble at school. He argues with adults, lies, gets angry easily, blames other people, and becomes defiant. Tony has ODD.

A variety of studies have demonstrated that kids with ODD as well as CD (see the following section), have a lower resting physiological arousal level (for example, lower pulse rates) than kids without these problems. Physiological arousal is often considered a sign of anxiety and is in fact higher in kids who have anxiety disorders. Perhaps a "little" anxiety could be a good thing and help prevent problems with aggression.

Conduct disorder (CD)

In the vast majority of cases, conduct disorder (CD) is preceded by ODD (see preceding section, "Oppositional-defiant disorder [ODD]"). However, compared to CD, ODD waxes and wanes over time and may or may not persist. CD, on the other hand, tends to be somewhat more stable over time, after it has become established and entrenched.

CD is a *severe* form of aggressive and antisocial behavior. These behaviors are not something to take lightly.

Prevalence figures for CD vary significantly from one study and population sample to another. However, it is not rare, apparently occurring in something under 10 percent of children below the age of 18. It most often occurs after age 9. The age at which CD begins matters, so CD has two subtypes:

- ✔ **Childhood onset:** Professionals give this label to those who show at least one significant symptom of CD before the age of 10. This type is much more frequent among males than females. And when it occurs at this early age, CD tends to be more chronic and difficult to treat. Incredibly, you can sometimes see the signs of childhood onset as early as the age of 2 or 3. Some of these kids show a remarkable lack of a conscience and inflict surprising harm on siblings and others. Later they sometimes exhibit even more serious problems.

- ✔ **Adolescent onset:** Males and females demonstrate this type of CD more equally in numbers. They are somewhat less aggressive than kids with childhood onset CD, and more of them show signs of improvement over time.

Although the majority of kids with CD do show improvements over time, they are at relatively high risk of developing an antisocial personality disorder (APD) as adults. That's especially true of kids with a childhood onset for their CD. *Antisocial personality disorders* demonstrate profound disregard for society's rules; they are seen as callous, manipulative, narcissistic, impulsive, and lacking in remorse for their various transgressions. The diagnosis is applied when the behavior demonstrates a persistent, entrenched pattern after the age of 15 when a child has previously shown signs of CD. Antisocial personality disorders are seen in an overabundant supply in the prison system. They literally represent society's worst.

The next two sections provide a more detailed description of what CD looks like in kids generally along with a real world example. See Chapter 17 for information about treatment of behavior disorders.

Introducing the symptoms of CD

There are four major symptom categories of CD behavior listed in the professional *Diagnostic and Statistical Manual of Mental Disorders* (DSM), each of which come in various forms. Those individuals with CD have typically engaged in a majority of these categories at one time or another. The major forms include:

- ✔ **Aggression targeting people or animals:** Kids with this type of CD behavior often start fights. They bully other kids and threaten them. They often have actually employed weapons in their fights. They display cruelty. Sometimes they derive pleasure from torturing or killing animals. They sometimes rape. Or they may mug, steal, and extort their victims.

- ✔ **Deceit:** This category of CD is more indirect, but still involves antisocial behavior that violates other people's rights. They may break into houses or cars, lie to get what they want, con people, or shoplift.

- ✔ **Property destruction:** Many of those with CD set fires to homes, cars, buildings, or other property. They may also "key" cars, shoot out windows, destroy public art, or seriously vandalize school property.

- ✔ **Major rule violations:** This category covers behaviors such as staying out well beyond parental rules starting before the age of 13. It also includes truancy from school beginning before 13 as well as running away from home and staying away overnight or longer.

In addition to the four serious symptom classes of CD, people with CD demonstrate a wide range of other problematic behavior. They tend to

- ✔ Lack empathy and concern for others.
- ✔ Engage in early, risky sexual behavior.
- ✔ Smoke, drink, and abuse various substances with some frequency.
- ✔ Be drawn to gangs.
- ✔ Become pregnant at earlier ages, for females.
- ✔ Attempt suicide at an increased rate.

Getting a feel for CD in the real world

Although CD is more prevalent in boys, girls can have this disorder as well. The following example of Hannah (age 13) illustrates what CD can look like.

> **Hannah** kicks at the dirt in the field behind her school while she waits for the other kids to join her. The bell rings in the distance announcing the beginning of first hour. Hannah and a few of her friends decided yesterday to ditch school. She looks up across the field and sees Luke walking toward her.

She asks, "Where's the rest of our gang? Did they chicken out, Luke?"

Luke replies, "Yeah, they're too scared they might get caught — especially after we all got suspended last time. So I guess it's just us. What do you want to do?"

Hannah says, "How about going over to the mall and pick up some music. That one store over there has lousy security; we can steal a bunch of CDs and then sell them at school like we did last month. Do you know something? I love to steal; it makes me high."

"Great idea," Luke smiles, "this time though I won't get caught at home with the cash. Last month I had about 50 dollars, and my mom started asking me lots of questions about where I got the money."

"Tell your mom you found it at school or something. My mom doesn't ask me questions anymore," Hannah confides, "I think she's scared of me. Last time we got into a fight, she made me so mad that I started pushing her around and broke her stupid lamp. Then I walked out and didn't come back for two days. I don't think she wants to mess with me anymore — she's so weak. She starts crying practically every time I talk to her. I can't stand that; she makes me sick."

Hannah has conduct disorder. She ditches school, shoplifts, and has run away from home. She intimidates her mother with threats of violence and has no remorse.

Sleuthing Substance Abuse

Substance abuse and behavior disorders often go hand in hand. Professionals categorize substance abuse separately from behavior disorders. However, we include it in this chapter because obtaining and consuming drugs in youth is largely an illegal activity, and it is highly associated with other behavior disorders as well as delinquency. The precise ways that mental disorders are categorized is somewhat arbitrary.

The abuse of substances — alcohol, tobacco, marijuana (hashish), inhalants, hallucinogens, cocaine, prescription drugs such as pain killers and tranquilizers, and even over-the-counter medications such as nonprescription cough medicines — has always occurred at high rates among youth. Alcohol, likely because it's fairly easy to obtain, has consistently remained the most commonly abused substance. And the substance that has demonstrated the greatest long-term health risk is tobacco, generally in the form of cigarettes.

According to the National Institute on Drug Abuse (NIDA) in 2009, almost half of all twelfth graders acknowledged having tried some type of illicit drug (not including alcohol and cigarettes), over a third in the year prior to the survey, and almost a fourth in the previous month. The percentage of twelfth graders who have consumed alcohol is almost three-fourths at some point or another, two-thirds in the year prior to the survey, and somewhat less than half in the previous month. Again, such surveys are probably conservative estimates because not everyone openly reports on their own illegal behaviors even when anonymity is assured.

Although alcohol is often not categorized under "illicit drugs," it is a drug because it alters brain functioning and behavior artificially just as other drugs do. Furthermore, it's generally "illicit" for teenagers simply because they are not old enough to purchase alcohol legally.

Pre-adolescent and adolescent kids don't need to have a full-blown diagnosis of substance-use disorder (see the next section for more information) to end up in trouble. Just one serious episode of drinking or taking drugs can lead to highly dangerous behaviors due to disinhibition and impaired judgment. Furthermore, death from overdose is always a risk as well.

Substances exert a wide range of effects on kids and cause them all sorts of problems in their lives. And a wide range of factors increase the risks of kids taking this route. The next two sections review these issues.

Identifying the effects of substance problems

Substance-use disorder involves a pattern of substance abuse that creates significant distress or dysfunction over a 12-month period of time or more. Thus, substance abuse leads to at least a couple of the following types of problems:

- ✔ **Problems with school, family, and other obligations:** These issues include frequent absences, failure to complete schoolwork, expulsion, fights with parents or siblings (including failure to adhere to household rules), and so on. Sometimes the youth withdraws from extracurricular activities and other types of healthy recreation.

- ✔ **Dangerousness:** Abusing substances often occurs in situations that are dangerous, such as when teenagers drive or operate machinery when drunk.

- ✔ **Tolerance and withdrawal:** *Tolerance* involves needing increased amounts of the substance to obtain the same effect. *Withdrawal* refers to various symptoms that occur when ceasing consumption of a substance and the actual symptoms tend to be specific to each type of drug. However, youth do not display tolerance or withdrawal problems as often because they generally don't have access to the substance on the same regular, sustained basis as do adults.

- ✔ **Increasing consumption:** Over time, the person consumes greater amounts than intended, largely due to the fact that the body habituates or becomes accustomed to lower amounts and thus requires more to obtain the same effect.

✔ **Desire to reduce intake, but failure to do so:** This aspect of substance-use disorder is less common in adolescents who are generally in the early stages of the pattern. Yet, a few kids start abusing substances in their pre-teen years and are deeply into an addiction pattern by adolescence.

✔ **Time:** People with substance-use disorder often spend a lot of time trying to obtain the substance and in overcoming the effects of intoxication.

✔ **Cravings:** The young person generally has a driven desire to continue use of a particular substance.

The chances that teenagers will develop a serious problem with substances appear to decrease significantly with each year of delay before they begin. For example, studies show that the risk of ultimately becoming dependent on alcohol decreases by close to 10 percent each year after the age of 14. Drinking in early adolescence is also considered more dangerous than later adolescent years because the brain is still undergoing critical development during this time.

Reviewing risks and protective factors

It turns out that most, if not all, of the risks for developing behavior disorders in general (see earlier section "Considering the Risks for Behavior Disorders") also increase the risks for substance abuse. Following are some of the most common risks with substance-use disorder:

✔ **Genetics:** Alcoholism and substance abuse run in families.

✔ **Poor family functioning:** High conflict, hostility, and poor monitoring of kids' behaviors creates a risk of kids turning to substances.

✔ **Negative modeling:** When parents drink or abuse substances, they provide powerful models to their kids for doing the same. Friends and peers can also serve as models.

✔ **Early experiences with drugs or alcohol:** The younger a kid experiments with drugs, the more likely the experiment will turn into a lifelong habit.

On the other hand, there are a few factors that provide some degree of protection or risk reduction for turning toward substances. Some of these include:

✔ The degree to which teens are connected to their school community seems to make a difference in whether or not kids turn to substances.

✔ The extent to which parents communicate their expectations about substance use and how much they monitor their kids' behavior makes a real difference.

✔ If kids are highly involved in extracurricular activities such as clubs, sports, or religious groups, kids tend to be less inclined to experiment with substances.

Detecting delinquency

It's worth noting that *juvenile delinquency* is not a psychological term; rather, it's a legal issue. Most, but not necessarily all, juvenile delinquents probably have conduct disorders. Thus, a child who shoplifts a minor item once or who slips into a concert without paying is technically a delinquent if arrested, but probably doesn't have CD. Furthermore, many youths who could be diagnosed with CD may not have an arrest record and thus not be considered a juvenile delinquent even though their behavior may be more outrageous than the minor, first-time offender.

Juvenile arrest rates have declined somewhat since the mid 1990s. It appears that a significant portion of this decrease is likely due to less use of lethal weapons on the part of youth. In addition, schools, homes, cars, and businesses have tightened security considerably in the last decade or two. We would like to think that improvements in risk factors such as sensation seeking, family conflict, and improved attachments have contributed to the decrease in juvenile crime statistics, but we don't have data available at this point for answering that question.

The best time to prevent substance abuse is before kids become addicted. Ideally, before they've even experimented with them. Strong healthy families and communities can do a lot to prevent serious problems. Families that experience conflict or strife should seek help from a mental health therapist before more serious problems arise.

Chapter 16

Looking at Trauma and Abuse

Children look to the adults in their lives for basic survival. They need food, clothing, and shelter. Children also look to adults for love, comfort, and protection. Sometimes, adults are unable to prevent bad things from happening. Accidents or natural disasters happen. At other times, adults abuse or neglect the children they are charged with taking care of. When traumatic events occur in the lives of children, they feel unsure and unsteady. If trusted adults can't keep them safe, the world must indeed be a dangerous place.

In this chapter, we look at the difficult issues of child abuse and trauma. Too many children are abused or neglected by their parents or caregivers. We discuss the types of child abuse, as well as physical and emotional signs in children that may indicate abuse. Children are also victims of other traumatic events, such as car or other accidents, acts of terror, war, medical trauma, crime, and natural disasters.

When children experience trauma, they are at greater risk than adults are for experiencing psychological distress following such events. This distress can be short lived or persist into adulthood. Some children, however, seem to be able to withstand horrific events without appearing to suffer serious long-term effects. We look at the factors associated with this strength, which is often called *resilience*. Finally, we discuss some of the emotional disorders specifically associated with the experience of trauma.

Watching Out for Abuse and Neglect

Child abuse occurs in every neighborhood — in homes ravaged by poverty and in huge mansions. Children are abused in homes where caregivers are doctors, as well as homes with high-school dropouts. Abuse can be inflicted by parents, relatives, family friends, coaches, or next-door neighbors. Those who abuse drugs or alcohol, whether they're rich or poor, are more likely to abuse children. And, abuse comes in many forms, including physical, sexual, emotional, and neglect.

When child abuse is suspected, any concerned adult can make a report, and it's arguably the most ethical thing to do. Such reports can be made anonymously. The Childhelp National Child Abuse Hotline is staffed 24/7 and can assist with reporting; call 1-800-4 A CHILD (1-800-422-4453). Calls are staffed by professional counselors and toll free. Some professionals — such as nurses, doctors, teachers, psychologists, counselors, and social workers — are required by law to report suspected child abuse. States vary somewhat on who is required to report abuse, but it's always the right thing to do.

If you are considering reporting child abuse, leave the actual investigation up to the agency. Don't directly confront the abuser or try to intervene or assess the situation yourself. You don't need to have documentation although if you do, by all means, give it to the agency you report to. If you're the abuser, the Childhelp National Child Abuse Hotline (see preceding paragraph) also offers help for abusers.

Uncovering physical abuse

About five children die every day as the result of child abuse in the United States. Most of those who die are under the age of 4. Someone calls authorities to report child abuse every 10 seconds, and almost 6 million children are involved in reported allegations every year. Of those cases in which abuse is confirmed, about two thirds involve babies. These statistics are believed to be underestimates of the true incidences of abuse because child abuse occurs most often behind closed doors; therefore, most cases of abuse likely go undetected.

The most common types of child abuse include the following:

- ✔ **Physical child abuse** is an injury inflicted by another person. Injuries can range from minor bruises to severe damage or even death. Incidents of physical abuse sometimes occur when a parent attempts to discipline a child or when a child is fussy, irritable, or misbehaving in some way. Many times, however, physical abuse occurs when a *parent* is fussy, irritable, or misbehaving in some way.

- ✔ **Shaken baby syndrome** is a form of physical abuse that happens when a baby is shaken violently. The syndrome is caused by brain damage that occurs when the brain is repeatedly bounced against the skull. The results may include bleeding in the brain, bruising, bleeding in the retinas, damage to neck and spine, and broken bones. The injuries can lead to seizures, coma, death, or permanent brain damage. Diagnosing shaken baby syndrome is somewhat complex and at times has resulted in courtroom controversies.

- ✔ **Abuse resulting from impaired parents** occurs when caregivers expose children to danger because of their own drug or alcohol use. A pregnant mother is abusing her unborn child when she uses unsafe substances during her pregnancy. Furthermore, it is considered to be child abuse when someone drives a motor vehicle while intoxicated with a child as a passenger or a child ingests drugs or alcohol available in the home.

Signs of possible physical child abuse include

- ✔ **Bruises:** The child may have lots of bruises in different stages of healing without obvious causes. (Many kids have bruises from falling while playing, but the cause is more apparent.)

- ✔ **Burns:** When a child has burns that she has no explanation for, further investigation often reveals that abuse has occurred. Such abuse frequently involves burns from cigarettes or from immersion in hot liquid.

- ✔ **Cuts:** The child has numerous cuts that aren't explained by everyday activities.

- ✔ **Swelling:** The child's tissues are swollen, especially around the face.

- ✔ **Broken bones:** Particularly when the explanation for the injury seems to be unlikely, the child may have been abused.

- ✔ **Wearing clothing inappropriate to the weather:** The child may come to school or day care wearing long sleeves in warm weather to hide injury.

- ✔ **Fear:** The child seems to be afraid of caregivers, parents, or most adults and doesn't want to go home.

Looking at neglect

Not providing adequate care is the most common form of child maltreatment. Child neglect really involves *not* doing something rather than doing something to a child. The parent or primary caregiver is responsible for providing basic necessities to a child. Failure to do so is deemed neglectful. It is not considered neglect when caregivers are unable to provide adequate care because of poverty or lack of resources, or when the parents' religious beliefs prohibit certain medical procedures, although this latter issue can be quite controversial.

Types of neglect include

- **Physical neglect** involves a failure to provide sufficient food, clothing, or shelter. It can also involve allowing a young child to be unsupervised either because a parent is absent from the home or because the parent is impaired and unable to care for a child. Children who are physically neglected may steal or hoard food, report that they were left home alone, or fall asleep in school.

- **Abandonment** happens when parents leave a child and fail to provide support or leave without providing information about their whereabouts. It can also occur when a parent leaves a child somewhere (such as a babysitter's home, a relative's home, or sometimes at a hospital) and does not return. It is also considered abandonment when parents direct children or teens not to return home.

- **Medical neglect** occurs when a child does not receive adequate preventive care, care for illness or injury, dental care, vision care, or mental-health care. Kids who experience medical neglect often suffer preventable or untreated illnesses and have dental cavities or various other unmet health needs.

- **Educational neglect** happens when parents allow children to stay home from school (or fail to provide an alternative, such as home school) or when parents don't allow a child with a handicap to attend an appropriate program. Children whose parents engage in educational neglect often miss school and are at risk for early school dropout.

- **Emotional neglect** can be similar to physical neglect because it often involves allowing a child to be unsupervised. Parents who emotionally neglect their children do not give them sufficient love and attention. They may ignore a child's emotional needs, abuse substances in his presence, engage in criminal or violent acts in front of him, and allow him to use unsafe substances. Unfortunately, emotional neglect often goes undetected and is difficult to document.

Encountering sexual abuse

Child sexual abuse involves engaging in sexual activity with a child, such as fondling, penetration, rape, or sodomy, or having a child participate in sexual activity with another person. Sexual abuse can include any acts that exploit a child for the purposes of pornographic materials or for prostitution. In addition, it is considered sexual abuse to expose a child to pornography or to sexually explicit and developmentally inappropriate material. Engaging in exhibitionism or voyeurism that involves a child is also considered sexual abuse.

Signs of sexual abuse in children vary depending on the type of abuse and the age of the child. Physical signs may include sudden trouble sitting down or walking, genital pain, frequent urinary infections, or bruises or bleeding in the genital area. Behavioral or psychological signs sometimes include nightmares, bed wetting (in children who have already mastered toilet training), sudden unexplained changes in weight, knowledge of sexual activities beyond what is age-appropriate, seductive sexual behavior, suicide attempts, or running away from home.

In this day and age, many children are accidentally exposed to sexually explicit material. Therefore, they may have some sexual knowledge that seems beyond their age. Children also get urinary infections for reasons other than sexual abuse. One or two possible signs do not necessarily mean that a child has been abused.

If you have concerns that a child may be a victim of sexual abuse, make a referral to either the child's doctor or to a local protective-services agency. Don't attempt to interview the child yourself unless you have professional training in this type of assessment. There have been unfortunate instances when sexual abuse was suspected but did not occur and innocent people were accused. When children are interviewed by people who do not have proper training, the information that children give sometimes becomes contaminated or tarnished. When sexual abuse is suspected, the child should be evaluated by a professional highly trained in procedures that have been shown to elicit accurate information.

Listening for emotional abuse

Emotional abuse may be the most common form of child abuse. We don't know for sure because it is rarely reported and can be incredibly difficult to detect or prove. This type of abuse almost always accompanies other forms of abuse and by itself can cause years of suffering for its victims. Like any type of child abuse, emotional abuse should be reported. Emotional abuse can take various forms, some more obvious than others, but it often falls within the categories described in the following sections.

Ignoring

Parents who do this can be especially cruel. Unlike parents who are a bit neglectful, these parents purposely punish their kids through extreme withdrawal. Usually, they become angry and then stop speaking to or showing affection to a child. This behavior can go on for hours or sometimes days or weeks at a time. Children feel guilty and lost when this happens. The kids desperately desire a connection and can't understand why their parents aren't speaking to them. They assume that they've done something horribly wrong and somehow deserve the silent treatment.

Humiliating and rejecting

Humiliation and rejection hurts — especially when it comes from someone a child looks up to and loves. Caregivers or parents (and sometimes even teachers) may call a child names, put her down, use cruel sarcasm, blame her for messing up somehow, and make her feel profoundly ashamed. Words such as *ignorant, worthless, stupid, foolish, lazy, inadequate, incapable, evil,* and *bad* are commonly used.

As you would surmise, children who suffer this type of abuse are likely to have low self-esteem. They lack confidence in their abilities, feel inferior, and may do poorly in school. Problems with sleep, asthma, and depression often occur. Later, delinquent behavior may develop.

Criticizing

This form of abuse often comes with humiliation and rejection but is more specific to a particular behavior that a child may have engaged in. Parents or caregivers who continually criticize a child target whatever tasks or behaviors the child is doing and then tell him that he's doing it wrong, ineptly, sloppily, too fast, too slow, or carelessly. Sometimes, these parents expect too much from their kids and criticize them when they are unable to comply.

Before children master toilet training, for example, they will *almost always* have a few accidents. Parents may react with anger and rage, telling their children that they are lazy or stupid for having an accident. When children are harshly criticized for their efforts, many of them stop trying. If there is no way to please a parent, why bother? Some kids do find ways to persevere despite these assaults on their self-esteem — usually when another adult in their lives gives them hope and encouragement.

When children do something wrong because of lack of effort or deliberate carelessness, it is fine to let them know. We are not suggesting that criticism is all bad. When giving critical feedback, however, it is important to target the specific problematic behavior and to do so with tempered disapproval accompanied by information about what children can do to improve. What parents and teachers want to avoid is passing harsh judgment or making global evaluations of children's worth.

Bullying and intimidating

Some adults get a sick kick out of bullying children. They may threaten children with physical harm, exploitation, or severe punishment. Adult bullies may grab children (without leaving marks or causing physical injuries) and yank them around. They sometimes tower over kids, yelling and screaming. One particularly horrible way that bullies terrify their victims occurs when they frighten children by abusing a family pet or another family member in their presence.

Looking at Other Sources of Trauma

Children around the world experience trauma, which comes in many forms. Children can experience physical trauma, such as being injured during an earthquake, a car accident, or highly painful medical procedures (see Chapter 11 for information about illnesses, pain, and hospitalization). Children can also suffer psychological trauma from witnessing others being hurt, watching traumatic events unfold on television, or even overhearing discussions about frightening events. In addition, children who lose a parent or other close relative to illness, violence, or accident experience trauma. In other words, most kids face emotionally distressing or painful experiences at one time or another.

In this section, we explore various types of trauma. (For info on trauma from abuse, see "Watching Out for Abuse and Neglect," earlier in this chapter.)

Noticing neighborhood crime

It is hard to shield today's children from the reality of crime. Whether they see reports on the local news or have to deal with crime in their schools and neighborhoods, most kids today understand that there are bad people out there who may want to hurt them. Kids learn early about not talking to strangers and good touch versus bad touch.

Crime burdens and steals freedom from children. Many parents keep their kids unintentional prisoners. They shelter them inside the house and drive them from place to place. These anxious parents feel too afraid to let their kids outdoors to run and play. Children pick up on their parents' fear. When crime is too close (whether in reality or in the imagination), children can't concentrate on learning and enjoying life.

In spite of parents' best intentions, children sometimes witness violent crimes; a close friend or family member may become a victim of crime; or they themselves become victims. In those instances, they may suffer a variety of emotional disorders. On the other hand, many children show incredible resiliency and seem to come through these difficult experiences relatively unscathed.

Parents can't always keep kids safe. They need to provide their kids appropriate freedom whenever possible. Kids need supervision and guidance in dealing with bullies and other threats, of course, and when neighborhoods are dangerous, letting kids out unsupervised is not warranted. But safety must be balanced with reality. Therefore, it's important to allow children some independent experiences so that they can learn to handle the real, sometimes scary, world on their own. It's a tough balancing act.

Attending to accidental trauma

Accidents are by far the most common reason for death and serious injury among children ages 1 to 18. Car accidents are responsible for the majority of deaths and injuries in children although accidents also occur in playgrounds and at home. Child safety seats substantially reduce the risk of death and injury, and their increased use has certainly saved lives. Nevertheless, many children are either not restrained or improperly restrained. Unfortunately, even when children are contained in safe car seats, some drivers run red lights, text or talk on cell phones while driving, turn illegally, or drive while impaired, and sometimes, accidents just happen.

Every community has programs to assist parents in the proper installation of car seats for their kids. The installation of some of these seats appears to require a PhD in engineering, so we highly recommend getting some help. See www.nhtsa.gov for information about programs near you.

Following an accident, children often have increased worries and fear. After a child's physical needs are addressed, parents need to be on the lookout for emotional problems. Kids who have prolonged symptoms of anxiety or irritability, or who have trouble sleeping or eating following an accident, may need treatment. If you're concerned, discuss the issue with the child's pediatrician or a mental-health professional.

Considering terrorism and war

Adults are completely responsible for acts of war or terrorism, but children are often the victims. When children witness disasters that are intentionally caused by adults (who are supposed to take care of children), they are more likely to suffer psychological distress than when a disaster occurs naturally. Those children who lose a parent, relative, or caregiver to the violence or whose parents are physically injured are more likely to have especially severe reactions. In addition, when adults have their own normal emotional reactions to the disaster, they may be less available to care for the emotional needs of the children around them. Therefore, it's important that the mental-health issues of caregivers be treated so that they may be more present in the lives of children who are experiencing the effects of trauma.

Psychological problems can be made worse by physical vulnerabilities. Babies born in lower Manhattan in the nine months following the World Trade Center attack of Sept. 11, 2001, for example, weighed significantly less than babies born in Manhattan farther from the site. Low birth weight is associated with increased risk of developmental problems. Also, children who lived close to the World Trade Center have a much higher rate of asthma than kids without the exposure. Asthma attacks often lead to fear and panic in addition to posing daily stress and made the adjustment to post-Sept. 11 life more difficult for many kids.

Noting responses to natural disasters

When natural disasters occur, children and their families lose lives, are physically hurt, displaced, or emotionally scarred. Many of our country's biggest disasters occurred before researchers started tracking the mental health of the youngest victims. That oversight changed with Hurricane Katrina, one of the greatest disasters in U.S. history. The immediate effect of the hurricane itself paled in comparison to the storm surge and flooding that destroyed homes, neighborhoods, and a way of life for those who lived in the region. Following Katrina, the mental health of survivors has been studied extensively.

It is estimated that more than 160,000 children lost their homes for more than 3 months as a result of Hurricane Katrina. Many of the children affected by Katrina came from homes in which other stressors were present, such as high rates of neighborhood crime, poverty, and family problems. Those other difficulties piled on top of the trauma of Katrina probably explain why researchers report that more than 37 percent of the children in the affected areas have been diagnosed with a serious emotional disturbance.

Recovery from such incidents usually requires professional help and time. Parents can help by encouraging kids to discuss their fears and feelings. And they can help their kids by making sure that their own emotional issues are addressed.

Losing loved ones

When children lose someone they love, they feel sad but often guilty or angry as well. Whether the loss is because of death, divorce, imprisonment, hospitalization, or another reason, such as job transfer or military service, children tend to personalize their loss. Kids may believe that someone left because *they* were bad or had angry thoughts.

Those who care for children after a loss need to be sensitive to these feelings and help children interpret their loss realistically. Here are a few ideas for discussing these issues with children:

- ✔ **Tell the truth.** Children have an uncanny ability to see through deception. You don't want to talk to very young children about the details, but don't try to lie about the separation. Similarly, if you tell children that someone will return in a while and that isn't going to happen, they may be worried about other people in their lives disappearing.

- ✔ **Watch your language.** If you tell children that someone dies because of illness, they may believe that colds or sore throats can cause death. Be sure that you choose words that kids can understand.

- ✔ **Let children lead the conversation.** Don't offer more than a child wants to hear. Let children know that you are available if they have questions. Sometimes, kids need time to digest difficult information. Long-winded lectures will probably be tuned out.

✔ **Expect children to react differently.** Some kids talk openly about their feelings; others clam up; still others act angry or aggressive. Allow children time to grieve the loss, but when they show signs (longer than a couple of weeks) of difficulty sleeping, changes in appetite, loss of interest in activities, or avoidance of activities, it's time to ask for help. Contact the child's medical provider or a mental-health professional for more advice.

Seeing What Happens to Traumatized Kids

The effects of trauma on children range from small to large. How children react reflects a variety of influences and support systems. Some kids' reactions to trauma appear to be surprisingly small and transient; others find themselves shattered by what happened to them. See `http://www.cdc.gov/ace/index.htm` for more information about the effects of various types of trauma on later life and well being.

In this section, we cover common reactions to trauma, as well as factors that affect how severe a child's reaction is likely to be.

Note: Both abuse and trauma can cause problems with mental health other than the diagnoses we review here. Sometimes, trauma and/or chronic stressors or abuse cause kids to get depressed. Other kids fall into a pattern of chronic anxiety and/or worry. Still others become oppositional and defiant, and others try to manage their difficult feelings with drugs or alcohol. See Chapter 14 for more information about depression and anxiety, and Chapter 15 for more about defiance and substance abuse.

Factors that affect how well a child copes

The following factors are critical in influencing how children ultimately adapt to traumatic events:

✔ **Location of the trauma:** Close proximity to trauma makes it harder for children to deal with. When trauma occurs in the home or at school, children are more affected than if the trauma occurs at some distance.

✔ **Time exposed to the trauma:** As the time of exposure to a traumatic event lengthens, kids tend to experience greater emotional distress. Thus, a child who is repeatedly abused over time is likely to be more affected than one who experiences abuse in a single event.

✔ **Beliefs about the trauma:** Children's beliefs or perceptions about how threatening a trauma is makes almost as much difference as the objective nature of the trauma itself. Also, kids' beliefs about the trauma are greatly influenced by their caregivers' beliefs about or perceptions of the trauma.

✔ **Extent of injury to the child:** When trauma results in significant pain and/or injuries, the impact is increased. In addition, children who are either scarred or disabled from their trauma are likely to have more trouble coping than kids exposed to traumas that don't have lasting physical effects.

✔ **Extent of injury to others close to the child:** Children can be hurt emotionally almost as much by injuries that occur to their parents, siblings, and loved ones as they are by injuries to themselves.

Resilience

It's important to note that children cope unexpectedly well with traumatic events with surprising frequency. *Resilience* refers to the ability to adopt and function effectively in spite of adverse circumstance such as trauma, serious handicaps, and challenges. Studies have found that both kids and adults demonstrate resilience more often than experts used to think. Sometimes, kids get through horrific events and manage to prosper, have good relationships, and achieve success.

Some of the major factors thought to contribute to resilience include

✔ **Family support:** The support that kids receive from their families following a trauma makes a big difference in how they cope later. Children whose parents are emotionally unavailable or depressed don't do as well as those whose parents can provide emotional support and caring.

✔ **Support from community and extended family:** Not all support must come from a child's parents. Sometimes, a concerned neighbor, pastor, big brother or sister, grandparent, aunt, uncle, or teacher can reach out and help kids in surprisingly effective ways. In addition, school counselors and mental-health providers can play an important positive role.

✔ **Child factors:** In general, younger children are more gravely affected by traumatic events than older kids, but extremely young kids (those younger than 2 years old) may not perceive the meaning of trauma, although they may still be affected by it. In some cases, if their basic care is not interrupted, they may not experience a large negative effect. Kids' mental health before the experience of trauma also affects how they will respond. Kids who have a history of traumas are likely to struggle more than those who have no such history. Finally, it is generally thought that genes likely contribute to determining how well any given child reacts to traumatic events.

Immediate responses to trauma

Children who experience traumatic events often show signs and symptoms immediately after. These symptoms may go away within a month or two, or they may become chronic, depending on the child's resiliency and the nature of the trauma. The following indicators are common following traumatic events but may resolve:

- ✔ Problems sleeping
- ✔ Changes in appetite
- ✔ Clinging
- ✔ Immature behavior for the child's age
- ✔ Increased irritability
- ✔ Anxiety upon separation from caregiver
- ✔ Temper tantrums
- ✔ Increased fears
- ✔ Problems in school
- ✔ Withdrawal
- ✔ Fatigue

If such symptoms are not too severe, you can often provide support, love, and attention while keeping close tabs on a recently traumatized child. Given a couple of months to adjust, the child may regain her former high level of functioning without further intervention. If symptoms continue or substantially interfere with the child's life, professional help should be sought.

Post-traumatic stress disorder

Post-traumatic stress disorder (PTSD) occurs in some kids when they have been exposed to a severe stressor and, for various reasons, their reactions to the stress fail to resolve within a month or so. The stressor can happen to the child or to a close relative or friend. The child's initial response includes extreme fear about actual or threatened death, sexual abuse, or serious injury. Kids may be extremely stirred up and agitated. In addition, they are likely to have memories, flashbacks, and very upsetting dreams and/or imagery and thoughts about the event. They may react with repetitive play involving themes of the event, and they get quite upset when they're reminded of the event.

Furthermore, kids with PTSD try to stay away from reminders of the event, such as people, places, or things associated with it. They may have trouble remembering what happened. They may blame themselves or others even when the trauma was unavoidable. They often feel separate from other people and seem to lose interest in usual activities. They also seem to be unhappy and express pessimism.

Kids with PTSD often have trouble sleeping. They can be self-destructive and jumpy. Finally, they frequently scan their worlds for signs of possible danger. Thus, they have trouble concentrating and focusing on tasks.

When a child shows significant signs of PTSD, treatment should be sought. This condition is treatable but can become chronic if not dealt with.

Reactive attachment disorders

Babies are prewired to form attachments with their primary caregivers. Sometimes, attachment — the process of learning to love and trust — is largely unsuccessful due to persistent neglect, abuse, or repeated changes in caregivers (such as what often occurs to children in foster care). When babies or very young children do not have opportunities to develop attachments (see Chapter 3), later adjustment can be negatively affected, sometimes severely.

Children who do not develop normal attachments to caregivers can develop reactive attachment disorder (RAD). RAD is quite uncommon but profoundly problematic because it prevents kids from forming normal relationships with other kids and adults.

RAD comes in two types:

- ✔ **Inhibited:** Children with this type of RAD do not seek comfort from others when distressed and are not comforted when others attempt to provide it. These kids seem to be disinterested and disengaged from other people. They can appear to be irritable, sad, or afraid without clear reasons.

- ✔ **Disinhibited:** Children with this type of RAD will approach almost anyone indiscriminately. They may seem to be *too* friendly, willing to sit in a stranger's lap or go with anyone anywhere any time. They fail to understand usual boundaries.

The next edition of the *Diagnostic and Statistical Manual of Mental Disorders* will likely divide RAD into two separate diagnoses: Reactive Attachment Disorder of Infancy or Early Childhood, which parallels the current category of inhibited RAD, and Disinhibited Social Engagement Disorder, which is analogous to disinhibited RAD.

Dissociative disorders

Dissociative disorders involve disruptions in usual consciousness, identity, memory, and sense of connectedness to the world. These disorders are usually thought to occur as a result of repeated exposures to traumatic or abusive events. Dissociative disorders can be a bit tricky to diagnose in young children, because they are not easily distinguished from other problems such as inattention, learning disorders, being oppositional, and memory gaps that would be expected at certain ages.

Children with dissociative amnesia, for example, may demonstrate striking gaps in memory that go beyond typical childhood forgetfulness. Furthermore, a few adolescents may at times demonstrate dissociative problems with identity, such as presenting with two or more clear-cut personalities, with the different personalities seemingly taking charge of the teenager's behavior at various times. Finally, a small number of adolescents demonstrate problems with dissociative depersonalization, in which they have persistent problems with feelings of detachment, as though they were observing themselves outside their bodies or feeling like they are living within a dream state.

The effects of certain drugs can mimic the symptoms of dissociative disorders. If a child exhibits signs of dissociation, you should look into whether substances are causing the problem. Professional help is likely called for.

Part V

Getting the Right Therapies

"How can you not feel confident? You're wearing Versace sunglasses, a Tommy Hilfiger sweater, Calvin Klein jeans, and Michael Jordan gym shoes. Now go on out there and just be yourself."

In this part . . .

We look at how to get help for children when normal development is interrupted. Kids should get care from well-trained professionals as soon as trouble is spotted. It's also important to be sure to ask for effective treatments backed by research. We describe the types of professionals who offer treatment and some of the strategies that they use.

Helping kids with problems works best when the members of the treatment team work together. We describe ways that schools identify kids with special needs. Then we show how parents can support the efforts of professionals to help their precious children.

Chapter 17

Types of Therapy That Work

Lots of kids grow up uneventfully, without major physical, psychological, or learning problems. In Part II of this book, we lay out what normal development looks like. Kids are different and grow at different rates, so there are many variations of normal. Some children, however, don't meet developmental milestones on time; have troubling learning or paying attention; or experience emotional problems. Throughout Part IV, we discuss the early signs, symptoms, and causes of these difficulties. In Part V we discuss the ways professionals, parents, and teachers can help children overcome or meet their challenges.

In this chapter, we turn to treating problems, whether mild or severe. When a child has a problem, parents, relatives, and teachers want to help. Fortunately, an array of effective options can help children manage or sometimes overcome their difficulties. Unfortunately, some "solutions" for helping kids are based on hype, not hope. Buyer, beware. We provide you a guide to treatments that work and a few that don't.

When someone promises a quick, spectacular fix for a childhood problem, it's pretty unlikely to work. Helping children takes time and effort. No pills, books, computer programs, diets, or CDs have been shown to be totally effective in treating childhood disorders, but plenty of marketers stand ready to sell you those so-called cures.

Getting Help: The Earlier, the Better

Before we discuss the specific types of intervention and therapies that work for children, we want to make a very strong pitch for early intervention. Years and years ago (and sometimes even now), professionals involved with babies and young children were quite cautious about diagnosing or labeling a child with a possible disability. Many took a wait-and-see approach, telling parents not to worry. That's pretty understandable, because babies and young children have their own individual timetables for development, and lots of kids who start slow eventually catch up.

That wait-and-see approach has a huge problem, however. Over at least the past 50 years, evidence tells us that *early* treatment of developmental issues — including motor problems, speech and language problems, emotional problems, and learning problems — not only helps young children in the short run, but also has long-lasting benefits. These benefits include reduced need for special-education placement, less risk of dropping out of school, improved physical functioning, higher levels of academic achievement, and improved overall emotional and behavioral functioning. The cost of early intervention is quite cheap compared to the long-term costs of untreated disabilities.

Early intervention doesn't require a child to have a specific diagnosis, which is why the rather general term *developmental delay* is often used to describe a wide variety of potential problems (see Chapter 12). Early intervention often targets specific problems such as delays in motor skills or speech as opposed to waiting until the development of a fully diagnosable condition. Early-intervention programs are often based in a child's home and generally include the child's caregivers as well as a team of professional care providers. These professionals come from a variety of fields, including

- ✔ Physical therapy
- ✔ Occupational therapy
- ✔ Speech therapy
- ✔ Psychology
- ✔ Medicine
- ✔ Education
- ✔ Social work

When parents have any concerns about the development of their children, they should first check with their primary medical care providers. These providers or their staff almost always know the local agencies that provide assessment and treatment for kids. Multiple providers collaborate and coordinate the care they give kids with various developmental delays and problems. The following sections review how each of these fields brings important strategies and therapies to bear on helping kids of all ages.

Understanding Types of Treatment

Getting the right treatment for a child with a problem can seem overwhelming to parents. In the next sections, we talk about specific professionals and their roles in helping kids. But first here are three guidelines for parents to consider:

- ✔ **Prior to getting therapy, make sure your child gets an assessment to identify specific problems.** The assessment can provide information about how the child is functioning and be used again to measure progress after treatment has started.

- ✔ **Understand that the therapies for kids should address symptoms.** For example, a girl who has trouble expressing herself in words likely requires a speech therapist. A boy who has trouble walking can probably benefit from physical therapy.

- ✔ **Verify that your child and the therapist have a good working relationship.** The relationship between kids and therapists must be good in order for progress to be made. Professionals who choose to work with children are usually well liked by the kids they work with. If your child doesn't like the therapist (or if you don't like the therapist), then be sure to talk this over and see whether it can be resolved.

Improving everyday functioning: Physical and occupational therapy

Problems with development or learning often show up early in the form of delays in motor development. These delays may involve difficulties with fine or gross motor skills, as follows:

- ✔ **Fine motor:** Involves small movements, such as grabbing, grasping, moving the lips, or holding a pencil.

- ✔ **Gross motor:** Requires big movements, such as crawling, walking, running, or jumping.

Motor problems are common in kids who are born prematurely and those who are later diagnosed with learning problems. In addition, kids with genetic disorders, birth defects, or prenatal exposure to toxins are more likely to have difficulty in fine or gross motor development. Kids with autism-spectrum disorders can also be delayed in motor skills. Motor problems can be present in kids who have experienced brain injuries, severe illnesses, injuries, or even abuse. Many times, the exact cause of motor problems can't be determined; sometimes, the child seems to be just slightly uncoordinated or clumsy. Nevertheless, professional help can be beneficial.

Physical therapists (PTs) and occupational therapists (OTs) are professionals who help children who have problems in the areas of motor development and motor skills. PTs and OTs work with children of all ages, providing services in early-intervention programs, at schools, at health clinics, and at hospitals. Although many times, their services seem to be confusingly similar, OTs and PTs have a slightly different emphasis:

- ✔ **Physical therapists** help children with motor problems or injuries perform as well as possible. Therapy involves increasing strength, endurance, balance, and flexibility. PTs promote improving movement and reducing pain, and look at preventing future physical problems. Their services may involve physical activities as well as technology and equipment (such as wheelchairs, walkers, or ultrasound or electrical stimulation to improve circulation).

- ✔ **Occupational therapists** are more concerned with how children function or navigate in their environments as opposed to improving motor skills per se. They help kids with disabilities learn to adapt and compensate rather than change their situation. OTs may help children learn to use equipment such as computers to help them communicate. They can also help classroom teachers adapt their instruction or classroom to promote learning. They may use many of the same strategies as PTs, but they focus on how to help children function better with limitations.

OTs and PTs both help children maximize their abilities to engage in developmentally appropriate tasks, such as learning, communicating, eating, toileting, dressing, and playing. A PT, for example, might work with a child who has stiff muscles due to cerebral palsy stretch and loosen the muscles. An OT might help the same child learn to use a specially designed pencil for writing.

Infant massage therapy

Infant massage involves gentle stroking and rubbing of babies' bodies. It has been part of child care in traditional cultures. Most mammals massage their young by grooming and licking them. What has been natural for living creatures over many centuries is now being studied by human scientists. In many published studies, infant massage has been found to benefit babies. Healthy babies who are given regular massages are less irritable, sleep better, and grow faster than babies who don't receive regular massages.

The effect of massage on premature babies has been an area of much research interest.

Premature babies' temperatures rise during massage. Babies who are given massage also gain weight faster and have better bone density and improved overall development. Infant massage has become a regular part of treatment in most neonatal intensive care units.

Parents or caregivers don't need to be licensed massage therapists to practice infant massage; neither do babies need to be taken to an expensive spa. Babies love being touched. You can get oil or lotion (designed for sensitive baby skin) and rub away. Like adults, babies enjoy a bit of pressure, and most love having their backs rubbed.

Teaching communication: Speech-language therapy

Children learn to communicate with others quite early. From the serious gaze of the newborn to the first word, language and communication skills develop quickly throughout childhood. Some kids have problems in this area, however. Speech and language therapists are professionals who help children improve the following skills:

- **Eating and swallowing:** Kids may have trouble chewing or swallowing. The therapist uses different exercises to improve muscle tone around the mouth.

- **Articulation:** These children have trouble pronouncing certain sounds or words. Therapy includes practice and modeling of correct sounds.

- **Fluency:** Problems in this area may include stuttering or stopping the flow of language with pauses or filler sounds such as "uh" or "er." Stuttering can be a complex disorder that requires individual diagnosis and treatment planning. A speech and language therapist (with support from family members) can help a child improve or eliminate this problem.

- **Vocal:** Problems with the voice can include quality (such as being too nasal), volume (too loud or too soft), and pitch. After ruling out a medical cause such as allergies, a hearing problem, or other physical problems, the therapist uses practice, modeling, and positive reinforcement to help a child with vocal difficulties.

- **Expressive language:** Problems with expressive language include difficulty forming sentences, using correct grammar, having trouble remembering words, using pronouns, or using vocabulary. Therapy for expressive-language problems includes exposure to appropriate language, as well as opportunities for practice.

- **Receptive language:** Kids with receptive-language problems may have difficulty understanding what is being said (their hearing is fine) or be unable to follow oral directions. Therapists help children with receptive-language problems develop listening skills through practice and direct instruction.

Disorders or delays in language can interfere with almost all areas of life. If a child can't be understood by others, relationships will be difficult, or if a child can't pronounce sounds, learning to read will be very challenging. Furthermore, kids with language problems can become anxious or depressed or may develop behavioral problems as a result of their problems with communication.

Speech therapists work with small groups of children or with a single child. Sometimes, they work within a classroom; at other times, they work in an office. They help children practice skills to improve their abilities to communicate with others. As with other therapies, if a child has some problems in these areas, early intervention works best.

Using psychological strategies to help kids

Psychological strategies are delivered by a range of professionals. These services may be delivered in a private office, at school, or at home. They may come in the form of individual therapy, family therapy, or school-based approaches. The following sections discuss the types of professionals who deliver these services and review effective psychological treatments.

Meeting the pros

Professionals in the fields of mental health and education are particularly likely to employ psychological strategies for helping kids. These professionals have various titles and educational backgrounds, and sometimes parents, teachers, and child-care providers aren't sure who's who in these fields. To clarify the situation, we list some of the most common professionals you're likely to encounter:

- **Clinical psychologists:** Clinical psychologists generally must have a doctoral degree (PhD) in psychology. This degree generally requires a minimum of four years of graduate-level education. Psychologists also complete a yearlong internship in clinical psychology. Many clinical psychologists are especially well trained in the area of assessing emotional and behavioral disorders, and some specialize exclusively in such assessments.

  If a child you care about has received a diagnosis, and you have any concerns about whether that diagnosis is correct, you may very well want to see a psychologist who specializes in the assessment of children (which will likely include psychological testing). Incorrect diagnoses can lead to inappropriate interventions.

- **School psychologists:** School psychologists typically have a master's degree, which usually requires a minimum of two to three years of graduate education. Some school psychologists have a PhD in either clinical or school psychology. School psychologists are usually well trained in child assessment, psychological testing, and psychological interventions. They understand learning disabilities as well as emotional and behavioral problems that commonly affect kids. They are often a great resource for kids who are experiencing problems in school for whatever reason.

- **Counselors:** Counselors usually have a master's degree, which also requires a minimum of two to three years of graduate education. Counselors are trained to treat emotional and behavioral problems but typically don't have advanced training in psychological testing, which is often of great value in diagnosing complex issues.

✔ **Psychiatrists:** Psychiatrists first obtain their medical degree and then usually participate in a four-year residency program that trains them in the diagnosis and treatment of emotional and behavioral problems. Most psychiatrists specialize in the medical and biological treatment of emotional and behavioral problems. Some also have training in psychological intervention, but you have to ask. Only a small number are trained in psychological testing.

✔ **Social workers:** The majority of social workers have a master's degree in social work, which requires a minimum of two to three years of graduate education. A few have a doctoral degree in social work (DSW). Social workers sometimes take the role of case managers for children who require services from a variety of professionals and social agencies. Some of them are also trained in diagnosing and assessing emotional and behavioral problems in kids. Social workers don't have training in psychological testing.

✔ **Special-education teachers:** These professionals generally possess a bachelor's degree in special education. Many of them also have additional graduate training and/or a master's degree. They can carry out individualized educational plans (see Chapter 18) to help kids overcome learning difficulties as well as manage their emotions and behaviors.

✔ **Behavior management specialists and behavior analysts:** Qualifications for this title vary considerably across settings and states. Most behavior management specialists have at least a BA degree in psychology or a related field and additional specialized training in the nuts and bolts of certain types of behavior therapy programs (see next section). Typically, they aren't trained in the diagnosis of emotional and behavioral problems, but they can be very useful in providing critical assistance at school or at home in setting up or carrying out behavior management plans. Some people go through a credentialing program and become Board Certified Behavior Analysts (BCBAs). The BCBA designation indicates they have received this level of additional training in behavioral analysis.

Clinical psychologists, counselors, psychiatrists, and social workers may specialize in the treatment of children or may provide services only to adults. You have to ask. School psychologists, special-education teachers, and most behavior management specialists typically specialize in working with children.

For referrals to mental-health professionals, consider talking to your primary health-care provider or contacting the psychology department of a local university or college, the psychiatry department of a local medical school, or state associations for mental-health professionals. (Just search online for the name of your state and the profession you're interested in, along with the phrase "state association.")

No matter what type of professional you choose, be sure that you feel comfortable in communicating with that person. Your child also needs to feel respected and valued by the therapist.

When consulting professionals to provide a child psychological help, we recommend that you ask about *evidence-based treatment* — interventions supported by scientific studies. If you select treatments without sound evidence to back them up, you run a substantial risk of wasting a great deal of time and money. Currently, most evidence-based treatment is known as behavior therapy or cognitive behavior therapy, as explained in the next two sections.

Discussing behavior therapy:

Behavior therapy (BT) often encompasses a variety of strategies, all of which are based on scientifically validated approaches designed to change behavior. You may see the terms *behavior therapy, behavior modification, behavioral activation,* and *applied behavioral analysis* used almost interchangeably. These therapies incorporate essential principles about how kids learn. In other words, these therapies operate on the assumption that kids do what they do in large part because of

- What they observe other kids and people doing (known as *observational learning* or *modeling*)
- Associations they've made between events that cause them to have reflexive emotional responses to events *(classical conditioning)*
- Consequences that influence their behavior to increase or decrease in the future *(operant conditioning)*

See Chapter 2 and Chapter 8 for more information about these learning principles and how they work.

Considering cognitive behavior therapy

Therapies known as *cognitive behavior therapy (CBT)* and *cognitive therapy (CT)* are compatible with the learning principles that undergird the various subtypes of behavior therapies. However, to a greater degree, cognitive therapy and cognitive behavior therapy emphasize strategies designed to alter how kids perceive or interpret events in their world by their thinking processes. Thus, these therapies attempt to address the distorted ways in which kids perceive themselves, their worlds, or their futures. These thoughts or perceptions are overly negative, which then causes emotional difficulty. A depressed teenager, for example, may mistakenly believe that she's an inherently inferior person whom others don't and couldn't like. A CBT or CT therapist would try to help her see that she has both strengths and weaknesses and that any social problems she is having could be improved.

Cognitive behavior therapy and cognitive therapy are administered in the form of individual psychotherapy, whereas BT for kids generally involve manipulation of the environment by parents, teachers, and others in ways that will help bring about changes in behavior. Both behavior therapies and cognitive behavior therapies have been applied successfully to a wide range of problems, as illustrated in the sections that follow. Behavior therapy tends to be the treatment of choice for most kids up to the age of 10 or 12, after which either cognitive behavior therapy or cognitive therapy may be equally useful.

Interpersonal psychotherapy (IPT) has also shown potential for helping kids with depression, and studies have demonstrated that multisystem therapy appears to be effective for conduct problems. At this time, IPT and multi-system therapy have only been used to treat a limited range of problems. Therefore, we discuss these approaches, under the later section "Seeing What Works for What Problems."

Looking at medication

Psychotropic medications are used to treat the symptoms of mental illness. Unlike antibiotics, which cure infections, psychotropic medications, when they work, improve symptoms so that someone suffering from a disorder is less distressed. Medications target specific chemicals in the brain and either increase their availability or suppress them.

All this sounds pretty straightforward. Unfortunately, every brain is different. Some people are helped by one type of medication, and for others, the same medication has no effect. Also, there's no easy way to predict who will ben-efit from what drug, so there tends to be lots of experimentation to find the right treatment. Furthermore, children and adolescents may have completely different responses to medications than adults do. Finally, long-term effects of medication on the growing body and brain are just not that well known. Those are some pretty good reasons why prescribers of psychotropic medi-cations need to be well trained and good at solving problems.

The purpose of this section is *not* to provide the latest stats and research about new drugs or new uses for drugs, or to tell you how to pick the right medication for a particular child's specific problem. Instead, we want to give you some guidelines on who prescribes psychotropic medication and what questions to consider when making a decision about medication. Drugs are being developed and evaluated for effectiveness every day, so if you want to learn more about a particular drug, we encourage you to go to the U.S. Food and Drug Administration Web site (www.fda.gov) for current information.

Previewing the prescribers

Medications can be prescribed by many professionals. Most of those profes-sionals are competent and comfortable in treating a wide variety of disor-ders. When seeking consultation about medication, feel free to ask about the provider's background and training in mental health. The provider should be able to answer questions about the effectiveness of medication as well as other options for treatment. The following professionals are the ones most likely to write prescriptions for children:

- **Primary-care providers:** These providers include physicians, physician assistants, advance practice nurses, or nurse practitioners. Most prescriptions are written by primary-care providers.

- **Psychiatrists:** These folks are physicians who have received additional training in the diagnosis and treatment of emotional and mental disorders (see "Meeting the pros," earlier in this chapter). Primary-care providers often refer complicated or difficult cases to these specialists.

- **Psychologists:** A few states allow psychologists to prescribe medications after additional training. Psychologists (see "Meeting the pros," earlier in this chapter) have training in the diagnosis and treatment of emotional or mental disorders. Psychologists who don't prescribe may be consulted for a comprehensive assessment of a child or adolescent.

Exploring concerns about medication and kids

In this section, we introduce some of the worries, concerns, and controversies that are being discussed by parents, teachers, and child-care providers, as well as those who prescribe drugs to children and the scientists who are looking at the pros and cons of prescribing for kids.

The ten years that began in 1990 were called the Decade of the Brain in a presidential proclamation by President George H. W. Bush. This hopeful proclamation was based on the stunning developments in research about how the brain works in healthy people as well as in people with mental or physical illness. Optimists believed that science was close to figuring out how the mixture of chemicals in the brain could be changed to combat depression, anxiety, and other disorders. A huge amount of information has been accumulated during the past two decades, but not enough to explain how or why certain medications work for certain populations and types of problems.

Research on the long-term effects of medications on the developing brains of children continues to be sparse. Yet prescription pads fill with orders for designer antidepressants, stimulants, atypical antipsychotics, mood stabilizers, and even sleeping pills for kids from preschool to college age. Unfortunately, many children are prescribed powerful medications without comprehensive psychological assessments. In other words, all too often, kids are being given medications without really knowing what's wrong with them. It's as though you went to your doctor and said, "I don't feel good," and the doctor wrote out a prescription for a drug without doing a physical exam or running any tests. For adults, this experimental approach is often harmless. When adults get medication that doesn't relieve their symptoms, they can go back to their doctors and discuss how they feel. When children are given medications that don't work, they're less able to describe their experiences.

So why do kids end up on medications without proper diagnosis? One reason is the lack of highly trained mental health professionals — in particular, child psychiatrists and psychologists who often work in isolation from other professionals involved with children's care. Furthermore, when professionals are available, they often have insufficient time to provide the comprehensive diagnostic and treatment that children and adolescents need. We suspect that another reason is due to the view that mental health problems are diseases (or chemical imbalances) that can be fixed with medication.

We strongly recommend that before children are prescribed medication for any type of emotional or behavioral problem, they have a comprehensive evaluation by mental health professionals who specialize in the assessment and treatment of children and adolescents.

The following example illustrates how a child can be misdiagnosed and then prescribed medication when other forms of treatment or intervention could be more effective.

> **Alana** can't wait for sixth grade to start. She recently moved with her family to a new city, and she hasn't met any neighborhood kids yet. She finds her classroom and smiles at the faces as she makes her way to an empty seat. She's wearing a shirt with her favorite band splashed all over it. She looks around at the kids and notices that a couple of girls are pointing at her. She returns their glance, and they start giggling and pointing. Soon, other kids are talking about her. She realizes too late that her shirt displays a band that's no longer popular in her new town. Alana, the new kid in school, becomes the victim of cruel teasing. Not all the kids in her class participate, but those who don't stay away from her.

> After a few weeks of being rejected, Alana dreads going to school. Her parents notice that she seems to be down and depressed. She withdraws, loses her appetite, and has difficulty sleeping. When her parents discuss their concerns, Alana tells them that nothing is wrong; she just doesn't feel like doing anything. After a few months, Alana's doctor diagnoses her with depression and treats her with medication.

Alana is certainly sad; she's also quite anxious. But will medication relieve her sadness and anxiety? Unlikely. Alana is getting bullied at school. Her reaction is *normal,* not a disorder or disease. If Alana were cheerful in these circumstances, that would be abnormal. Understandably, her parents and doctor are concerned and want to help her, but they don't know all the details. In her case, counseling would have been a better first step. She might have been able to talk to a counselor about the reasons for her sadness. Appropriate interventions at school would make more sense than medication for a normal human reaction to bullying.

Here's another example to help you understand how kids can end up with the wrong treatment. In this case, the child has already been diagnosed as having a learning disability, but more is going on.

> **Lucas** receives extra help in his fourth-grade class because of a learning disability. His special-education teacher works with him in a small group for reading and writing for a couple of hours a day. Despite lots of support from the school and at home, he has trouble completing schoolwork during the time he spends in his regular classroom. He's quiet and well behaved, and his teachers report that he tries; he just can't seem to keep up with the work. A conference is held at school, and the recommendation is to increase the amount of time Lucas spends in special education.

> At Lucas's next physical exam, his mother discusses her concerns about her son's lack of progress in school with the pediatrician. The physician evaluates Lucas and has his mother, father, and teachers fill out questionnaires about Lucas. After carefully reviewing the information and discovering a family history of attention problems, his doctor makes a diagnosis of attention deficit disorder (ADD). (See Chapter 12 for information about ADD and ADHD.) The doctor explains that Lucas isn't hyperactive, but inattentive.

> A trial of medication starts, and Lucas seems to be a different child. The doctor also refers Lucas to a child psychologist who works with his teachers on implementing some behavioral strategies to help with his ADD. He is able to stay focused in school and complete his work. His progress is amazing, according to his teachers and his family.

Although some children get medication when other options are more appropriate, other kids don't get medication when that choice is appropriate. Unaddressed attention problems can contribute to poor school achievement. Both examples illustrate the need for careful diagnosis.

Making medication decisions

The decision to give children medication that affects their moods, behaviors, and brain functions is a serious decision that should be made with great deliberation. Parents and caregivers need to be aware of the risks and benefits of various treatments before giving their consent. They should be able to openly discuss their worries and concerns with a health-care provider. The following questions and issues should be considered when making a choice:

- ✔ **Health:** A thorough physical should be part of a diagnostic evaluation. It's possible that underlying health concerns are affecting mood or behavior. Are there other health issues that might interfere with treatment?

- ✔ **Effectiveness:** You need to know whether the medication has been studied on populations of children or adolescents. How effective has the medication been found to be? Are there other methods of treatment that might have similar or better effects?

✔ **Interactions:** Are there any medications that should be avoided when taking this medication? How about foods that might cause problems?

✔ **Side effects:** What are the side effects of the medication? Do side effects go away over time? What are the remedies for side effects that linger? How will side effects interfere with daily life? Are there increased risks associated with the medication?

✔ **Long-term effects:** Have there been studies on the long term effects of the medication? What happens if or when the medication is discontinued? Are there problems with relapse?

✔ **Follow-up:** If medication is agreed to, what kind of follow up appointments will be provided? Are there regularly scheduled follow-ups to check on progress?

✔ **Collaboration:** How will the treatment be coordinated? Kids with emotional or behavioral problems often have difficulty at school as well as at home. Will there be opportunities for communication? Are other forms of treatment such as psychotherapy indicated?

✔ **Cost:** What are the costs of treatment? Will they be covered by insurance?

✔ **Options:** If medication does not work or is not indicated, what other treatment options are available?

There are no right or wrong answers to the previous questions. Some families after consulting their medical providers will decide that medication is not an option or at least not at the top of the list. Others will decide that medication is an appropriate treatment. The answers to these questions can change over time. The important message for parents, caregivers, and for children (when developmentally appropriate) is to be informed and communicate with health-care providers.

Seeing What Works for What Problems

Part IV provides an overview of the wide range of problems that today's children all too often must face. Whether a child is dealing with developmental delays, learning problems, emotional issues, autism, or behavioral problems, a wide array of interventions are available to help. This section gives you an overview of what such interventions look like and how they work.

Motivational problems sometimes occur by themselves but frequently accompany one or more of the problems that we discuss later in this chapter. Kids with depression often lack the motivation they need to do well in school, for example, and kids with conduct problems typically don't seem to care about making changes.

Motivating kids

Most kids with motivational problems don't pay attention to their teachers; they don't do their homework and show little interest in persevering on tasks. All such cases should be evaluated for the possibility of learning disabilities, ADD, or slow learning. (See Chapter 12 for more information about these childhood problems.)

Sometimes, altering a child's educational plan to address the learning problems and/or intellectual disabilities will improve motivation. Kids with low motivation also need to be assessed for the possibility of behavioral disorders, emotional disorders, autism, and/or trauma (see Chapters 13, 14, 15, and 16 for more information). BT and CBT can also be employed for those issues, and motivation improves as a result.

In some cases, however, poor motivation stands out either as the sole issue or as something in need of attention in addition to other problems a child may have. In these cases, BT has been shown to be quite effective. A behavior therapist or a teacher can design a plan that includes giving unmotivated kids rewards (or reinforcements) for completing assignments and staying on tasks while making sure that the kids don't receive attention and reinforcement for going off task. Although most good behavioral programs emphasize positive rewards, sometimes they're structured so that kids will lose something they value (rewards) if they fail to engage in the desired behaviors.

Good behavior therapists are aware that what's rewarding for one child may not be to another and that some events most adults would find unpleasant might actually be rewarding to some kids. Thus, some kids actually respond to disapproval and admonishments by increasing their problematic, off-task behavior. Careful monitoring of any behavioral program put in place can determine whether any such unintended effects are occurring so that adjustments can be made.

Attending to autism

Autism (see Chapter 13) is a neurodevelopmental problem in children that affects the way kids relate to other children, the nature of their play, the way they communicate with other people, and a host of other problematic behaviors. Autism often restricts the ability of such children to cope and function independently, although those with very mild symptoms may function quite successfully. Because most children with autism suffer profoundly in terms of their relationships and ability to function, professionals have worked hard to develop treatments for this problem.

Behavior therapy for autism

Dr. Ole Ivar Lovaas was a pioneer in developing strategies designed to ame-liorate the symptoms of autism. He took a behavioral approach described as applied behavioral analysis. His program emphasized early intervention, with most kids receiving it being between the ages of 3 and 8, although older kids were shown to benefit as well. A few of the strategies employed in most applied behavioral analysis programs for autism include

- Redirection of the child to interrupt and reduce repetitive behaviors as well as self-stimulation
- Positive reinforcement of carefully defined, specific behaviors
- Carefully shaping behaviors by rewarding small steps in the right direction
- Modeling of desired behaviors
- Prompts to encourage appropriate behaviors

These strategies are aimed at increasing positive behaviors and decreas-ing problematic behaviors. These behaviors are selected as the ones most important for a child to have to function effectively in school and in life. Common behaviors targeted for treatment include

- Social skills
- Decreased repetitive behaviors and self-stimulation (**Note:** Early approaches used some unpleasant aversive strategies for reducing these problematic behaviors but have been abandoned in favor of other techniques.)
- Imitation skills
- Academic skills
- Verbal and communication skills
- Play skills
- Ability to follow directions

Behavior therapy for autism generally is intensive and may require up to 35 or 40 hours per week. Usually, parents and teachers are taught how to apply these strategies in the child's home and school. Applied behavioral analysis appears to work on a long-term, enduring basis. Most kids show considerable improve-ment in functioning, reduced need for special education, and decreased inap-propriate behavior. A significant minority of kids treated with this approach become virtually indistinguishable from kids without an autism diagnosis.

Other therapies for autism

Other psychosocial and educational interventions for autism have been devel-oped and look as though they may have significant potential. Most of these programs at least appear to have some behaviorally based components.

These interventions haven't received as much research support as approaches based on applied behavioral analysis, but that doesn't mean they won't eventually do so.

An incredibly wide range of so-called alternative therapies (approaches that don't fall under conventional professional or medical practice and may lack scientific basis) for autism including various supplements, dietary regimens, and facilitated communication, among others are available. At this time, research support for their efficacy is lacking. Perhaps in time, research will provide that support, although in the case of facilitated communication, the approach has been denounced by several professional organizations as invalid. In the meantime, the consumer needs to be cautious and careful before spending lots of time and/or money on these strategies.

The Combating Autism Act Initiative supports training and research on behavioral and biological interventions for autism. Go to www.aucd.org to stay up on the latest developments.

Addressing Attention Deficit/Hyperactivity Disorder

Attention deficit/hyperactivity disorder (ADHD or ADD) is one of the most common childhood disorders. (See Chapter 12 for more information about ADD and ADHD.) Kids who have ADHD often struggle in school, at home, and with relationships. The disorder is chronic. Behavior therapy and medication have been found to help children and adolescents with ADHD.

Behavior therapy for ADHD

Behavior modification is used in school settings to help kids complete assignments, stay focused, and increase motivation. Parents are trained to understand the challenges of ADHD and improve their own use of behavioral principles to help kids with ADHD. Kids can also benefit from behavior therapy to help them cope with problems of impulsivity, inattention, and hyperactivity. Here's an example of how the principles of behavior modification can work for a girl with ADHD:

> **Charlotte** has ADHD. She is disorganized and forgetful, and has trouble staying focused. Every morning, her mother begs her to get ready for school. She forgets where she put her homework and can't find her shoes. By the time she's supposed to be ready for the bus, she and her mother are angry and irritable. A psychologist discusses these problems and helps Charlotte and her mother make a plan to improve their daily start. Together, they develop a structured checklist with all the activities Charlotte needs to complete to get ready for school. When she completes each task, her mother puts a check next to the item. This helps Charlotte stay focused on what she needs to do. When Charlotte is able

to complete all the items in a morning without her mother reminding her, she can earn a reward. Charlotte needed the structure of the list to help her overcome her natural distractibility. This helped her and her mother start their days without arguments, and Charlotte enjoyed the reward of completing her tasks.

Medication for ADHD

Stimulant medication (think of a cup of heavily caffeinated coffee) improves attention. The most common stimulants are amphetamines and methylphenidates. Stimulants can be used to help children and adolescents with ADHD and are usually quite effective. Most kids have few side effects that can be managed with proper dosing. There are concerns, however, about side effects such as decreased appetite and problems sleeping. Some kids experience moodiness. Stimulants, especially when abused, are addictive, and withdrawal symptoms include trouble sleeping and fatigue. Due to concerns about side effects, other options, such as antidepressants, are also used to treat ADHD. The downside to medications for ADHD include the issue of side effects, the fact that many kids don't benefit from them, and questionable long-term effectiveness. Thus, we usually recommend that behavior therapy be tried first.

Defeating depression

Depression is relatively uncommon in young children and increases significantly in adolescence. (See Chapter 14 for a detailed review of what depression looks like in children.) Depression greatly impairs the quality and overall satisfaction of kids' lives and warrants treatment when it appears. Parents and teachers shouldn't ignore significant episodes of sadness, withdrawal, and avoidance in kids and teens. Fortunately, treatment for depression usually works.

Treating depression with therapy

Cognitive behavior therapy (CBT) for depressed kids usually includes a component known as *behavioral activation,* which typically looks for areas that depressed kids have been avoiding due to their depressed moods. Thus, depressed kids and adolescents typically withdraw; avoid friends; drop previously enjoyed activities; and pull back from homework, lessons, and sports. Behavioral activation tracks this avoidance and attempts to slowly but surely get kids moving again. Therapists using this approach collaborate with kids in setting up doable goals. They problem-solve together when obstacles seemingly stand in the way.

CBT also usually attempts to address distorted thinking, which most depressed children and adolescents demonstrate. This treatment component teaches them to collect evidence that might refute their depressed thoughts while helping them look at things more realistically. A depressed child who had been seeing herself as incompetent, for example, would be guided to realize that she actually has superior artistic and musical skills, even though she's struggled in school. CBT has been given with good results in both a group format as well as individually for depressed kids and adolescents.

Interpersonal psychotherapy (IPT) focuses on four major issues that are assumed to lie behind much of what causes kids, adolescents, and adults to become depressed. This therapy is quite structured and teaches clients how to deal with problems involving interpersonal conflict, transitions from one phase of life to another (such as from elementary school to middle school), grief due to various types of losses, and problems with interpersonal skills. The approach has been shown to be quite effective, and some of its components are somewhat similar to certain aspects of CBT.

Giving kids antidepressants

Professionals often prescribe antidepressant medication to treat depressed kids. Studies have typically shown that antidepressant medication is effective.

A wide range of types of such medications is available. A few cautions are in order before giving a child medication for depression:

- ✔ Antidepressant medication has been shown to increase suicidal thinking and actions in children, adolescents, and young adults.
- ✔ As is the case with most medications, we don't know yet what effects antidepressant medications may have on a young, developing brain. The younger the child, the greater the concern.
- ✔ Side effects can be significant, uncomfortable, and troubling in some cases.

Therefore, we usually recommend that CBT or IPT be attempted before starting most kids on antidepressant medications. Furthermore, therapy has the potential to prevent relapse of depression, because the skills learned in therapy last a lifetime. In especially severe cases or if therapy fails or doesn't bring a child far enough along, antidepressant medication may be indicated. If it's prescribed, careful monitoring is strongly recommended.

Bashing bipolar disorder

Bipolar disorder, also known as manic depression (see Chapter 14 for more information), is a serious emotional problem that involves mood swings and (usually) intense periods of anger in children and adolescents. Kids can go from euphoria to despair in a matter of minutes or days.

Treatment for children with bipolar disorder should include family-focused education and psychotherapy that stresses ways to manage this chronic disorder. CBT strategies have been found to be effective for helping kids with bipolar disorder improve their functioning.

Medications are almost always required to help decrease symptoms. Because of the complexity of the symptoms, multiple medications are frequently required. Medication management usually calls for the specialized training of a psychiatrist, because finding the right mix of these medications can be rather tricky. Common medication choices include mood stabilizers, antidepressants, antipsychotics, and sedatives.

The diagnosis of bipolar disorder in children and adolescents has skyrocketed in recent years. Some professionals think that this increase is due to increased awareness of the disorder, but many worry that part of the increase may be caused by inaccurate diagnoses. Kids can be moody, angry, and easily irritable just because they're ornery. Bipolar disorder should be diagnosed only after careful evaluation and assessment that includes ruling out other possibilities. If in doubt, get a second opinion.

Attacking anxiety and trauma

Cognitive behavior therapy has been applied successfully to a wide range of anxiety problems in children. (See Chapters 14 and 16 for information about anxiety disorders and anxiety resulting from trauma or abuse.) In general, most treatments for child or adolescent anxiety include some of the following major components:

- Relaxation training

- Education about the nature of anxiety and how one copes with it

- Gradual, repeated exposure to whatever arouses anxiety in the child

- Learning to think less negatively and/or catastrophically

- Training parents to respond to anxiety in their kids

- Reinforcement for children's attempts to master anxiety

When child anxiety problems involve fears of social situations, children are also often also trained in social skills. They practice these skills and learn how to gradually apply them in social situations. Group therapy can be an especially good format for learning such skills.

When kids' anxiety problems come in the form of obsessive-compulsive disorder (OCD) (see Chapter 14 for more information), a behavioral treatment known as exposure and response prevention is generally given either alone or in conjunction with other CBT strategies. Exposure and response prevention essentially guides a child to expose himself to whatever triggers his OCD behavior and asks him to refrain from engaging in his usual compulsions. Exposure and response prevention are carried out in a graduated fashion, starting with relatively easy triggers to more difficult ones. An adolescent might gravely fear germs and compulsively wash his hands for hours each day. Exposure and response prevention would systematically have him touch feared objects such as doorknobs, dirt, and carpets without washing his hands. The technique is surprisingly effective.

When kids' anxieties stem from trauma in the form of post-traumatic stress disorder (PTSD) (see Chapter 16 for more information), a specific form of CBT known as trauma-focused CBT has shown significant promise. Trauma-focused CBT teaches kids many of the same skills as other CBT treatments for anxiety, but in addition, it instructs kids on how to cope with and process their emotions. Trauma-focused CBT also shows kids how to master situations that remind them of their traumas. In addition, this approach usually involves some sessions conducted jointly with parents and their kids so that they can learn how to talk with one another in a healthy way about what happened to the child.

Interested parents and professionals may want to visit the National Child Trauma Stress Network site at www.nctsnet.org for information about treatment of traumatized children.

Medications are sometimes prescribed for children's anxiety disorders. The antidepressant medications are among the most commonly prescribed, in part because they don't have as much potential for addiction as some medications originally formulated to reduce anxiety (such as alprazolam and diazepam). Such medications can be effective, but we generally recommend them only for especially serious cases of anxiety or when other treatments have failed (refer to "Giving kids antidepressants," earlier in this chapter). Severe cases of OCD are somewhat more likely to require antidepressant medication in addition to exposure and response prevention.

Some antidepressant medications are quite ineffective for OCD, but fluvoxamine, paroxetine, fluoxetine, sertraline, and clomipramine seem to be helpful for especially stubborn cases.

Busting behavior problems

Kids with behavior problems cause havoc in schools, at home, and sometimes in the neighborhoods. (See Chapter 15 for specific information about behavior disorders.) CBT principles are used to treat behavior problems such as oppositional defiant disorders or conduct disorders. CBT strategies to support changes in behavior must be implemented within the greater context of the family, school, and neighborhood.

In other words, kids with behavior problems usually don't improve much with individual therapy by itself, even though many parents try that approach. Family therapy or parent training helps extend and support individual work. In fact, sometimes intervening with the family or parents will be sufficient to extinguish behavior problems without requiring individual therapy for the child. In addition, behavioral strategies are frequently implemented at school to improve compliance with expectations.

Medications for behavior problems have not been found to be effective. Sometimes, however, children or adolescents with behavior problems have underlying problems with attention or mood. In those cases, medication is one possible treatment option.

In the case of more serious conduct problems associated with juvenile delinquency, multisystemic therapy (MST) addresses problems within the family, helps the teen stay away from poor role models, engages the teen in vocational training, promotes healthy recreation, and helps the family access community services. This intensive program usually lasts several months and involves multiple hours of treatment every week. MST, when implemented with all its components, has been found to be quite effective at decreasing serious conduct problems, but treatment takes a considerable amount of financial resources that are often not available.

Seeing psychosis

Kids with psychosis (see Chapter 14) are out of touch with reality. They may be paranoid, believe that they have superpowers, or perceive things that aren't really there. Psychosis is extremely debilitating; fortunately, it's very rare in children. The first signs of schizophrenia, a disease that involves psychosis, usually appear during adolescence, however.

Treatment for psychosis should be comprehensive in scope, including education for the family and the child as well as medication. Medications are usually managed by a psychiatrist. School-age children require specialized day programs.

Cognitive behavioral therapies and strategies can help improve the daily functioning of the child as well as help families cope with the illness. Schizophrenia is chronic, and symptoms tend to wax and wane over a lifetime; therefore, treatment should include planning for future care.

Tackling tics and habits

Lots of kids (and adults) have habits. Some twirl their hair; others tap their fingers or clear their throats. Most of the time, these slight peculiarities are of no particular consequence. When they cause discomfort, distress, or deformity, however, treatment is indicated.

Hair-pulling (trichotillomania) can result in bald patches; skin picking can lead to infections and sores; and tics such as grimaces or throat clearing can lead to self-consciousness or embarrassment. Habit-reversal training is a form of behavior therapy that has been found to be useful in treating these problems.

Habit-reversal training involves four steps:

1. **The child is asked to become aware of when the habit that she wants to change occurs.**

    Kids don't always realize that they engage in these habits during school or while watching television. This step helps the child increase awareness.

2. **The child learns some brief relaxation strategies, such as deep breathing or muscle relaxation.**

    These skills are practiced.

3. **A new behavior to replace the old behavior is taught.**

    This new behavior shouldn't have any negative consequences for the child. Some common strategies include making a fist and squeezing or holding on tightly to a pencil. Some children do deep breathing. These new behaviors should be practiced when the desire to do the other habit is strong.

4. **Whoever is delivering the treatment (therapist or parent) monitors progress and reward success.**

    This critical step can help improve motivation and compliance.

Habit-reversal training can be used for just about any habit that needs to be changed. Research has shown it to be particularly effective in the treatment of tics, hair pulling, and skin picking.

Dealing with miscellaneous problems

Part IV of this book reviews a host of other problems experienced by children. A few of these problems are relatively rare and thus have not received extensive study using randomly assigned groups of children. However, limited studies have indicated that certain strategies appear to be effective. Here's a quick overview of additional specific problems and what appears to work for each of them:

- ✔ **Childhood eating disorders:** A significant number of studies have shown that a package of cognitive behavior therapy techniques accompanied by nutritional information has great value in the treatment of childhood obesity, anorexia nervosa, and bulimia. This therapeutic approach appears to work best by including the parents in the program as well as helping parents deal with their own eating issues if that is a problem, which it frequently is.

- ✔ **Miscellaneous problems with eating:** Feeding disorder of infancy, pica, and rumination (see Chapter 14 for a discussion of these problems) have not received extensive large-group study at this time. BT and learning principles are often used to treat these problems, however, and numerous anecdotal, clinical data suggest they can be highly effective.

✔ **Selective mutism:** We aren't aware of large randomly controlled group studies for the treatment of selective mutism, but the learning principles of BT are used for treating this problem, and anecdotal data suggests that they are effective.

✔ **Elimination disorders:** *Enuresis* involves a lack of control of urination, most commonly at night but also during the day, and *encopresis* refers to a lack of control of feces. (See Chapter 11 for more information about these problems.) Enuresis is treated with a technique known as the pad and bell, which is based on the principles of operant and classical conditioning. (See Chapter 2 for information about these learning principles.) Ideally, the pad and bell is combined with other behavioral strategies designed to provide kids for success while minimizing stress and shame. This approach is highly effective; in fact, it's much more effective and enduring than the administration of Desmopressin (DDAVP), a hormone that restricts urine output. DDAVP is actually prescribed much more often by pediatricians than the pad and bell even though it's less effective.

We strongly recommend that you work with a child or pediatric psychologist on the use of the pad and bell before considering the use of DDAVP, which, although relatively safe, can have significant side effects.

Encopresis has not been studied as extensively as enuresis has, but a number of reports indicate that a combination of behavior therapy involving reinforcement of the child's efforts and coping strategies combined with dietary changes, mineral oil, and increased intake of fluids appears to work effectively.

✔ **Recurrent abdominal pain:** This complaint is particularly common among children and always must be carefully evaluated by a pediatrician. Quite often, no physical basis can be found for the problem, and several studies have suggested the value of behavior therapy programs that include the parents and family as a way of improving the condition. These programs teach kids coping strategies and relaxation techniques, and provide reinforcement for efforts at coping. They're often combined with increases in the child's fiber intake. Other types of chronic pain in children appear to respond well to similar programs, though changes in diet usually wouldn't be part of the plan.

✔ **Substance abuse:** Adolescents all too often turn to alcohol and drugs as a way of coping with the stressors that this stage in life often brings along. Various combinations of cognitive behavior therapy techniques have been shown to have significant value in teaching adolescents alternative ways of coping and thinking in a more healthy way. Adolescents are taught to understand the triggers and high-risk situations for drug use and learn alternative behaviors. They learn how to assertively deal with pressure from peers and construct a healthy social network. Techniques for increasing their motivation to change are also employed.

Finally, we should note that behavior therapy has been used successfully for the treatment of various other disorders, although carefully controlled studies have been made more difficult due to the rarity of these problems. Nonetheless, behavior therapy appears to be effective for treating kids to cope with problems associated with chronic illness as well as genetic disorders (see Chapter 11). It may have potential for treating reactive attachment disorders (see Chapter 16 for more information), but research of treatments for this problem is in an early stage.

Various therapies that have been promoted for reactive attachment disorders appear to be quite unpleasant and involve evoking rage, extreme physical restraint, or other highly confrontational techniques. To date, no data support the effectiveness of these approaches and they have been highly criticized. At this time, there appears to be little or no justification for using highly aversive strategies for kids with this problem.

Chapter 18

Enhancing Educators' Efforts

*W*hen children have problems such as learning disabilities, emotional disturbances, developmental disorders, or physical disabilities, they often need extra help at school. In addition to their schoolteachers, many children with disabilities have medical or other service providers who participate in their care. In order to best meet the overall needs of children, caregivers and service providers must cooperate and communicate.

In this chapter, we describe how to support optimal communication between school, home, therapists, and medical providers. You can discover how to avoid misunderstandings and defensiveness whether you are a parent, caregiver, outside provider, or educator. We also take a look at the common ways that children are evaluated and how to interpret test results. Although the focus of this chapter is on enhancing education efforts, open communication among all service providers is the most direct path toward meeting this goal.

Children with problems sometimes qualify for special education in order to address their disabilities or challenges. The evaluation process can seem complicated and overwhelming. We discuss the laws regarding special education services and the making of an individualized education plan (IEP). Finally we lay out some alternatives to special education that can be found in the regular classroom.

Communicating About Children

Kids do better when the adults who care for them talk to each other. Good communication between home and school and outside providers is particularly important when children have disabilities. Even though parents, educators, medical providers, and therapists almost always want what's best for kids, they all have different perspectives. Those diverse perspectives some-times lead to discord. Thus, a physician may determine that a child needs med-ication, and a family may decide that they don't want their child on medication.

Decisions about care can be particularly problematic when communication is poor. When effective communication breaks down, conflicts between home, school, and other providers increase and children lose out. Disagreements sometimes occur because of limited resources. For example, a parent may want her child to receive speech therapy twice a week, and a school adminis-trator has to balance that request with the fact that the school's only speech therapist already has a full caseload.

The following two sections discuss ways of making communication more effective, whether it's between teachers, parents, school administrators, counselors, speech and other therapists, or doctors. First, it's important to know how to reduce the all-too-common problem of defensiveness. Then, we discuss the importance of consistency in communication efforts.

Tackling defensiveness

One major obstacle to effective communication is defensiveness. Defensiveness occurs when people feel unsafe, unheard, or vulnerable. When people become defensive, they don't hear what's being said and lose the abil-ity to problem solve. Tempers flare, and communication stops. Parents natu-rally feel protective of their children and can easily become defensive when discussing what is most important to them — their kids. Teachers or other providers can also get defensive when they feel attacked by parents.

When defensiveness creeps into conversations, people say things they fre-quently regret later. Think of defensiveness as an understandable reaction to fear. If you or someone you're talking to slips into defensiveness, try to prac-tice forgiveness and use the skills in the following sections.

Seeing the signs

Avoiding defensiveness requires acknowledging that it exists and recogniz-ing it when it occurs. Most people become defensive from time to time. Defensiveness happens more frequently when people are exhausted or depressed.

Signs of defensiveness include

- ✔ Anger
- ✔ Tension
- ✔ Blaming others
- ✔ Verbal attacks

- ✔ Increased hostility
- ✔ Sarcasm
- ✔ Failure to stay on topic
- ✔ Rapid speech
- ✔ Higher pitched voice
- ✔ Flushed face
- ✔ Increased heart rate

Relaying a response

If you are on the receiving end of defensiveness, try to slow the conversation down. Let the other person talk without interruption. And when there is a pause, encourage the person to clarify and give you more detail. Often times, people need a bit of time to vent, and when given a chance, they calm down and lose their defensive stance.

Here are a few questions or comments to make when you believe someone is getting defensive:

- ✔ "Sounds tough; how does that feel?"
- ✔ "Help me understand more about your point of view."
- ✔ "No wonder you're upset."
- ✔ "Tell me more about that."
- ✔ "I can see your point."
- ✔ "Anyone in your shoes would feel strongly about that."

Reigning yourself in

When you feel a conversation is getting out of control and that *you* may be getting a bit defensive, some of the same strategies noted in the earlier section "Relaying a response" can work to calm yourself down too. Slow the conversation down, ask more questions, and get more details. Be honest with yourself. Everyone gets defensive from time to time. Additional things you can try include:

- ✔ Take a few deep breaths.
- ✔ Ask for a break (get a drink of water or use the restroom).
- ✔ Reschedule to talk another time.
- ✔ Admit that you're feeling upset.
- ✔ Apologize for getting a bit defensive.

Keeping in-touch consistently

Keeping the lines of communication open between home and school and home and health-care professionals is very important. The caregiver is the link to tell teachers if a medical issue is occurring, to find out from school whether a problem with schoolwork or peers exists, or to give teachers and health-care providers information about changes at home. The following sections go into more detail about how to keep the communication lines clear.

Sending information to and from school

Oftentimes, report cards are the main vehicle for communication between school and home. However, report cards do not always mean the same thing from school to school or from teacher to teacher.

So, an "excellent" in one classroom may mean that a student is working at grade level and turning in homework. "Excellent" in another classroom may mean that the student is performing well above grade level. "Excellent" in still another classroom may mean that the student is doing the best that can be expected of her although below grade level. All three teachers could give valid reasons for providing the same feedback to reflect different realities. Periodic report cards do not provide enough information for parents to know what's really going on.

We recommend *brief* and *frequent* communication to supplement intermittent report cards. Technology makes that easier than ever. These exchanges should be planned out ahead of time and agreed upon by all parties. Here are some ideas for communication shortcuts:

- ✔ **Text messages:** Brief messages from the teacher or parent to say what kind of day the child is having.

- ✔ **E-mails:** Notes about what troubles or accomplishments the child is having in school or at home.

- ✔ **Notebook:** A place for the teacher to jot down situations that are occurring and for parents to ask questions — the notebook can travel between home and school on a daily basis.

Don't solely rely on technology or written messages for communicating with your child's teacher. Also, request in-person meetings whenever you have a concern.

Parents or guardians need to grant permission for teachers to communicate with other providers. This process is usually done with signed permission to release and/or exchange information forms provided by the school or outside agency. See the following section "Keeping in contact with health-care providers" for more info.

Putting technology to task

A great way to use today's technology is in the form of a communication tool between teachers and caregivers. Using e-mail and text abbreviations and symbols allow teachers and caregivers to communicate with one another in brief and frequent formats. Following are some ideas to keep communication concise.

From the teacher to home:

✔ Great day: J

✔ Has homework: HW

✔ Poor attention today: Lattention

✔ Had trouble getting along: L + L

From home to teacher:

✔ Didn't get enough sleep: L Zzzz's

✔ Change in medications: MChg

✔ Had trouble on homework: L hw

✔ Charged up today: J ++

Keeping in contact with health-care providers

Busy doctors rarely have time to have much of a discussion with a child's teacher. But there are ways for doctors, teachers, parents, and therapists to stay in touch. Increasingly, doctors are open to brief e-mail communication, but it's important you don't abuse the privilege if that's available.

Doctors also frequently request information about children's behavior and functioning at school. They love to receive hard data in the form of observation rating scales when it's available. Or, teachers can send them clear, concise summaries of how a child is doing. Most doctors want to be informed; so don't leave them out of the loop for fear of taking too much of their time. Just be concise.

Understanding the Meaning of Test Scores

Testing is part of life for the vast majority of school-aged children whether they attend public or private schools. Many states also require children who are homeschooled to participate in some form of testing or assessment. So people interested in kids need to know something about testing and test scores. Besides, test results communicate a lot to parents, teachers, and counselors about how a child is doing.

The maze of testing conducted across the country is downright complicated. Some school districts use tests that compare students' progress to a national sample of children, others use tests developed by the state in which they operate, and some employ tests designed by the school district. Then of course, teacher-made tests also give information about how well students in the classroom are doing on a particular subject. Other tests that are given by a school psychologist or educational specialist determine whether a child has a learning disability. Most schools use a mixture of different types of tests.

With all the different scores and ways of reporting results, it's no wonder parents and the public are often confused. With literally thousands of different tests available, we can't possibly tell you what each one means. However, we can give you some general principles to help you figure them out.

Knowing what's average

Many times parents are given results indicating that a child has performed at, below, or above average. But, the meaning of *average* can vary widely depending on what comparison group average refers to. Here are some examples of what we mean:

- **Teacher-made tests:** Say that three fifth-grade teachers — Mr. A, Mrs. B, and Ms. C — all give their students the same math test. The test consists of 100 questions. Table 18-1 shows you the scores obtained for each classroom.

  As you can see the "average" (calculated by adding up all scores in a given class divided by the number of kids taking the test) is quite different for the three classrooms. Yet, parents told that their children obtained an average grade would all assume that their kids were right on target. In other words, you have to know the comparison group to know what average really means. By the way, which teacher's classroom would you like your kids to be in?

- **Statewide tests:** Tests given on a statewide basis have a larger comparison group and thus the results are likely a little more meaningful. Statewide tests can identify schools or towns that aren't doing as well as others in that particular state. But they don't tell you how the state is doing compared to other states. That's because statewide tests vary from state to state. So, the state test in New York may be harder or easier than the state test in Nevada. A student with what looks like a high score in one state may not look as good if he'd taken a test in a different state.

- **National tests:** Tests that are given nationwide, or even across many nations, have an even broader, more-meaningful comparison group. Scores based on these tests are often seen as more important to college admissions offices. Thus, kids in Georgia probably score differently than kids in New York or Minnesota. Some states score quite poorly compared to other states.

The bottom line is that if you see an "average," "above-average," or "below-average" score, it doesn't mean much until you know what the comparison group consisted of. So when you see such descriptions, be sure to ask about the nature of the comparison groups. Teachers or counselors should have the answer and be able to communicate this information clearly to you.

Table 18-1	How "average" means different things		
	Mr. A's Class	*Mrs. B's Class*	*Ms. C's Class*
All Scores	95, 93, 93, 91, 87, 76, 71, 55, 48, 40	100, 98, 98, 95, 94, 90, 90, 89, 87, 86	90, 83, 81, 80, 62, 59, 51, 45, 38, 35
Class Average	74.9	92.7	62.4

Freaking out over tests

High-stakes tests are tests that are used to determine something important or of consequence for a child or an adult. For example, tests required for getting a driver's license are high stakes — you can't drive without passing. Other high-stakes tests include college entrance exams, high school competency tests, and many tests required by local schools. Results may be used to evaluate school districts, individual schools, administrators, teachers, and children. These tests are high stakes for those giving and taking the tests.

High stakes often means that parents, kids, and teaching staff feel stressed. Before schools begin yearly testing, teachers send notes home to parents reminding them to make sure that their kids have a good breakfast and get enough sleep (In bed by 8 p.m.? Check. Oatmeal, fruit, and milk? Check.). In addition, many hours of classroom time are dedicated to making sure that kids know how to fill in the little bubbles. How many times does real life require you to fill in hundreds of bubbles? Okay, forgive us for a little editorializing.

Setting the standard (score)

If you review a child's score on a statewide or nationally administered test, you may very well run into a concept known as a standard score. A *standard score* is a way of converting the child's actual *raw score* (the total number of correct responses) into a score than indicates where the child falls in relation to other kids' performance. The standard scores for many tests (such as most IQ tests) are set with 100 as the average.

You can find various types of standard scores. Some set the average at 0, some at 50, others at 5, and so on. Discussing the meaning and nature of standard scores with a child's school counselor or school psychologist is important in order to understand what you're looking at. See *Statistics For Dummies* by Deborah Rumsey (Wiley) for more information about standard scores and what they mean, if you really want the full scoop on standard scores.

So yes, some tests involve rather high stakes. However, you don't want either you or your child to get too worked up and worried about them; high levels of anxiety can impair performance. Here are some ideas to consider for keeping anxiety about high-stakes tests in check:

- ✔ If a poor score is received, the student can usually take the test another time.

- ✔ Don't put even more pressure on your child by saying it's important that she do really well. Tell her it's just one test of many that will come along in life. And remind her, as with all tests, just do the best she can.

- ✔ The results of a single, high-stakes test are usually not the only piece of information considered for many important decisions such as college admissions.

Keeping test scores in perspective

Test scores represent *estimates* of a child's skills or abilities. They are not chiseled in granite and scores may vary some over time. Tests measure a child's performance during the time of testing. So, if a child is unmotivated, sick, sleepy, or distracted, that measurement can be an underestimate of the child's true skill level or ability. Less frequently, a child's score may represent a slight overestimate of her abilities because she frankly got a little lucky and filled in just the right bubbles.

Consider test results only as one part of a larger picture of the child over time. Test scores represent one piece of the puzzle. Classroom observations, parent reports, teacher's insights, the child's past history, all come into play when evaluating any given child. Most tests measure in part what the child has been taught. So if during third grade a child was sick and missed school or if the third- grade teacher was sick a lot and missed school — a child's score on a third-grade achievement test may be low because of lack of instruction.

Knowing What to Do When Kids Need More

Children have problems in schools for lots of reasons. Sometimes the method of teaching doesn't work well with a particular child. Other times a teacher may not be a good match for a child. And sometimes the school administration doesn't work well. All these possibilities must be honestly considered prior to holding children responsible for problems with learning.

When a child struggles in school, national laws require schools to take action. The first step is to take a close look at the classroom. Does the teacher use scientifically validated methods for teaching? If not, perhaps the child doesn't really have a problem, the classroom does. You can find information about curriculums that work at: `http://ies.ed.gov/ncee/wwc`.

The following sections outline the steps schools, caregivers, and third parties take to help a child who is not doing well in school.

Initial interventions

After problems with the teaching method, the classroom, and the school environment are ruled out, a team of educators discuss the child's case. Those educators, depending on the resources in each school, may be joined by a school administrator, a counselor, a school psychologist, a speech therapist, or another education specialist. The purpose of getting together as a group is to generate ideas about how to help a struggling student.

Strategies developed by the team may include

- ✔ Giving extra attention in the classroom
- ✔ Providing different teaching methods
- ✔ Having the child receive tutoring
- ✔ Giving the child more structure
- ✔ Changing seat assignments
- ✔ Moving the child to a different classroom

The group agrees upon strategies to try out and the give these strategies a chance to work (the timeline varies depending on the unique needs of the child). If the child makes reasonable progress, then the group keeps track of the child to make sure that progress continues and further formal evaluation may be unnecessary.

Getting a formal evaluation

If a child *continues* to have problems despite classroom interventions, then more extensive help may be required. Before that happens, the child undergoes a comprehensive evaluation. The purpose of the evaluation is to better assess why a child is having difficulties and to develop a plan to intervene, as you can see in the following sections.

Gathering information

A comprehensive evaluation involves a team of professionals, which usually includes a school psychologist. In addition, the evaluation team typically involves the child's classroom teacher and primary caregivers. Information is gathered and written up in a report. The content of an evaluation depends on the problems the child is having in school.

Evaluations include some or all the following information which is gathered prior to meeting to decide whether the child will require special education services:

- **Background information:** Such information includes any problems with the pregnancy, birth, or early development of the child as well as family history of learning problems. Problems at home or in the neighborhood are taken into account. School attendance and prior school achievement are also considered.

- **Classroom observations:** These firsthand accounts help the team see how the child responds to the classroom. The teacher and parent may be asked to complete rating skills that look at specific behaviors, problems with attention, or emotional problems.

- **Intelligence tests:** Intelligence tests measure different abilities including reasoning skills, language skills, long-term memory, short term memory, visual-spatial skills, and speed of taking in information.

- **Language tests:** These tests look at specific language skills such as how well a child can listen to and understand spoken language as well as how a child uses spoken language. Other skills include how well a child can recognize sounds (which can affect spelling and reading), conversation skills, articulation skills, and knowledge of vocabulary.

- **Achievement tests:** These evaluations look at reading skills, math skills, and written-language skills. The tests are chosen to answer specific questions. For example, if a child does well in math but has trouble reading, the tests would focus on reading skills.

- **Processing skills:** Processing tests look at the way a child takes in information from the world and sends it back out. Think of the brain as a computer — when working well it's fast and efficient. But a computer can be slow, overwhelmed, or crash. Some kids struggle to process certain types of information such as sounds, visual-spatial information, body sensations, or sequencing.

The evaluation can also include other measures that are specific to the child's problem. For instance, if a child has physical difficulties, a physical therapist may participate in the evaluation. Or, if a child has emotional issues, psychological testing may be included. By law, school districts must conduct comprehensive evaluations on students who are suspected of having disabilities that impair learning. Parents can also request these evaluations.

Finding a reason

The evaluation process (see preceding section "Gathering information") hopes to uncover the reason or reasons a child is having trouble learning.

The Individuals with Disabilities Education Act (IDEA) identifies 13 categories of disability. They are

- **Autism:** This broad category includes children with autism, pervasive developmental disorder, or Asperger's disorder (see Chapter 13 for more information).

- **Deafness:** A severe impairment in hearing that cannot (at the time) be corrected enough to allow the child to process information presented by speaking.

- **Hearing impairment:** Less-severe hearing problems than deafness that negatively impact learning.

- **Deaf-blindness:** These children have both serious hearing and vision loss. The combination requires very specialized educational services.

- **Mental retardation:** Very low intellectual abilities as well as severe delays in everyday skills — also called intellectual disability.

- **Multiple disabilities:** This category is used when a child suffers from more than one disability, such as both a hearing impairment and autism.

- **Orthopedic impairment:** Children who have problems with their bones, joints, or muscles that negatively impact their ability to learn are orthopedically impaired. These impairments can be the result of genetic disorders, disease, or accident.

- **Other health impairment:** This category describes a wide range of problems that limit strength, vitality, or alertness and hinders a child's learning. Health problems such as asthma, attention deficit/hyperactivity disorder (ADHD), epilepsy, or childhood cancer are covered under this label.

- **Serious emotional disturbance:** Kids who suffer from chronic emotional problems such as schizophrenia, depression, or anxiety and have trouble performing in school are served under this category.

- **Specific learning disability:** A child who has a learning disability does not perform as well as expected in speaking, reading, writing, or mathematics (see Chapter 12). This disorder is assumed to be caused by differences in brain functioning of the children with learning disabilities. Their abilities in unaffected areas are often average or above average.

- **Speech or language impairment:** Problems with speaking (such as stuttering or difficulty pronouncing sounds), problems with understanding, or problems with communicating through language.

- **Traumatic brain injury:** An injury to the brain that occurs after birth and that negatively affects learning. This category does not apply to kids who have degenerative or congenital brain injuries.

Developmental delay is a term used to describe young children that have a delay in motor, language, social, or cognitive development, usually under the age of 8. After that time, if a child remains delayed, more specific and definitive terms from the preceding list are used.

Every profession has its own vocabulary along with unique definitions. IDEA lists 13 disabilities, each with specific requirements that must be met in order for a child to be considered disabled. The definitions have similarities and differences from those given by mental health professionals outside of the school systems. You can find out more about the regulations by visiting the web site of the United States Department of Education: `http://idea.ed.gov/`.

States and individual school districts may have slightly different ways of implementing federal laws. If you want more information about specific programs, contact your local school district.

Be aware that evaluations can also be done privately. Some psychologists in private practice specialize in assessment. Some parents prefer to have a second opinion or want more information than the school assessment provides. These private evaluations can be expensive although a few health insurance plans cover some of the costs in certain cases. In addition, when parents disagree with the assessment done at the school, the school district sometimes pays for an independent evaluation.

Reviewing the results

After a comprehensive evaluation is completed, the school personnel holds a meeting with the child's parents or guardians, classroom teacher, an administrator, a special education teacher, and a professional who can interpret the findings of the comprehensive evaluation. The purpose of the meeting is to determine two issues:

- ✔ Does the child have a disability as defined by federal law?
- ✔ If the child has a disability, does the child require specialized instruction in order to learn what other children are learning?

If the answer to both questions is yes, then the team begins the process of developing a plan to address the child's unique needs. This written plan, called an *Individualized Education Program (IEP),* establishes how special education will address the needs of the child. (For more on IEPs, check out the later section "Understanding the Individual Education Plan [IEP]." If the answer to either eligibility question is no, then the child is not eligible for special education services and the meeting is adjourned.

Many students enter public schools without English-language proficiency. Understandably, these kids often have trouble keeping up with children who speak English as their first language. Students for whom English is a second language do not qualify as having a disability unless they show significant problems in their native languages.

Understanding the Individual Education Plan (IEP)

About 13 percent of public school children are eligible to receive specialized services under the Individuals with Disabilities Education Act. Most of those children, almost 40 percent, have learning disabilities. An IEP is constructed for each of those children. IEPs are usually written once a year, but may be rewritten more frequently if the child's needs change.

The IEP is a written *promise of services*. The team members who write the IEP include the child's teachers, parents, therapists, and other education specialists. The team can also involve the child, especially as the child becomes more able to handle the complexities of the process. (For more on the evaluation process, see the section "Getting a formal evaluation" earlier in this chapter.)

Each school district may vary on how the IEP is formatted or written, but by law, all IEPs must contain the following elements:

- **Present levels of performance:** In this section, the child's strengths and weaknesses are described. Information from the comprehensive assessment, results of school-wide testing, reports from the classroom teacher, and observations from the child's parents or guardians are included. This section also details how the child's disability affects performance in the regular classroom.

- **Goals:** This part of the IEP spells out how the child will improve. Goals are specific. For example, "become more proficient in reading," is not specific. A better goal would be "will be able to answer reading comprehension questions at a third-grade level." This section also lays out how progress toward achieving the goals will be measured.

- **Services provided:** This section discusses the services that will be provided for the child as well as any adaptations in the regular classroom that may be made. Services may include various therapies, special transportation, equipment, and specialized instruction.

✔ **Time in program:** Children with disabilities must be given a chance to interact with nondisabled children. In this section of the IEP, the amount of time the child special education services provide and the time spent in activities in regular education settings is described. In addition, the schedule of services is spelled out. Examples include

- Speech therapy will be provided twice a week.

- The child will participate in regular education classes four hours a day.

- The child will be in a resource room for language arts instruction two hours a day.

- The child will be allowed to take tests in a quiet setting.

✔ **Participation in assessments:** This part of the IEP describes whether a child will take the mandated school-wide or statewide tests. If so, modifications such as extended time or having the test read out loud are considered.

Providing Equal Access to All

Most students do not require special education services. Some may have minor problems that affect their schoolwork, but just need a few changes in the regular classroom. Part of the federal law regarding individuals with disabilities, known as Section 504, prohibits discrimination against people with disabilities. This law ensures that children with disabilities, even if they do not qualify for special education, have equal access to an education.

School districts, by federal mandate, must provide a free and appropriate public education for children with disabilities. Experts have written volumes about the complex rules and regulations. Advocates for children have many resources available to help them navigate the maze of special education law. The following are some of the key parental rights and the school districts' responsibilities:

✔ **Prior written notice:** Schools must inform parents or guardians in writing when they propose to start a comprehensive evaluation, when they conduct an IEP (see the section "Understanding the Individual Education Plan [IEP]" earlier in this chapter), when eligibility is changed in any way, or when services are changed.

✔ **Informed consent:** School districts are required to provide parents information in a language they can understand and get parental consent before conducting an evaluation, giving a child special education, or making changes in services.

✔ **Discipline:** Students with disabilities are expected to follow school-wide rules of conduct. They may be suspended from school, like nondisabled students. However, if the student's misbehavior was possibly related to a disability, then the IEP team must meet to consider options and strategies.

> ✔ **Dispute resolution:** When the schools and parents disagree, specific procedures must be followed in order to resolve the disputes. These procedures include mediation by a neutral person with expertise in special education law and, if that process does not work, a formal hearing with an impartial hearing officer is held. In some cases, attorneys are hired, and a court of law reviews the disagreement.

Many children have either emotional, behavioral, learning, or health problems that may impact their school days but do not require special education. These problems can range from minor to serious. Reasonable accommodations must be made to allow children to access education.

Resources for parents and teachers

In this sidebar, we list a few of the thousands of Web sites where parents and teachers can find out more about certain conditions or problems that plague kids.

The ABC's of Child Development, `www.pbs.org/wholechild/abc`. This Web site is produced by the Public Broadcasting System (PBS). It contains considerable, detailed information on children's physical, social, emotional, and cognitive development.

American Academy of Pediatrics, `www.healthychildren.org`. This Web site provides extensive information about development, health and wellness, safety, and current concerns affecting children and their parents.

Institute of Education Sciences, `http://ies.ed.gov`. The U.S. Department of Education's Institute of Education Sciences has a Web site that provides education statistics and tons of information about schools, including colleges. If you go to this site, you can conduct a customized college search, or find out about high school dropout rates or adult literacy.

National Center for Learning Disabilities, `www.ncld.org`. This Web site has information about disabilities for parents, educators, and adults with learning disabilities. It provides articles about each type of learning disability and has blogs and free newsletters.

Anxiety Disorders Association of America, `www.adaa.org`. This Web site lists self-help groups across the United States and displays a variety of anxiety screening tools for self-assessment. It also provides an online newsletter and a message board.

Autism Speaks, `www.autismspeaks.org`. Autism Speaks is dedicated to promoting research on the causes, treatment, and prevention of autism. Its site provides a wealth of information for parents, professionals, families, teachers, and caregivers.

Center on the Social and Emotional Foundations For Early Learning, `http://csefel.vanderbilt.edu`. This site provides information about school readiness and development of children from ages birth until five. There are parenting training modules and tips for supporting optimal child development.

For example, students in wheelchairs must have access to classrooms. If a child has a hearing impairment and would benefit from sitting close to the front of the room, that accommodation has to be made. Some children are prescribed medication during the school day. The school must make provisions for administering and keeping the medications in secure locations.

If a child has a chronic illness that requires frequent hospitalization, then educational services must be made available either at home or at the hospital if the child is well enough to benefit. Adolescents that are placed in institutions such as jails, group homes, or psychiatric hospitals must also have access to education.

Chapter 19

Knowing What Parents Can Do

*N*o one can predict how any given newborn baby will develop. From the moment of conception and beyond, a dizzying array of influences bombard babies from all directions — genetics, toxins, peers, parents, siblings, poverty, wealth, diseases, culture, schools, trauma, and random events. (Chapter 2 discusses how all these factors influence whether development proceeds smoothly or hits bumps in the road.) All too often parents blame themselves when their children encounter problems, but parents obviously hold only a few of the cards that are dealt to their kids.

However, parents do have an important role to play in helping their kids as they run into obstacles. When parents take the right steps, they can collaborate with teachers, professionals, and healthcare workers to improve the odds. We've seen many cases of kids who faced formidable barriers yet overcame them because of due diligence demonstrated by their various caregivers.

In this chapter, we help parents navigate what they can do to best help their kids get through the tough times. We discuss how to adjust parenting attitudes and work effectively with their children's therapists. Then we describe actions parents can take when their children are diagnosed with some of the most common childhood disorders such as autism, anxiety, depression, or a behavioral disorder. Although this chapter focuses on what parents can do when their kids start running into real trouble, Chapter 8 gives you important foundational parenting principles that can prepare you for dealing with the tougher issues. If you haven't already read that chapter, you may want to check it out first, as it helps parents acquire important skills for helping your kids.

Acquiring the Attitudes You Need to Help

Being a parent and knowing how to react when problems arise isn't always natural. If your child seems to consistently be hitting a brick wall and needs help, you may feel a variety of emotions in your desire to help your young one. You may feel grief, anger, or refuse to believe the accuracy of an assessment of your child. Powerful emotions need to be sorted out because they can get in the way of parents being the best advocates they can be for their children. The following sections help you know how to handle these emotions and arm yourself with positive attitudes that can set the stage for your child's success.

Denying denial

When school counselors, teachers, doctors, or child-care workers tell parents that their kids are having problems, parents often react with resentment, anger, or denial. Denial usually includes an element of defensiveness (see Chapter 18 for a discussion about defensiveness), but goes even further. Parents have trouble even imagining the idea that one or more of their children are experiencing trouble. You can begin to navigate the denial waters in the following sections.

Demonstrating denial

The possibility that one's child has a genetic problem, a physical challenge, emotional difficulties, or behavioral issues isn't a pleasant thought. The following parental reactions reflect denial:

- "That simply can't be true."
- "Shelly behaves fine at home; it must be the school's fault."
- "No child of mine would ever have a problem like that."
- "I think that teacher must have it in for our son."
- "Autism?! That's crazy; Jake's smarter than most kids!"

We're not suggesting that parents should accept everything and anything that a professional might have to say about their kids. But blatant denial slams the door on communication and prevents the possibility of useful intervention.

Working through denial

The alternative to denial is to gather more information. In other words, ask questions — lots of questions. Here are just a few examples of the types of questions we recommend asking when you hear what sounds like bad news about a child:

✔ "Can you tell me what you're basing that diagnosis on?"

✔ "Would testing be appropriate for confirming this possibility?"

✔ "Are there any other possible explanations for this problem?"

✔ "Can you tell me where I can read more about this?"

✔ "What kinds of help are available for this issue?"

✔ "Do you see this as a temporary difficulty or something chronic?"

Such questions allow you to more fully explore what may be going on and why. You can seek additional information and deepen your understanding of the professional's concerns. Depending on what you discover, you may look for additional services or realize that you as the parent can do much to help. You may find that the problem is not as serious as you initially feared.

On the other hand, you may end up with remaining doubts. You may continue to have disquieting feelings that what you're hearing doesn't feel right. In that case, by all means seek a second opinion. Just don't reflexively ignore and deny that something could be going on if reasonable professionals tell you that they believe a problem exists.

Fending off fear

Feeling anxious and fearful if you're told that your child may have some kind of problem is natural. But if you hear terms like *learning disability, autism, obsessive compulsive disorder,* or *behavior disorder* applied to your child, allowing fear to spin out of control is easy. Parents often panic upon receiving news like that.

In some respects, fear and panic represent the opposite side of the coin from denial (see the earlier section "Denying denial" in this chapter). Parents who panic not only fully believe the "bad news," but they also believe the worst possible outcomes from what they've heard. They jump to dire conclusions. But fear and panic immobilize people. They don't think through and solve problems effectively when panic takes hold.

If fear or panic describe you, we suggest stepping back. If you get the news about your child during a meeting, ask for a few minutes to regain your composure. Take a walk, get some water, and breathe. If you find yourself unable to continue because of your emotions, it's perfectly understandable for you to ask to reschedule.

Focus on what you can do to help your child live life fully, despite any limitations. Realize that effective interventions exist for the vast majority of childhood problems. Even in cases where kids are likely to be profoundly affected for a lifetime (such as severe autism or serious intellectual disabilities), parents discover much to love and appreciate about their child who has problems. Every child is a gift.

If you panic upon hearing possible bad news about your child, give yourself a little time. Rarely does one have to take immediate action. If your panic does not subside, get help for yourself. As airline personnel so often advise, you have to help yourself with the oxygen mask in order to then help your child.

You can find numerous support groups for parents who have kids with all sorts of problems. If you're struggling to deal with your child's issues, look for such support groups. You can usually find them online or in your local newspaper.

Putting parents in charge

When parents find themselves in the position of needing to help a child with problems, sometimes they get confused about their roles. Parents find themselves wanting to help their kids, as they should. And because they feel great empathy for their children's problems, they sometimes slip into wanting to be their child's best friend. They want to listen, nurture, and be best buddies.

Listening, supporting, and nurturing are actually great things to do! Best buddies? Not so much. Especially when kids have problems, they need their parents to be leaders. Parents need to set limits and boundaries. Kids actually feel safer when an adult takes charge and provides clear expectations and structure.

Sure, parents feel empathy and compassion for their children's plight. But sometimes parents have to push — and that's a role that leaders play, not best friends.

When kids struggle with problems, allowing your protective instincts to run out of control is pretty easy. Parents naturally feel sorry for their kids when they experience trouble. Thus, they want to rescue them from difficult feelings in any way that they can. Sometimes that means they start letting their kids out of basic responsibilities such as chores around the house, cleaning up after themselves, doing their homework, and so on.

Even kids who are struggling with emotional difficulties or other problems need to have reasonable expectations for carrying out typical life activities, some of which (like putting their dishes away) can be a little frustrating. But learning to tolerate frustration is a critical goal of growing up. Working with the child's therapist to know what's reasonable and what's not is important, and then be sure to follow through and make sure such expectations are met.

Minimizing parental anger

Parenting is a tough job even when kids don't have diagnosable problems. But parenting kids with emotional and behavioral issues greatly increases

the difficulty. Sometimes parents end up feel
feel acute embarrassment about their child's
other people will think about themselves or t

Either embarrassment or frustration can easi
ally just makes things worse. Even when kids
activities (see the later section "Dealing with
chapter) parental anger usually just leads to

If your child has problems, realize that these p
reflect poorly on you as a parent. See the prob   a problem
with which you, your child, and your support team needs to tackle together.
If your anger feels uncontrollable, please discuss it with your child's therapist
who may recommend therapy for you.

Participating as Partners in Kids' Therapy

If you discover that your child has problems, you're likely to enlist the aid of
a specialist such as a speech therapist, occupational therapist, physical therapist, academic tutor, psychologist, psychiatrist, or other treatment provider
(see Chapter 17 for information about such professionals). Depending on the
nature of the problem, your involvement can range from brief meetings with
the therapist to actually participating in the therapy. The next sections help
parents ask the right questions and support their child's therapy.

Working with therapists

Parents often need to recruit therapists, coordinate appointments, and sometimes collaborate to make sure that their kids are getting the best treatment.
The following questions can help parents clarify goals, keep track of progress, and enhance treatment outcomes:

- ✔ Why does my child need treatment?

- ✔ What are the goals of treatment?

- ✔ How do I know that my child is making progress?

- ✔ How do I know that my child has achieved these goals?

- ✔ Are there any short-term or long-term effects related to the treatment?

- ✔ What can I do as the parent to help in between your sessions with my child?

- ✔ How do you as my child's therapist plan to communicate and collaborate with other professionals involved in my child's care?

All types of therapies for kids' problems work better when parents are actively involved. Don't be passive in the process. Ask lots of questions and carry out any suggestions the therapist gives you for enhancing the therapeutic efforts at home.

Collaborating with mental-health therapists

Mental-health therapists take various approaches to allocating therapy time between parents and their kids. Your child's age, type of problem, shyness, conversational skills, and maturity all contribute to whether a therapist spends most of the therapy hour with your child, both parents and child, or in a split fashion with part of the hour spent individually with the child and the balance of the time with the parents. Generally speaking, therapists usually see teenagers by themselves, with parents playing a relatively smaller role in the therapy hour.

However the time is divided, work with therapists needs to be a collaborative, confidential connection between the child and the therapist. That means that kids need to feel free to confide whatever they want to with a therapist. The therapist then informs parents about general therapy goals and progress, but they do not discuss details about confidences revealed to them by a child unless a child intends to inflict harm on herself or someone else.

Try not to worry about your child revealing family secrets or saying embarrassing things to her therapist. Therapists are good at being nonjudgmental, and they know how to take what they hear "with a grain of salt." After a child's therapy session, feel free to ask the child open-ended questions such as "How did it go today?," but avoid asking about specifics and don't push your child to reveal details that she doesn't want to.

Therapeutic goals emerge from a collaboration between parents, children, and the therapist. Everyone should be on board about the basic goals. Parents can play an especially important role by reporting on the child's progress and keeping the therapist informed about what's going on at home.

Addressing autism

Parents often feel both grief and relief following the diagnosis of their child with autism, Asperger's disorder, or pervasive developmental disorder (see Chapter 13 for detailed information about these disorders). They grieve the loss of a perfect child. At the same time, parents usually know that something was different about their child and so they may also feel some relief that they finally have a name for the problem. After the diagnosis, parents need to take a deep breath and take care of themselves emotionally. Experiencing strong feelings is perfectly normal.

Wanting results, right away

If you have a child who has a problem that requires help, you may find it pretty easy to become impatient. Parents often want to see improvements right away. Sometimes they complain when they don't see much change happening in the first few weeks of therapy. Therapy takes a while to work. Therapists often need time simply to build trust with a child. Psychotherapy is a process in which change can usually be seen over months rather than weeks.

If your child doesn't seem to be getting anywhere after three or four months of therapy, discuss your concerns with his therapist. If the therapist's response doesn't feel right to you, seeking a second opinion is always an option.

The best thing a parent of a child with autism can do is become educated about the disorder and stay highly involved by collaborating with the child's therapists and teachers. Parenting a child with autism takes extraordinary patience, hard work, and commitment. The first thing parents can do is to find out everything they can about autism and effective treatments for the disorder. Parents can get resources from several national organizations such as the Autism Society of America, The National Foundation for Autism Research, or Autism Speaks.

We recommend that parents join a support group (either in person or online). Other parents of children with autism can share knowledge about resources, advocacy, challenges, and opportunities. Parents also need to educate family and friends about the nature of their child's difficulties.

Autism affects children in many different ways. Each child with autism is unique and strategies for helping a child with autism vary depending on the child's strengths and weaknesses. Parents participate by being strong advocates for their child, arranging for early intervention, and by supporting the work being done in therapy.

Two strategies — behavior modification and motherese (also known as child-centered communication) — are particularly useful for parents of kids with autism. Here are some details about each technique:

- **Behavior modification:** These techniques are based on learning theory (which we describe in Chapters 2 and 17). Very briefly, one of these principles is based on the fact that behaviors that are rewarded increase in frequency. Parents can help therapists develop a system for rewarding specific behaviors by identifying what things are particularly rewarding to their child. But, for children with autism, finding out what rewards work to increase behavior can be challenging. They may not respond positively to praise or rewards based too far in the future.

✔ **Motherese:** This strategy is based on the way parents or caregivers talk to babies and is practiced throughout the world. This technique needs very little training. The method involves a high squeaky voice, slower pace, and intense enthusiasm. Babies prefer and pay more attention when people talk to them using motherese. Autistic kids sometimes seem quite disconnected from others and motherese seems to stimulate improved interactions between parents and the child. This technique may also help young autistic children pay more attention to social interactions with others.

Axing a child's anxiety

Anxiety in children comes in a variety of flavors (see Chapter 14 for more information about anxiety disorders). The good news is that the vast majority of childhood anxiety problems are highly treatable. Your child's therapist is likely to ask you to participate in at least two ways:

✔ Encourage gradual exposure.

✔ Avoid the reassurance trap.

The next two sections detail how these techniques work.

Encouraging gradual exposure

Most anxiety-related problems cause kids to avoid whatever is making them anxious. For example, if a child fears insects, he goes to great lengths in order to avoid any bugs. Or perhaps a kid avoids other kids and after-school activities if she has a social phobia. If she fears germs (as in obsessive-compulsive disorder), she tries to avoid dirt and contamination at all costs.

Cognitive behavior therapy (see Chapter 17) for anxiety attempts to break through avoidance. This method entails encouraging your child to make consistent, but gradual steps toward encountering and dealing with the things that are making him anxious. Most likely, you as the parent, your child, and the therapist will all collaborate to develop a step-by-step plan.

In cognitive behavior therapy, the therapist will also help you develop a list of a few incentives or rewards for your child to be given as he progresses through his plan. Rewards can help motivate your child to face his fears head on which is never easy to do.

When using rewards, it's important to not use excessive enthusiasm for each small gain. Sometimes kids actually start resisting because over-the-top encouragement starts to feel like pressure. In other words, you want to show that you're pleased, but don't go on and on.

If your child has autism in addition to anxiety, don't mute your enthusiasm. Autistic kids usually need higher levels of excitement and praise than kids who are merely dealing with anxiety. If in doubt, check with your child's therapist who can give you feedback on the approach that you're using.

Avoiding the reassurance trap

When kids have problems, parents want to do everything they can to help them feel better. No one wants to see a child struggle with anxiety and fear. However, the desire to reduce kids' distress can actually boomerang.

Here's how the boomerang can occur:

1. A child who has an anxiety disorder feels a sharp pang of disquieting insecurity.

2. He goes to one of his parents for reassurance in order to feel better.

3. His parent says something reassuring, such as, "There's nothing to worry about; you'll be fine."

4. The child feels an immediate drop in anxiety and distress, which feels good to him.

5. That brief drop in anxiety actually reinforces the child for seeking reassurance in the first place.

The child is more likely to turn to his parents whenever he feels upset rather than working through the problem himself. A cycle is set in motion in which the child feels anxious and dependent, seeks reassurance, obtains that reassurance, feels better, and then starts all over again.

What we're going to tell you now may likely feel counterintuitive. Stop giving your kids reassurance when they feel anxious! We realize that carrying out this advice can be a little tricky. Therefore, work with your child's therapist for developing alternatives to reassurance. Table 19-1 lays out a few examples of common reassurance-seeking behaviors along with good alternatives to reassurance. These alternatives are pretty effective for most any age child that is able to easily understand the vocabulary (probably ages 6 and up or so).

Don't start the alternatives to reassurance plan until you've talked it over with your child as well as his therapist. When you do start, expect your child's anxiety to increase for a week or two. If you persist, the odds are his anxiety will begin to decrease.

Table 19-1	Reassurance Alternatives
Reassurance request	*Reassurance alternative*
Is the food here really clean?	It's always possible that germs could be on anything.
Will the kids in the new school make fun of me?	I don't really know. How will you handle it if they do?
Will I do OK on the exam tomorrow?	That probably depends on how hard you studied. How will you feel if you don't do well?
Are there any bugs in here?	Gosh, I don't know. Bugs can be anywhere. What will you do if you see one?

If your child doesn't suffer from excessive anxiety, giving a little reassurance here and there is appropriate and unlikely to cause any significant problems. However, if your child does have a problem with anxiety, giving him reassurance is likely to add fuel to the fire. One more alternative to providing direct reassurance is to simply turn the issue over to the therapist by saying something like, "That sounds like something to ask your therapist."

Defeating depression

Depressed children withdraw from family and friends. They lose interest in activities that were previously enjoyable and feel tired and in the dumps. Kids with depression often have changes in appetite and sleep. They feel pessimistic about themselves, their worlds, and their futures (see Chapter 14 for more information about depression in kids).

When children show symptoms of depression, they need to be evaluated and treated by mental-health professionals. Parents should never attempt to take this job on by themselves. But, family members and caregivers can help depressed kids move forward and regain some of their previous enthusiasm for life.

A simple treatment that is highly effective for treating depressed children (as well as adults) is called *behavioral activation.* Another way to describe behavioral activation is "get moving." Depressed kids avoid doing things that they enjoy because they believe that their depression will keep them from enjoying things. But the more they avoid and withdraw, the more depressed they become. Parents can help kids get moving again.

Assuming your child is working with a therapist, be sure to ask how you can help your child implement behavioral activation plans. Here are a few guidelines:

✔ **Don't push too hard.** Depression can lead to sluggishness and lack of motivation. When beginning behavioral activation, you may find your child resisting. Back off. Don't force the issue. Take another run at it another time. Consider trying some other idea. But if resistance continues, talk to your child's therapist.

✔ **Start short and small.** Kids with depression feel overwhelmed. If your child loved to hike mountains before getting depressed, don't start with a 14,000 foot climb. Start with a 15-minute walk together.

✔ **Gradually increase frequency.** Don't suddenly announce a hectic schedule of activities. Go slow, start with once a week, and then add activities. You don't have to schedule a specific activity for every day. All kids need some unstructured time.

✔ **Choose noncompetitive fun.** Feelings of inadequacy often go along with depression. Don't put a depressed child on a highly competitive baseball team. Sports are great when they encourage fun, safety, and fair play.

✔ **Choose mastery activities.** In other words, focus on things that your child can succeed at. Don't sign up a girl with depression for classical ballet if she tends to be clumsy. Instead, if she wants to dance, start with line dancing. You don't want to add failure to depression.

✔ **Pair up.** Spend time with your child. Even rides in the car with a bit of conversation can help boost your child's mood. If other friends or family members are willing, enlist them to spend a bit of time with your child. Depression leads to withdrawal. Having understanding people around helps.

✔ **Offer rewards.** We're not suggesting that you reward your child for "getting over depression." But work together to set up a small achievable goal (such as helping clear the table after dinner without complaining, getting homework done, or doing another simple chore). After you both have agreed on one or more small goals, offer a special time together or another mutually agreed-upon reward.

Encourage your children to talk by providing a safe, comfortable atmosphere. Listen to what they say without harsh judgment. Never tell children that they have no right to feel a certain way. Kids and adults feel the way they do. Don't try to talk children out of their depression. Bring up your concerns to the child's therapist.

Cognitive behavior therapy helps depressed kids change the way they think about themselves and their worlds (usually in addition to behavioral activation) and has been shown to be quite effective for adolescents and pre-adolescents. However, leave the attempts to change your kid's depressed thinking to the therapist. Even if you as a parent say the exact same thing that the therapist would, your child is likely to resist your efforts. It's important to understand that parents play an important role, but they shouldn't try to duplicate what the therapist is doing.

Dealing with behavior disorders

Oppositional-defiant disorder and conduct disorders are challenging to treat (for a full description, see Chapter 15). Often times kids with these problems don't really want to get treatment. Despite regular conflicts at home and at school, they tend to blame others for their problems and see no reason to change. So parents of these children need support, usually from a therapist, in order to help their kids see the need for changing their behavior.

The first step is getting the child to treatment. Parents *must not negotiate* with their kids on this issue. Behavior disorders can lead to lifelong problems and without treatment get worse over time. When children are sick, they need to get medical treatment. The same holds true for kids who have behavior problems — they need psychological treatment.

Kids with behavior disorders get angry quickly. They frustrate parents and teachers with their defiance and disobedience. It's no wonder that many parents and teachers feel angry at them in return. However, when kids with behavior disorders have the power to get someone angry, they feel bold and powerful. That's not good. So parents and teachers must learn emotional neutrality. *Emotional neutrality* means keeping the emotions out of your interactions with your child — especially when employing discipline strategies.

Work with your child's therapist on developing structure, limits, boundaries, and discipline strategies. Your child may attempt to subvert these efforts by acting as though consequences don't matter at all. For example, you may threaten to take away a privilege, a cell phone, or an allowance. Your kid is likely to say something like, "Fine, I don't care at all!"

Don't believe it. Stick to your guns. Consistency of effort can get you there. Realize that change takes patience and time.

If your child reports something awful that her therapist said, check it out before you react. Often kids with behavioral problems come to their parents after a therapy session and report that the therapist said something bad about the family. As often as not, the therapist said no such thing. What the kids are trying to do is manipulate their parents into stopping the therapy. Parents who fall for this trap sometimes get angry at what the therapist allegedly said and occasionally terminate therapy. These manipulations are especially common in the first few sessions.

Part VI
The Part of Tens

The 5th Wave   By Rich Tennant

"They say your setting your bed on fire was a cry for help, pushing my car into the lake was a cry for help, and your failing grades are a cry for help. The next time you feel like crying for help, would you mind just crying for help?"

In this part . . .

We present ten ways to help calm kids down. These tricks can help when tough times challenge kids, parents, and other caregivers. Then we describe ten qualities to look for that may indicate giftedness in children. Finally, we give you ten signs that a kid may be in trouble and in need of professional help.

Chapter 20

Ten Ways to Calm Kids Down

Kids have many ways of expressing themselves when they're upset. Some kids get quiet and withdrawn; some cry; others kick; and some have loud, noisy tantrums. When kids have tantrums, heads turn. If you're the adult in charge, you want to calm the kid down. Now.

Strong emotions cause hearing loss. No, not really — but in a way it's true because when kids are very upset, they can't hear logical, reasonable alternatives. As a result, adults faced with an upset kid should act, not lecture. Frankly, lectures aren't heard (as in pretty much never heard). So the following ten strategies are alternatives for dealing with upset kids.

Not all these tips will work with every upset child every time. Pick and choose what you think may work. Most kids won't go for a hug in the middle of a tantrum, for example; temper tantrums usually require a time-out. You never know, however. Kids can surprise you.

Breathing

We generally recommend breathing to all our readers. It's sort of difficult to get around without it. Seriously, you can teach kids a quick breathing technique to help them calm down. Practice this strategy *before* you need to use it.

Here's how it goes:

1. **Tell your child to take a deep breath.**

2. **Have her hold that breath for a count of ten.**

3. **Tell her to release the breath very slowly while making a slight hiss-ing noise.**

    Making the noise helps slow the breath down.

4. **Repeat the breath two or three times.**

This simple strategy works for both kids and adults. Try it sometime!

Helping with Hugs

Hugs help. Get down on eye level with a child, and hold out your arms. When kids are very upset, they're often afraid. Having an adult wrap them up in their arms often settles them down.

If a child has been abused in any way by an adult, hugs may be frightening. If that is the case, a pat on the back is probably a better choice. In addition, most kids don't appreciate hugs from strangers. Furthermore, hugs aren't the first strategy to try with tantrums.

Playing in the Tub

Most kids enjoy bath time. Cover the floor with lots of towels, and let them go at it. Make sure that you include lots of plastic toys or tubs. Young kids can play endlessly; older ones may prefer a soak. Be sure to add some bubbles for kids of all ages. The warm water helps soothe troubled kids.

Oatmeal baths help soothe irritated or dry skin. Buy oatmeal, and grind a cup of it in a blender or coffee grinder, or buy preground oatmeal in packages made for baths. Dump the ground oatmeal under a running faucet, and you have a soothing bath.

Reading a Good Story

Reading a story helps calm children. If the child can read, have him read out loud to you. If he prefers you to read, go ahead. Good books take children to other places in their imaginations. Sometimes, distraction is a very good technique.

Young children often have a favorite familiar book that they associate with cuddling time before bed. Those books can be brought out during the day to help soothe emotions.

Running Around

Kids like to move. When they play actively, they're at their happiest, and when kids are happy, it's pretty hard for them to be upset.

Chase is a favorite game for most kids. Hide-and-seek is a big hit too. Busy, serious adults don't always take the time to play with children, so we encourage you to do that. Be careful, though; you might end up having fun when you do!

Doing Jumping Jacks

Performing jumping jacks makes kids giggle, especially if a grownup jumps too. Rigorous exercise gets the heart racing and the blood flowing. Aerobic activity is healthy, and as a bonus, it burns off anxiety. Don't worry too much about form. Jump away.

Making Music

Music sets a tone and can actually change moods. For kids, familiar songs, no matter what the content, can calm them down. Encourage your kids to sing along; it's a terrific distraction.

Experiment with the type of music. Some kids find certain music relaxing even though adults don't. Keep in mind that it's your child you're wanting to calm down when you select the music, not yourself. Sometimes, giving headphones helps them stay focused on the music and keeps you from going crazy.

Calling a Time-Out

See Chapter 8 for details on using a time-out as a strategy. In brief, if a child is in the midst of meltdown, we recommend that you promptly relegate her to a safe, observable place where she can settle down for a few minutes. If the tantrum occurs in a public place, remove the child at once, even if it's inconvenient for you. The lesson that inappropriate behavior results in swift action pays off in better behavior over the long run.

Going Outside

Getting some fresh air and a change in scenery calms kids. Babies in strollers almost always settle down. Desperate parents find that putting babies in car seats and driving around works surprising wonders. Older kids can also benefit from being outside. Lots of times, we go outside ourselves when we tire of writing. It helps.

Talking Together

Sometimes, kids just need to talk a bit. Obviously, if a child is in the middle of a tantrum, talking isn't the way to go. But if a child is upset but not out of control, talking can help a lot. Like adults, kids benefit from venting, complaining a little, and talking things out. Give them a chance to do so without telling them that they shouldn't feel the way they do. Lots of times when given a chance, children can solve problems in positive ways if you let them talk a while.

Chapter 21

Ten Signs of Gifted Kids

*I*t's fun to look for possible signs of giftedness in kids. We want to be clear about one thing: All kids are gifts to their parents! Giftedness can refer to exceptional talents, but also to anything you find special about a particular child. If you look hard enough, you can always find something special about *any* kid, such as curiosity, affection, or ability to make you smile. This chapter gives you a few specific talents to look for.

There's no definitive list of talents that reflect giftedness. If you see something particularly special or talented about your child, you're probably right!

If a child you care about shows one or more signs of giftedness, it's not a bad idea to ask the school about testing for gifted students. Many schools have programs designed to foster and encourage the development of special skills in kids. Testing can tell you whether your child may profit from such programs.

Being Curious

All kids have a certain amount of curiosity about their worlds, but kids who are gifted in this way seek answers to everything. They want to know how things work. They often develop avid interests in science, reading, history, and other topics. They're rarely satisfied with parents' initial quick answers to their questions. They probe and prod further until they really "get it."

Talking Talents

Some kids pick up on language before others do. Precocious kids start putting short sentences together before their first birthday. Their vocabulary develops rapidly and is advanced compared with that of other kids their own age. They quickly master the understanding and expression of ideas. When kids start speaking early, they're probably gifted, but you should know that sometimes gifted kids start speaking later.

Musing about Math

Kids gifted in math master math facts quickly and easily. Sometimes, they teach themselves how to add and subtract, and have an intuitive understanding of *more* or *less* as well as fractions and percentages. They're also fascinated by the meaning of mathematics. They may be drawn to books that contain lots of statistics and data. Children who are gifted in math are often bored during math at school because they're so far ahead of their classmates.

Having Humor

Some kids have an unusual knack for humor. They easily detect absurdities or ironies in situations and turn them into jokes. Their humor seems more mature than their age. They play with words in humorous ways. Unfortunately, their peers don't always follow their humor and may think that they're a bit odd. Their mature sense of humor makes some of these kids gravitate toward older children and/or adults.

Craving Creativity

Creative kids seek new, novel, and interesting activities. They often love to draw, for example. Their drawings may be more sophisticated than those of their peers, frequently containing rich detail, and they may use those drawings to tell stories. Their creativity may show up in other endeavors, such as music, writing, and storytelling.

Minding Memory

Kids with gifted memories may have strong skills in remembering visual details. These kids may be able to sit in the backseat of a car and tell the drivers how to get where they're going at an unusually early age. Our 3-year-old grandbaby recently told us to "Turn left, then right!" on our way back to his house, and he was correct. (Being our grandchild, of course, he *must* be gifted!) Other kids with masterful memories are able to recall a vast array of verbal information, such as conversations they've had or overheard, songs, poems, and commercials.

These strong memories often help kids do exceptionally well in school. Gifted kids sometimes don't have to study very hard to do well, but they often like learning and thus work hard anyway.

Finding Focus

Long attention spans aren't exactly the hallmark of early childhood, but some kids seem to have an unusual ability to stick with problems or activities. They aren't easily frustrated when they're challenged. Sometimes, gifted kids have unusually advanced focus on the topics that interest them but not so much on other subjects. This selective attention can be problematic in school, when gifted kids want to focus solely on what they like rather than on the teacher.

Understanding Others

Most young children are flat-out self-centered. That's perfectly normal. But some kids demonstrate advanced skills in understanding the perspectives of other people. They seem to have radar for detecting how and what other people are feeling. They have unusual ability to empathize.

These interpersonal skills often help kids relate to others and form good friendships. Gifted empathic kids may become involved in charitable work or the helping professions. On the other hand, being too attuned to other people's feelings sometimes causes these kids to be overly sensitive.

Thinking Flexibly

Kids with the gift of flexibility are able to respond effectively to a wide range of challenges. They may come up with two or three ways of solving a particular problem and don't get locked into one. They can analyze, synthesize, and reason to come up with novel solutions. When obstacles stand in their way, they have the ability to shift their perspective and try alternative approaches.

Precocious Perception

Giftedness also shows up in the way that some kids process visual and spatial information. Such kids often love to solve puzzles well beyond their years. They can construct elaborate buildings with blocks. They like to take things apart and put them back together. This skill usually comes along with good visual memory. Kids with such talent sometimes drive their parents crazy taking things apart, but eventually, they start hooking up the family entertainment system.

Chapter 22

Ten Signs That a Kid Needs Help

*W*e describe normal and abnormal child development throughout this book in some detail. Here, we give you a quick overview of ten of the most common signs that a child may be headed for trouble and needs help. For physical, emotional, and behavioral problems, the first place to go for help is the child's primary-care physician. Physicians usually know which types of professionals will be needed to help your child in the way that she needs. For problems in school and with learning, we recommend checking with the child's school teacher, counselor, or principal.

Delaying Development

When children aren't developing as expected, their pediatrician or an early childhood professional should look at them more closely for an evaluation. Significant delays in development are signs that something isn't right. Early intervention often improves the outcome considerably. When parents or caregivers have worries, those worries are often justified. It never hurts to check into things, whereas ignoring problematic signs can slow progress. See the Appendix for charts of normal development.

Lacking Interest

Teachers, parents, and caregivers should be concerned if any child seems to lack interest in his world and environment. Kids are naturally curious and involved. A child who seems to be oblivious to other people may be showing signs of a problem. A child who once was interested in play and activities but no longer is likely has a different sort of problem. Any general lack of interest should be investigated.

Kids get bored from time to time, which is pretty normal. A lack of interest means showing a global lack of connection with people or the world.

Withdrawing from Family

Kids sometimes pull away from their families. In fact, most adolescents pull back from their parents to a degree. When the withdrawal is pronounced or comes on suddenly for no good reason, however, it's best to check into what's going on. Sometimes, withdrawal is a sign of depression. At other times, it may indicate substance abuse or involvement in gangs. Occasionally, other factors cause a child to withdraw, but you should always investigate. Mental-health professionals are a good source of help in sorting out withdrawal.

Getting Poor Grades

Kids come home with poor grades for various reasons. In some cases, the child is having trouble learning (see Chapter 12 for information about learning disorders). At other times, emotional problems may cause a child to do poorly in school (see Chapter 14 for information about emotional disorders). Sometimes, poor grades reflect lack of motivation or effort that results from behavior problems (see Chapter 15 for information about behavior disorders). Occasionally, poor grades come about due to an intellectual disability, but when that's the case, struggles in school usually are apparent early on. Whatever the cause, poor grades are something that should never be ignored. Get to the bottom of it. How a child does in school determines a great deal about her future.

Complaining about Aches and Pains

All kids have aches and pains from time to time. Stomachaches, earaches, leg pains, sore throats, and such are part of childhood. When kids repeatedly and frequently complain about vague pains like stomachaches or just not feeling well, something else may be going on. You want to consult the doctor first, however. The physician may tell you that the pains are more likely due to emotional problems, such as anxiety about school or trouble getting along with other kids. When that happens, a mental-health professional should be consulted.

Feeling Fearful

Fear is a normal part of childhood, especially from ages 3 to 6 or so. (See Chapter 14 for information about when fears are normal and when they're not.) Any time a child's fear interferes with having normal fun, learning, or other activities, however, you have cause for concern. A visit to the child's doctor can rule out possible physical or medication-related causes; then a referral to a mental-health professional may be in order.

Getting Angry

All kids get angry. They don't call them the "terrible twos" for no reason. Young kids have temper tantrums now and then. But one of the goals of growing up is learning to control emotions and impulses (see Chapter 3 for more about the goals of growing up). When anger hurts others, gets a kid in trouble at school or elsewhere, or starts disrupting the family, you need to get help. This problem usually is pretty easy to deal with if you catch it early. Later on, it becomes a much larger problem.

Changing Appetites

Lots of kids are picky eaters; we're not talking about that here. But when a child displays a sudden, dramatic change in appetite (whether increased or decreased), it could be a sign of either a physical or emotional problem. Parents shouldn't try to force a child to eat. Instead, check the problem out with the child's physician.

Regressing

After you learned how to ride a bike, you probably never forgot how. You may feel a little wobbly if you get on a bike for the first time in years, but you'll pick it up fast. If kids master a skill such as reading, writing, language, arithmetic, stacking blocks, or bike riding, they shouldn't start to slide back downhill. If you notice a child regressing or backsliding on a previously mastered skill, have the problem checked into. Sometimes, it's a temporary setback that means little, but it can indicate a serious problem. Err on the side of caution.

Feeling Fatigued

Kids are usually full of energy. They can wear an adult out pretty quickly. At least, that's how it should be. Lethargy or sudden fatigue isn't normal for kids. Whether low energy seems to be related to a change in sleep habits or appears for no clear reason at all, it's something that should be investigated. This problem can occur due to emotional issues as well as various illnesses, so it shouldn't be ignored.

Appendix

Developmental Milestones

· ·

*T*his appendix provides a condensed, easy-to-use overview of the major developmental milestones that children pass through from birth through adolescence. We hit the highlights only; every detail would fill an entire book on its own. Table A-1 provides information about prenatal development. You can find more information about pregnancy in Chapter 4. Table A-2 gives you important milestones kids achieve at various ages. See Chapters 5 through 7 for more details about child development.

It's important to note that these milestones are merely approximations of what happens at various ages for most kids. Normal development varies from one child to another. Generally you shouldn't be concerned unless these milestones are significantly delayed. If you have concerns, you should always check with your child's pediatrician.

Table A-1	Development during Pregnancy
Stage	*Developments*
First trimester	Fertilization, rapid cell division, and implantation occur. Cells differentiate into internal and external organs. Toward the end of this stage, the fetus looks like a tiny human.
Second trimester	More rapid growth occurs. The mother begins to feel the baby's movements. The baby develops regular sleep and wake cycles. The baby may be able to live independently by the end of this trimester.
Third trimester	The baby prepares for birth by adding fat for temperature control, and its lungs develop further. The baby acquires immunity from the mother. Typically, the baby grows to between 5.5 and 9 pounds.

Table A-2	Developmental Milestones: Learning, Moving, and Interacting		
Age	*Learning (Language and Thinking)*	*Moving*	*Interacting (Socially and Emotionally)*
3 months	Makes noises, coos, tracks objects with eyes	Lifts head, grasps objects, kicks, and wiggles	Recognizes caregivers, smiles, responds to contact, maintains eye contact, quiets when caregiver interacts by talking, rocking, or singing
6 months	Babbles, laughs, shows pleasure and protest, starts to understand cause and effect	Rolls over, sits with help, reaches for objects	May respond to name, attempts to get attention, makes attempts to mimic others
1 year	Says first words, understands that people or things can exist when they're not in view, searches for objects that are out of view, shows intentions, understands basic directions, imitates sounds and actions	Sits without support, crawls, pulls up to a stand, walks with support or takes first steps, uses finger food, holds a bottle	Shows fear of strangers, is affectionate with familiar people, waves, uses gestures, follows a point
2 years	Strings two or more words together to make a sentence, identifies a few body parts, shows early signs of humor, uses mental processes to solve problems	Drinks from a cup, uses a spoon, runs, stacks blocks, negotiates stairs with help	Begins make-believe play, understands "No," appreciates approval, sometimes intentionally refuses or disobeys, enjoys being read to, expresses wants, begins taking turns

Age	Learning (Language and Thinking)	Moving	Interacting (Socially and Emotionally)
3 years	Speaks easily in three- or four-word sentences; may pretend to read; asks many questions; uses pronouns like *he* and *her;* uses prepositions like *over, under,* and *on;* matches and groups objects, knows own age, understands past and present	Walks on tiptoes, uses stairs unassisted, is toilet trained during the daytime, kicks a ball, turns book pages one at a time, draws a circle	Shares toys, takes turns, engages in complex make-believe play, makes up stories and games, acts friendly
5 years	Knows colors, counts, makes rhymes, makes up jokes, defines some words, uses correct tense, answers telephone, tells stories	Walks backward, catches balls, stands on one foot, copies shapes and letters, uses scissors, shows preference for using left or right hand	Has best friends, understands fairness, is aware of others' feelings, has improved emotional control (fewer meltdowns), enjoys making people happy, likes to play dress-up, begins comparing self with others
6 to 12 years	Learns to read, calculates, describes experiences, understands the concept of future, understands classifications and relations	Is completely independent in feeding and dressing self, runs, skips, jumps, writes, swims, draws, rides a bike	Develops growing independence from family, develops close friendships, has better emotional control, displays a strong sense of right and wrong, has more-ingrained self-concept and feelings of competence
13 to 18 years	Uses logical thinking, performs hypothesis testing, continues to develop problem-solving ability, able to understand the concepts of probability and possibility, continues to build academic skills	Undergoes rapid physical development resulting in sexual maturity, develops near-maximum athletic skills	Is strongly influenced by friends, develops sexual identity and body image, may rebel against family, develops advanced moral reasoning

Index

• V •

Notes

Notes

Apple & Macs

iPad For Dummies
978-0-470-58027-1

iPhone For Dummies,
4th Edition
978-0-470-87870-5

MacBook For Dummies, 3rd
Edition
978-0-470-76918-8

Mac OS X Snow Leopard For
Dummies
978-0-470-43543-4

Business

Bookkeeping For Dummies
978-0-7645-9848-7

Job Interviews
For Dummies,
3rd Edition
978-0-470-17748-8

Resumes For Dummies,
5th Edition
978-0-470-08037-5

Starting an
Online Business
For Dummies,
6th Edition
978-0-470-60210-2

Stock Investing
For Dummies,
3rd Edition
978-0-470-40114-9

Successful
Time Management
For Dummies
978-0-470-29034-7

Computer Hardware

BlackBerry
For Dummies,
4th Edition
978-0-470-60700-8

Computers For Seniors
For Dummies,
2nd Edition
978-0-470-53483-0

PCs For Dummies,
Windows
7 Edition
978-0-470-46542-4

Laptops For Dummies,
4th Edition
978-0-470-57829-2

Cooking & Entertaining

Cooking Basics
For Dummies,
3rd Edition
978-0-7645-7206-7

Wine For Dummies,
4th Edition
978-0-470-04579-4

Diet & Nutrition

Dieting For Dummies,
2nd Edition
978-0-7645-4149-0

Nutrition For Dummies,
4th Edition
978-0-471-79868-2

Weight Training
For Dummies,
3rd Edition
978-0-471-76845-6

Digital Photography

Digital SLR Cameras &
Photography For Dummies,
3rd Edition
978-0-470-46606-3

Photoshop Elements 8
For Dummies
978-0-470-52967-6

Gardening

Gardening Basics
For Dummies
978-0-470-03749-2

Organic Gardening
For Dummies,
2nd Edition
978-0-470-43067-5

Green/Sustainable

Raising Chickens
For Dummies
978-0-470-46544-8

Green Cleaning
For Dummies
978-0-470-39106-8

Health

Diabetes For Dummies,
3rd Edition
978-0-470-27086-8

Food Allergies
For Dummies
978-0-470-09584-3

Living Gluten-Free
For Dummies,
2nd Edition
978-0-470-58589-4

Hobbies/General

Chess For Dummies,
2nd Edition
978-0-7645-8404-6

Drawing
Cartoons & Comics
For Dummies
978-0-470-42683-8

Knitting For Dummies,
2nd Edition
978-0-470-28747-7

Organizing
For Dummies
978-0-7645-5300-4

Su Doku For Dummies
978-0-470-01892-7

Home Improvement

Home Maintenance
For Dummies,
2nd Edition
978-0-470-43063-7

Home Theater
For Dummies,
3rd Edition
978-0-470-41189-6

Living the
Country Lifestyle
All-in-One
For Dummies
978-0-470-43061-3

Solar Power Your Home
For Dummies,
2nd Edition
978-0-470-59678-4

Internet

Blogging For Dummies,
3rd Edition
978-0-470-61996-4

eBay For Dummies,
6th Edition
978-0-470-49741-8

Facebook For Dummies,
3rd Edition
978-0-470-87804-0

Web Marketing
For Dummies,
2nd Edition
978-0-470-37181-7

WordPress
For Dummies,
3rd Edition
978-0-470-59274-8

Language & Foreign Language

French For Dummies
978-0-7645-5193-2

Italian Phrases
For Dummies
978-0-7645-7203-6

Spanish For Dummies,
2nd Edition
978-0-470-87855-2

Spanish
For Dummies,
Audio Set
978-0-470-09585-0

Math & Science

Algebra I
For Dummies,
2nd Edition
978-0-470-55964-2

Biology For Dummies,
2nd Edition
978-0-470-59875-7

Calculus For Dummies
978-0-7645-2498-1

Chemistry For Dummies
978-0-7645-5430-8

Microsoft Office

Excel 2010 For Dummies
978-0-470-48953-6

Office 2010 All-in-One
For Dummies
978-0-470-49748-7

Office 2010 For Dummies,
Book + DVD Bundle
978-0-470-62698-6

Word 2010 For Dummies
978-0-470-48772-3

Music

Guitar For Dummies,
2nd Edition
978-0-7645-9904-0

iPod & iTunes For
Dummies, 8th Edition
978-0-470-87871-2

Piano Exercises
For Dummies
978-0-470-38765-8

Parenting & Education

Parenting For Dummies,
2nd Edition
978-0-7645-5418-6

Type 1 Diabetes
For Dummies
978-0-470-17811-9

Pets

Cats For Dummies,
2nd Edition
978-0-7645-5275-5

Dog Training For Dummies,
3rd Edition
978-0-470-60029-0

Puppies For Dummies,
2nd Edition
978-0-470-03717-1

Religion & Inspiration

The Bible For Dummies
978-0-7645-5296-0

Catholicism For Dummies
978-0-7645-5391-2

Women in the Bible
For Dummies
978-0-7645-8475-6

Self-Help & Relationship

Anger Management
For Dummies
978-0-470-03715-7

Overcoming Anxiety
For Dummies,
2nd Edition
978-0-470-57441-6

Sports

Baseball
For Dummies,
3rd Edition
978-0-7645-7537-2

Basketball
For Dummies,
2nd Edition
978-0-7645-5248-9

Golf For Dummies,
3rd Edition
978-0-471-76871-5

Web Development

Web Design
All-in-One
For Dummies
978-0-470-41796-6

Web Sites
Do-It-Yourself
For Dummies,
2nd Edition
978-0-470-56520-9

Windows 7

Windows 7
For Dummies
978-0-470-49743-2

Windows 7
For Dummies,
Book + DVD Bundle
978-0-470-52398-8

Windows 7 All-in-One
For Dummies
978-0-470-48763-1

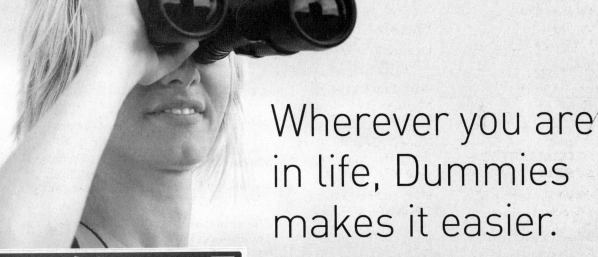

Wherever you are in life, Dummies makes it easier.

From fashion to Facebook®,
wine to Windows®, and everything in between,
Dummies makes it easier.

Visit us at Dummies.com

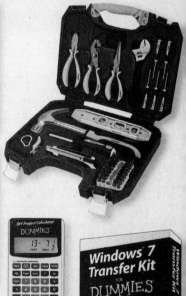